THE BIG OPEN

ALSO BY RICK RIDGEWAY

The Boldest Dream
The Last Step
Seven Summits (with Dick Bass and Frank Wells)
The Shadow of Kilimanjaro
Below Another Sky

THE BIG OPEN

ON FOOT ACROSS TIBET'S CHANG TANG

RICK RIDGEWAY

NATIONAL GEOGRAPHIC
WASHINGTON, D.C.

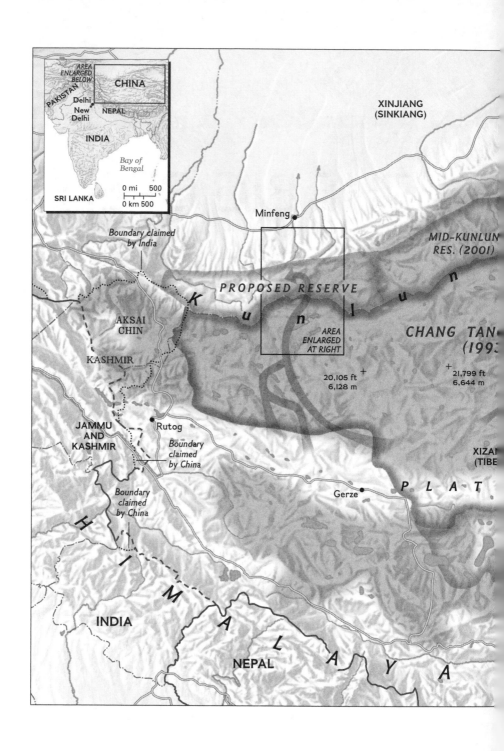

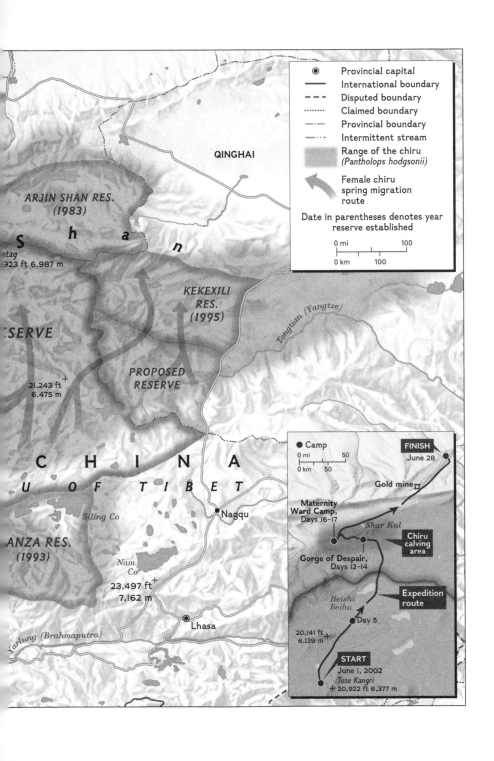

QINGHAI

ARJIN SHAN RES.
(1983)

...tag
...923 ft 6,987 m

S h a n

ESERVE

KEKEXILI
RES.
(1995)

Tongtian (Yangtze)

21,243 ft
6,475 m

PROPOSED
RESERVE

C H I N A

...U O F T I B E T

Siling Co

Nagqu

ANZA RES.
(1993)

Nam
Co

23,497 ft
7,162 m

Lhasa

Yarlung (Brahmaputra)

Legend

⊙ Provincial capital
— International boundary
- - - Disputed boundary
······· Claimed boundary
—·— Provincial boundary
—··— Intermittent stream
▨ Range of the chiru
(Pantholops hodgsonii)
⬅ Female chiru
spring migration
route

Date in parentheses denotes year
reserve established

0 mi   100
0 km   100

Inset map

● Camp
0 mi   50
0 km   50

FINISH
June 28

Gold mine

Maternity
Ward Camp,
Days 16-17

Shar Kul

Chiru
calving
area

Gorge of Despair,
Days 12-14

Expedition
route

Heishi
Beihu

20,141 ft
6,139 m

Day 5

START
June 1, 2002
Toze Kangri
20,922 ft 6,377 m

Published by the National Geographic Society

Printed in U.S.A.

Library of Congress Cataloging-in-Publication Data

Ridgeway, Rick.
  The big open : on foot across Tibet's Chang Tang / by Rick Ridgeway.
    p. cm.
  ISBN 0-7922-6560-2
  1. Ibex--Anecdotes--China--Chang Tang Plateau. 2. Mountaineering--Anecdotes--China--Chang Tang Plateau. 3. Ridgeway, Rick. I. Title.
  QL737.U53R54 2004
  508.51'5--dc22

                    2004001138

One of the world's largest nonprofit scientific and educational organizations, the National Geographic Society was founded in 1888 "for the increase and diffusion of geographic knowledge." Fulfilling this mission, the Society educates and inspires millions every day through its magazines, books, television programs, videos, maps and atlases, research grants, the National Geographic Bee, teacher workshops, and innovative classroom materials. The Society is supported through membership dues, charitable gifts, and income from the sale of its educational products. This support is vital to National Geographic's mission to increase global understanding and promote conservation of our planet through exploration, research, and education.

For more information, please call 1-800-NGS LINE (647-5463) or write to the following address:

National Geographic Society
1145 17th Street N.W.
Washington, D.C. 20036-4688 U.S.A.

Visit the Society's Web site at www.nationalgeographic.com.

In fond memory of
GALEN AND BARBARA ROWELL

क

CONTENTS

FOREWORD

क

CONRAD ANKER

IT'S BEEN A YEAR AND A HALF since I returned from our adventure walking across the uninhabited empty quarter of Tibet's Chang Tang Plateau, following on foot the endangered Tibetan antelope—the chiru—to their hitherto undocumented calving grounds. As a professional mountaineer, I go away on extended expeditions two or three times a year. I've been on climbing trips to Antarctica nine times, to Patagonia and the Andes six times, to the Himalaya sixteen times. A year and a half is enough distance on a trip to put it in perspective, and as Galen Rowell, one of my companions, said as we neared the finish line, our Chang Tang trek was the most fulfilling any of us on the team had ever experienced.

Back in 1978, the quintessential climber's mountain, K2, was ascended by a group of American climbers. One of them, Rick Ridgeway, later appeared on the cover of NATIONAL GEOGRAPHIC, wearing a protective aluminum sun mask. I was a teenager at the time, imagining myself on a Himalayan peak, climbing a ridge so close to the sun that I too would have to wear an aluminum mask. These were my boyhood dreams, and Rick was my hero. In 1996, a part of my dream came true when I joined my hero for a climbing expedition to Queen Maud Land, in Antarctica. Never mind that during the trip

Rick told me the aluminum mask was experimental, and that he had worn it only for a couple of hours before he found it so uncomfortable he packed it away, never to use it again.

Our goal in Queen Maud Land was simple: to climb a peak. Somehow the expedition became more than that when on the vertical wall we watched snow petrels nest and we marveled at the staying power of lichen, when on the icecap we came across the frozen remains of a seal nearly 100 miles from the ocean. Even in Antarctica, where winter never leaves, we were in awe of nature's diversity.

Several years later Rick invited me to join the board of the Conservation Alliance, a consortium of companies in the outdoor equipment industry dedicated to giving back to the wilderness; participating companies tithe to a fund that makes grants to small grass roots groups working on projects like protecting a backyard forest or removing an obsolete dam. I welcomed the opportunity to contribute to environmental organizations that have the same attitude toward protecting wildlands that we have toward climbing mountains: Even though the proposition from afar seems daunting, you get to the top by taking one step at time.

Our trek across the Chang Tang was the same sort of endeavor that required the same type of tenacity, as well as the same type of teamwork, communication, and preparedness. The environmental crisis is going to be solved by many dedicated individuals working toward the same goal. There will be no grand solution that will culminate in a perfectly balanced and healthy environment, but rather thousands of small steps toward the goal of a healthy planet home for all animals and by extension all humans.

In The Big Open, Rick describes such a focused campaign: the effort of a few individuals around the world to save one of the singularly unique creatures on our planet, the chiru. These rare animals live on the remote Chang Tang of the Tibetan plateau—a place that is frozen ten months of the year—and to survive they have evolved very fine wool, the finest in the world. Humans, in our pursuit of luxury and vanity, have found this wool can be woven into shawls of unparalleled lightness and warmth. These shawls have become a fashion craze, and the chiru have by the tens of thousands given their lives for a simple rectangle of cloth that fetches up to $15,000. The Big Open chronicles our contribution to this international effort to save the endearing chiru from extinction.

Despite our success, I will always remember the Chang Tang trek with sadness as well. One month after we returned, Galen Rowell, with his wife, Barbara, perished in a plane crash. We dedicate this book not only to their memory, but also in recognition of the photographs and books that together they produced. Their images and words celebrate the wilderness they cherished, and perhaps most important, they inspire us all to safeguard the remote places and wild animals that will nourish the generations to come.

PROLOGUE

क

IN JUNE 1999, I REACHED THE SUMMIT of a snow mountain
nearly 21,000 feet above sea level. Buffeted by cold wind, I stood overlooking the Chang Tang, the "northern plain," the high steppeland of
Tibet inhabited in places by *drokpa*—the leather-skinned nomads still
found living in yak-hair tents—and in other places by no human beings
at all. Today, these uninhabited tracts are the last strongholds of the
wild animals that once roamed freely across the Plateau of Tibet: Tibetan
gazelles, Tibetan brown bear, kiang—the Tibetan wild ass—wild yaks,
and chiru, known also as Tibetan antelope.

The mountain I had climbed had no name. Indeed, since the turn
of the previous century, the entire range had been visited by only one
other Westerner. This was the eminent wildlife biologist George
Schaller, who as part of a long-term study of the Chang Tang's wildlife
had journeyed on three occasions to Aru Basin—a broad valley on
the east side of the range—and on one of his visits had ascended into
the mountains searching for blue sheep. Schaller later described the
Aru as a "haven where human intrusion has been brief, where wolf
families can raise their cubs, and wild yak herds spread over golden
pastures. Here lakes absorb color from the deep blue sky and glaciers
shine among surging peaks, filling the basin with waves of light."

I had come to this sanctuary at Schaller's suggestion. Now, from the vantage of my rarified aerie, I could see to the north and east—beyond the limit of the nomads' summer pastures—the tips of distant glacial peaks peering above the horizon, mountains that were a hundred or more miles distant. Looking down, the great turquoise expanse of Aru Lake called forth the memory of a hike a few days before along its shoreline. Cotton-white clouds had floated in an azure sky, and melting snow from a recent storm revealed a patchwork of green-gold feather grass. I had lunch on a small hilltop, and then I sat still until the wildness of the place became tangible. Other than my breathing, the only sound had been the distant chirp of a snow finch, and the only movement a small group of male chiru in the middle distance galloping over the snow-patched alluvium. [i]

Once descended from my climb, I had wanted to stay longer in the Aru, but an early summer storm threatened to swell streams that could strand the two vehicles that had brought me there. Once back home, images of the Chang Tang—the open rangelands with snow peaks like white islands rising in a sea of gold grass, the enormous dome sky, what I had come to think of as "The Big Open"—filled my dreams and even my waking hours, appearing in my mind's eye like an unannounced but always welcome guest. I wanted to go back, and that desire was crystallized when, reviewing an article Schaller had written describing his work in the Chang Tang, I had an idea how I might assist him filling in a missing but key piece of his study of the natural history of chiru, the endangered Tibetan antelope.

Schaller first visited the Aru in 1988, the only Westerner to see the region since the turn of the previous century.[ii] He returned again in 1990, and it was then his work began to focus on chiru. "They intrigued me more than any other creature in the Chang Tang," he wrote in a description of that visit. "They look as if they have somehow strayed from the African plains—their lanky legs seem designed for striding toward the horizon, and their large, bright eyes are ideal for sweeping the steppe for danger." He noticed that in July the basin was filled only with small groups of males, distinctive with long rapier-like horns. Where were the females? Then in mid-August he saw on a hillside a "strange, tan, almost pinkish mass." With binoculars he brought into focus a scattered herd of some two thousand female chiru, half with small colt-legged calves at their heels.

"In June the pregnant females had hurried north," Schaller later wrote in the NATIONAL GEOGRAPHIC article that had kindled my own desire to return to the Chang Tang. "Moving silently over shimmering plains and past snow-swept mountains, [they had followed] an ancient migration route to some mysterious place to give birth. It is a place so remote that even nomadic herdsmen do not venture near it. It is so bleak that the animals find little more than the dry leaves of a sharp-tipped sedge to eat. We had tried to follow the herds, but severe blizzards stopped us."

How could I resist? "An ancient migration route to some mysterious place...so remote even nomadic herdsmen do not venture near it...we had tried to follow the herds." I called Schaller, and he confirmed the location of the calving grounds was still unknown; he also stressed that finding the nursery was an increasingly urgent concern. Elsewhere in the chiru's range poachers were slaughtering the animals, selling the wool to couriers who smuggled it to Kashmir, where it was woven into shawls called shahtoosh that had become a haute couture rage among the fashion elite. British Vogue had called the garments a "survival tactic to get through the parties and holidays," and Harper's Bazaar ran an advertisement for a New York boutique selling the shawls for nearly three thousand dollars each. Schaller sent me an article from Vanity Fair that described the shahtoosh craze and quoted a "Park Avenue hostess" who told the article's author she had, early in the fashion trend, resisted buying one of the shawls. "Twenty-eight hundred for a scarf—no way...[then] I broke down and bought my first shahtoosh. And let me tell you, once you own one shahtoosh, you want more and more and more. They're so light that you don't feel them hanging around your neck, and they drape in this special way that is extremely luxe."

Along with the Vanity Fair piece, Schaller also sent me photographs taken by wildlife patrols in the Arjin Shan and Kekexili Nature Reserves—in the eastern end of the chiru's range where there had been some effort to contain the poaching. In one image, reminiscent of photographs from World War II of frozen soldiers on the Russian front, the stiff bodies of dead female chiru were scattered across the steppe. In another shot, a patrolman tried to coax a baby chiru, whose mother had been shot by poachers, to drink rehydrated milk from a jury-rigged baby bottle; the caption said the calf died, as did the dozens of other orphans the officers had discovered standing next to the skinned carcasses of their mothers.

Schaller told me that to make one woman's shawl of standard length and width, between three and five chiru had to be killed. He estimated that the Chang Tang region once supported a chiru population of more than a million, and that by the 1990s perhaps 75,000 survived. At the same time, Chinese officials estimated as many as 20,000 a year were being shot.

"Any woman who wears a shahtoosh shawl," Schaller said, "should be deeply embarrassed. It's not a shawl; it's a shroud."

क

SCHALLER TOLD ME THAT IF THE CALVING GROUNDS of the western population of chiru—thought to be the largest of what he had determined are four migrating populations of the animals—could be documented, he might then be able to persuade the Chinese to establish a new nature reserve to encompass the area, and that way protect it before the poachers could discover it. To fulfill this goal, I asked him if he thought it would be possible to follow the animals on foot. He thought that would be difficult: The distance to get to the south side of the Kunlun Mountains—the area he suspected harbored the calving grounds—and then to get out would be two hundred to three hundred miles, and further, it was a region that, in addition to being inaccessible by vehicle, was also entirely uninhabited and therefore impossible to resupply. Making the proposition even more daunting, Schaller estimated there would be stretches fifty miles and more between streams, making it necessary to carry water. I penciled out the logistics of such a trek, and, assuming a team brought a minimum of camera and video gear, each person would need about two hundred pounds of supplies—an impossible weight to carry in a backpack.

Then I had an idea. I recalled reading about two Germans who had successfully crossed a section of the eastern Chang Tang pulling carts mounted on bicycle wheels. I also recalled that in the middle of the nineteenth century, Mormons, in a series of caravans, had crossed the American plains to Utah pulling rickshaw-type carts. In Tibet—indeed, all across China—I had seen peasants use rickshaw carts to carry heavy loads of feed to their animals, fertilizer to their gardens, produce to their markets. What if a rickshaw were made of lightweight aluminum with roller-bearing mountain bike wheels and disc brakes? Would it be possible to carry two hundred or more pounds two hundred or more miles?

Schaller thought it might be, but when I asked if he would be interested in joining such an adventure, he seemed amused by the thought. "Oh no," he laughed, "I might be able to do the walk, but not pulling a heavy cart. But someone young and fit like you should be able to do it." I also found his comment amusing: I'm past fifty and have more gray hair than brown.

Still, the idea remained just that until one day while attending a festival for outdoor films in Telluride, Colorado, I had lunch with three mountaineering friends, Conrad Anker, Galen Rowell, and David Breashears. I told them that my interest in adventuring was shifting from climbing to long walks across wild places. They asked if I had any such journeys in mind, and when I described the idea to follow the chiru on foot to their unknown calving grounds, their response was immediate: Let's do it.

Meanwhile, Schaller had come up with an alternative strategy to locate the calving grounds: to approach from the north by caravan, beginning in the great Taklimakan Desert of Central Asia, then crossing the Kunluns with donkeys and camels. He left in early summer 2001, and when he returned he reported mixed success. His caravan, crossing one pass through the Kunlun and coming out through another, had taken forty-five days. Halfway, in foothills on the south side of the high peaks, he and his team had seen herds of a thousand and more female chiru, nearly all pregnant. By then, however, some of his pack animals, with only scant forage, had collapsed from exhaustion. He had to leave before he could witness the birthing, but he was certain he had found the general area of the chiru's calving grounds.

Yet to achieve the larger goal of persuading the Chinese to protect the area in a nature reserve, he needed proof, preferably on film and video, that the area he found was indeed the calving grounds. Further, Schaller said it would be an important contribution to the knowledge of the chiru's natural history—and with it, the international efforts to save these animals from extinction—if the migration route of the chiru could be traced beginning to end.

Conrad, Galen, David, and I resolved to turn our handshake commitment into action. On foot, pulling custom-made rickshaws, we would try to follow the female chiru as they migrated north. Unlike nearly all our previous expeditions, our proposed adventure had the potential to help save these creatures, and with them, the land they inhabit. It was an opportunity to use our skills to give back to the wild earth that had so sustained and nurtured us. Then, as we were developing the carts, researching the logistics, designing the timetable, David had to drop out because of conflicting responsibilities promoting a large format film he had recently produced. Conrad suggested in his stead we invite Jimmy Chin, a young mountaineer who recently had accompanied Conrad on a difficult ascent in the Karakoram. When we asked Jimmy he took about two seconds to say, "Yes!"

क

LOOKING BACK ON THE TRAVEL that in my life I have been fortunate to experience, the best journeys have been those that answered questions that at the outset I never thought to ask. Even though I didn't realize it at the beginning of this expedition, our adventure in the Chang Tang would, for me, engender a meditation on our species' history of driving animals to extinction—in this case to feed a need, common to most of the animals we displace, to strut and display—

as well as our species' unique ability in the animal world to control and even reverse behavior that otherwise may have its roots in those basic biological imperatives. Even while it is understandable to feel despair, in view of what sometimes seem insurmountable challenges facing the long-term survival of what remains of the wild regions of our planet, I would find this expedition would ultimately leave me with a sense of hope and even inspiration. Once I realized how the restoration of the Chang Tang may come as the result of the collective work of a small number of individuals around the world dedicated to controlling the poaching of the chiru, to banning the weaving of the shawls, to enforcing the laws against selling them, and to bearing shame on those who choose to wear them, I then would become guardedly optimistic that not only chiru, but many others of the world's endangered species, do have a chance of surviving through the critical test of this current century, when it is very likely we will see whether or not our species hoists itself by its own petard.

"The unsatisfactory thing about despair," the nature writer David Quammen has observed, "is that besides being fruitless, it's far less exciting than hope."

PART ONE

THE MIGRATION

CHAPTER ONE

क

MAY 25

WITH THE CIRCADIAN CLOCK IN MY BRAIN still set to the other side of the world, I wake in the dark of early morning and enjoy for a moment that sense of suspended weightlessness you get when you don't know where you are, much less how you got there. Before I can locate myself either in time or place, my half-awake mind settles on a sweet smell that is at once familiar yet distant, like incense wafting from the joss sticks of some past life. I know that smell, but from where? I breathe in, and with the perfumed air comes a vague memory of youth, and a sense of setting out fresh into the world. The smell: It's from my first trip to the Himalaya, when I was twenty-six and had joined an expedition to Everest. There was the same smell at base camp, when we used to wake, as I have now, in the predawn. It would still be dark when we entered the great icefall, stopping at the small Buddhist altar outside camp to breathe the smoke so our souls would be cleansed. The Sherpas had told us you have better luck when your soul is clean.

Yes, of course, the smell is incense. It's juniper smoke coming through the open window of the hotel room, wafting over the rooftops from the urnlike ovens positioned on the cardinal corners of the Jokhang. I'm in Lhasa; we arrived yesterday on the long flight from

California to Tokyo to Beijing. I breathe again, my mind clearing as I recall today is *saga dawa*, the full moon in May that celebrates the triple anniversary of the Buddha's birth, death, and enlightenment. I look at my watch: 4:00 am. Even now, I imagine, the pilgrims are gathering to make the sacred *kora* around the most sacred temple in all of Tibet.

"Good morning, Rick."

"Hey, Galen, you're awake too."

"I heard you taking a deep breath."

"Smelling the juniper. Must be from the Jokhang, the pilgrims stoking the incense ovens."

"Oh, that's right, it's saga dawa. There'll be thousands of them this morning doing the kora. That should be some great shooting."

Galen gets up, turns on the nightstand light, and walks to the bathroom. He's naked save for his Speedo-type underwear—what Conrad refers to as "banana hammocks"—and the dim lamp reveals his sinewy muscles under skin textured with that fine wrinkling that comes from age and a lifetime of exposure to wind and sun. His black hair is only beginning to gray where it frames the top of a face that, like his body, is sharp and defined, with dark, close-set eyes that move quickly, revealing his energy. Galen looks mid-fifties but is actually sixty-two, and he is widely regarded as one of the finest adventure photographers in the world; indeed, many credit Galen Rowell with having invented the genre. I've been with him on enough outings—most to his beloved Sierra Nevadas in his home state of California—to know that a significant portion of his success hinges on a relentless work ethic that, in turn, is rooted in an inexhaustible font of enthusiasm. In the field, Galen is invariably the last one to bed and the first one up.

"You want to come along?" he asks as he comes out of the bathroom, water dripping from his face.

"To the Jokhang?"

"It's either that or lying in bed."

I decide that I shouldn't reveal to Galen, especially at the beginning of our adventure, that lying in bed, at the moment anyway, sounds pretty good. Even though I am ten years younger than Galen, I know from experience it is a challenge to keep up with him. Despite our different ages, however, we still consider ourselves from the same generation of mountaineers who came of age in the sixties, and we have in common many friends who, like us, happily accepted poverty in trade for the freedom to climb. Even though many of these friends—some who still affectionately call themselves dirtbags—now have families and successful careers, they still find time to climb. As one of our early comrades put it years ago, "on both ends of the social spectrum there lies a leisure class."

"Okay," I tell Galen. "Time to walk off a few sins."

As I get up and dress, I look out the window and see that in the adjacent room the light also is on.

"Conrad and Jimmy must be awake, too," I say to Galen.

"Great. We can all go to the Jokhang together."

क

NEKHOR, THE TIBETAN WORD FOR PILGRIMAGE, means literally "the circumambulation of a sacred place," and it is a purifying ritual of Buddhists in India, Nepal, and Tibet to circle all sacred places—temples, mani walls, stupas, prayer flag poles—clockwise, or at least to pass them, on foot or in vehicle, on your right. Temples, especially old and venerable ones like the Jokhang, are encircled with pathways for this purpose, and by first light Galen, Jimmy, Conrad, and I follow the endless loop of pilgrims, our feet among the thousands of padding feet so imperceptibly eroding the polished stone pavers. We walk behind two old monks in burgundy robes, both with hands clasped at the smalls of their stooped backs, fingers advancing their prayer beads in harmony with their sotto voce chanting.

When we complete our lap we pause at the large double doors of the main entrance. Dozens of pilgrims prostrate themselves in front of the six columns that support the portico, kneeling, clasping hands over heads, lowering to the ground, and prostrating, rising again to repeat the cycle. A friend told me these prostrations and the chant that accompanies them are actually a form of yoga: As every bone and joint touches the ground you are supposed to think of a specific visualization, attempting perfect harmony of body, speech, and mind. Tibetans believe if you do one such prostration perfectly, you will gain instant enlightenment. Watching these celebrants, I wonder what would happen if one of them did succeed in doing a perfect prostration. What does somebody look like who just gained instant enlightenment?

Galen takes photographs and Jimmy shoots video while Conrad and I, visible in the background, watch the worshipers. When we signed Jimmy Chin on the team to replace David Breashears, I told him he was going to have to shoot the video National Geographic wanted us to produce of our journey. "So I'm supposed to take the place of David Breashears?" he asked, a slight inflection of incredulity at the end of the sentence that had something to do, I suspected, with the fact he had only once used a video camera while David, with several Emmy statues on display in his house, is considered the foremost adventure filmmaker in America. "Don't worry, you'll figure it out," I had told him. On the long flight across the Pacific, while the rest of us had our noses in our compelling novels, Jimmy read "Operating Instructions for the Canon X-1."

Before this trip I had never met Jimmy, but I took an instant liking to him. He is of medium height and build, although his shoulders and back, shaped by years of climbing, are broad and strong. He is second-generation Chinese American. His mother grew up in Harbin, where her father was a progressive doctor trained in Japan who moved the family to Taiwan when the Communists became ascendant following World War II. Jimmy's father was from Wenzou, south of Shanghai, and as his father was a provisional governor under the Nationalist government, they also fled. Jimmy's mother and father met at Vanderbilt College, where their families had sent them to study, and after they married they moved to Minnesota so the kids could be raised in what the parents considered a friendly environment for immigrants. Jimmy's father was nevertheless a disciplinarian, forcing the kids to speak Chinese at home, and refusing to answer their questions in English.

"Like lots of Chinese parents," Jimmy told me, "we were pushed hard academically, with lots of extracurricular activities, martial arts, swimming, violin. I always wanted to go out and play, but I wasn't allowed to do that very often. Now I'm making up for lost time."

Jimmy wears his long black hair in a ponytail that he often tucks inside his jacket or shirt, not from diffidence but rather from modesty. For the same reason, in a group he is often off to the side, watching and listening. He also owns a perpetual smile that seems to reveal an equally perpetual state of amusement. That's not to say he doesn't take things seriously, but rather that he frames them in his optimistic temperament; in the vernacular, he's a glass-half-full type of person. He also has a sense of humor, an important attribute on a journey that doesn't require a palmist to see hardships in the future. Since we have no film crew, and since also we want Jimmy to be in the film, Conrad and I will be taking the camera from him on occasion. In a taped interview I asked Jimmy how he felt about our upcoming adventure. "Well, I'm really excited," he said with a mischievous grin, "to be on such a unique trip where I'll also have a chance to go out with the three old goats—I mean the three veterans." At twenty-eight, Jimmy is young enough to be a son both to Galen and to me.

When Galen and Jimmy have finished shooting, we head back to our hotel, pausing at a vendor to buy prayer flags that in the weeks ahead we will position at our various camps. This is Jimmy's first visit to Tibet, and it's Conrad's first visit to Lhasa. On a previous expedition to the Tibet side of Mount Everest, Conrad had crossed the border from Nepal, but then had traveled directly to the peak. He is considered perhaps the greatest alpine climber in America, and on that expedition to Everest, aided by unusually stable weather that had cleared slopes that in normal years remain covered with snow, Conrad had discovered at twenty-seven thousand feet the astonishingly well-preserved body of George Mallory, the Englishman who had disappeared in a summit attempt in 1924.

Unlike Jimmy, I already knew Conrad Anker, having shared two previous journeys. He has an athlete's build—long, muscled legs, broad shoulders, strong arms, and large hands. His face, like his body, is long and angular, and his strong chin, marine-blue eyes, and light-brown hair that bleaches easily in the sun reveal the German part of his heritage. His father's relatives homesteaded Priest Station, a small settlement near the entrance to Yosemite, in 1853. Conrad's father met his mother, who is from a small town near Dresden, when he was stationed in Germany. As an investment banker, Conrad's father took the family with him when he was posted overseas, and Conrad spent parts of his youth in Hong Kong, Japan, and Germany. He also spent summers at the family homestead, and Conrad started rock climbing in Yosemite Valley when he was sixteen. In high school he was a boarding student at Colorado Mountain School, near Aspen, where kayaking, skiing, and climbing are the extracurricular activities of choice. Now at age thirty-nine, he has spent so many years on big walls and steep alpine climbs that his arms seem to have lengthened, and when he walks they swing in fluid balance with his legs in a kind of swagger that has nothing to do with ostentation and everything to do with owning the body of a champion gymnast.

My first expedition with Conrad was to Queen Maud Land, in Antarctica, where I had filmed him and his best friend, Alex Lowe—who was then regarded as America's foremost alpine climber—on the first-ever ascent in the frozen continent of a big wall. A year later Conrad, Alex, and Dave Bridges were ascending a peak in Tibet when high above them an avalanche broke loose. Conrad ran to the side and was thrown by wind and debris more than fifty feet, while Alex and Dave ran downhill, perhaps trying to reach a crevasse to dive into. Conrad suffered cuts on his head, broken ribs, and a dislocated shoulder, but Alex and Dave were hit by the main force of the avalanche and their bodies were never found. When I saw Conrad two weeks later, he was aged, the ordeal visible in the strained lines on his face and the new intensity in his eyes.

My second journey with Conrad—a hiking and horse-packing trip to Mongolia—was two years later. I was with my youngest son, and Conrad was with Jenny Lowe, Alex's widow, and Jenny's three young sons, all by Alex. The next year, with whispers and innuendos among some people we knew, Conrad and Jenny wed. During our three weeks in Mongolia, Conrad dedicated each day to those boys, playing with them, reading to them, hiking with them, disciplining them with verbal directives when necessary. On a clear day under a crisp blue sky Jenny and I went on a hike, stopping to rest on a hillside overlooking a broad grass valley with our camp—on the bank of a trout river—visible below. She reached down and picked a tiny blue flower.

"An alpine forget-me-not," she said. "Alex used to pick them for me when we went hiking. It was our favorite flower."

In the years I have known her it is one of the few times I've seen her cry. She wiped the tear and said, "Conrad is so good to me and to the boys. I don't know, you lose and then you gain and you count your blessings." She gave me the flower and later I placed it in my journal, a reminder that love may be the only true balm against the pain of the loss of those we love.

क

AT MIDMORNING WE LEAVE OUR HOTEL for the outdoor market near the Jokhang where we will purchase fresh produce. On the way I spot a Tibetan woman—dressed traditionally in a floral-print blouse with a sleeveless black dress to her ankles that is fronted with an apron colored in bright green and pink bands—pulling a wooden rickshaw loaded with baskets of vegetables. Her cart, riding on bicycle wheels and pulled by two wood trace-poles—is not unlike the design of our own rickshaws, and I tell Jimmy, who is carrying our video camera, that it would be fun to give her cart a test drive. Jimmy grins, and when the Tibetan woman passes, he stops and speaks to her in Chinese. With a mixture of confusion and amusement, she trades places with me at the trace-poles, and I pull her cart the rest of the way to the outdoor market as she walks by my side and the passersby in the street stop and giggle.

"It's well-balanced," I tell Jimmy, who is videotaping me, "and easy-pulling, on the pavement anyway. I'm not sure how it would fare across a boulder field in the middle of the Chang Tang, though. As far as that goes, I'm not sure how our own rickshaws are going to fare."

I refer to the worrisomely short amount of time we had to field-test the final version of our carts. Early in our planning, we had scheduled weeks if not months to do this, and we had even discussed the possibility of making a multiday shakedown trip across a Nevada desert. Since the carts were going to be a wholly new design—and for purposes of our trip, if not a completely new concept then at least an innovative one—we had started the design process debating the basic consideration of whether to go with a two-wheel rickshaw or a four-wheel wagon.

Our first prototype, manufactured in South Korea by a company that makes aluminum frames for backpacks, was a four-wheel wagon, and it was so heavy and cumbersome we opted to shift to the two-wheel rickshaw concept. Two months later the next prototype arrived, and Conrad and I tested it behind my house in the coastal foothills of southern California. We loaded the cart with one hundred and fifty pounds of rocks, and we were a hundred yards up a hiking trail when the traces began to bend. To ease stress on the aluminum poles, I pushed the cart while Conrad pulled, but then suddenly both wheels folded, and we had to unload the rocks and carry the cart home.

By then we were three months behind our design schedule. Galen and I tested the next prototype in the hills near his house in Bishop, California, and this time we got about an hour up a trail before the wheels hit a rock while I was pulling, and the cart flipped, driving my head into the dirt so hard my hearing in one ear was impaired for three days. This time, both the wheels and the wheel frames collapsed. Now we had only enough time to return the cart for one more round of revisions before we would have to leave for the expedition, and any thought of an extended shakedown had to be abandoned.

When the final version of the carts arrived, we hired a designer who specialized in custom racing bicycles to modify the wheel frames and traces, fit the carts with disc brakes and install the strongest downhill mountain bike racing wheels he could find. When he had the first cart retrofitted, we loaded it with heavy bags of fertilizer and took turns pulling it through the neighborhood, where twice we were stopped by passersby who thought we were the first on the block with some new kind of fuel-efficient gardening vehicle; one woman wanted to know where she could buy one.

Once all four carts were retrofitted, we took them to Bishop, where we had only enough time, before leaving the next day to Tibet, to pull them for two hours in the hills behind Galen's house. While the carts seemed stronger than the previous models, we were all apprehensive that we had such a short amount of time to test them. We all knew once the truck and SUV that we would hire in Lhasa had taken us literally to the end of the road, and then left us facing one of the largest uninhabited sections of the planet, we would be so utterly on our own that the difference between survival and disaster could be as thin as the aluminum we had selected for our trace-poles, or as simple as whether we had chosen the right tools and spare parts for our repair kit.

क

AFTER PURCHASING VEGETABLES, we continue to a street where a dozen or more double-wheeled trucks, all available for hire, are parked cheek by jowl, their drivers standing in front of their vehicles smoking cigarettes and gesturing—like barkers in a red-light district—for us to consider their trucks. Accompanying us are the Tibetans we have hired to help us organize the first stage of our expedition, the difficult drive to the northwest Chang Tang that will be partly on rough dirt roads and partly across hardpan where at best we may encounter faint tracks of the infrequent vehicles that have traveled that region before us. Our plan is to take one Toyota Land Cruiser for us, and one of these Dong Fengs (the most prominent manufacturer of trucks in China) for our food and equipment, the six boxes that contain our rickshaws, and the six large drums filled with gas and diesel we must carry; once we enter the Chang Tang there will be no fuel for a thousand miles.

This is the same configuration of vehicles I used in 1999 on my previous journey to the Chang Tang, and I have cautioned Galen, Jimmy, and Conrad we need to take care selecting the truck: On that last trip we spent days coaxing the truck through mud and snow against which its asthmatic engine had been no match. In a previous life—back in his twenties when he was a dirtbag climber—Galen was also an auto mechanic. He used to build hot rods, and even now he gets a kind of crazed look when he gets behind the wheel. We are counting on him to make a discerning appraisal of any trucks we consider.

Galen reports the first Dong Feng we examine has a miss in the engine; the second, large hunks of rubber missing from its tires; the third, leaf springs held together with baling wire. I am despairing when we all spot at the same time an orange Dong Feng. All the other trucks are green or blue, and this one looks new; we guess (correctly, as it turns out) that the color of the newest Dong Fengs has changed, as it seems to do every ten or so years.

"If only we could get a truck like that," I sigh to one of our Tibetans.

"Maybe we can," he replies.

"You mean that one is for rent?"

"I think so."

"Then how come we've been looking at these others?"

"I don't know."

The driver, who is also the owner, confirms that it is for rent, and that yes, he would be willing to drive to the Chang Tang, and do it for a sum within our budget. We ask him to pop the hood, and Galen and I both whistle when we look in: There isn't even a hint of grease or dirt.

"You have no idea how lucky we just got," I tell my companions.

"That's because it's saga dawa," Conrad says. "An auspicious time to start our journey."

May 27

WE SPEND AN ADDITIONAL DAY purchasing supplies, then the following morning the truck, the driver, and driver's assistant arrive at our hotel only an hour late, also an auspicious sign. As we load our gear, including the large cardboard boxes containing our rickshaws,

I comment that it looks like a major expedition "when basically it's just a long walk."

"But that makes it true to the word 'expedition,'" Conrad replies, "meaning 'to leave on foot.'" He smiles and then adds, "As opposed to the more modern meaning of Expedition, as in Ford, which means 'to push down with foot.'"

Conrad tilts his head and flicks his hand in an imitation of that Indian gesture that seems to be the Hindu recognition of the point where absurd irony intersects predestined fate; and it's a gesture Conrad will use many times in the weeks ahead. Norgay, a young Tibetan we have hired as cook, helps Conrad load the last baskets of fresh vegetables purchased the day before, then with his endearing smile the Tibetan climbs in the truck's cab between the driver and the driver's assistant. The doors close, the engine starts on the first crank, and the truck departs with the clattering roar of a well-lubed diesel. We have a second driver for the Land Cruiser, and when the four of us have our cameras and daypacks in the back of that vehicle, we also depart, driving down the main thoroughfare past the new department stores with gleaming gold pillars and bright windows with mannequins dressed in the latest fashions, passing the shining blue-glass windows of the twenty-story headquarters of China Telecom.

Other than the Potala and a few other temples such as the Jokhang, Lhasa has so thoroughly modernized that any visitor who hasn't seen it for twenty years would likely fail to recognize it. Watching the passersby on the downtown streets, I am guessing most of the younger Tibetans, some of whom are talking on their cell phones, welcome the transformation, but I wonder about the older people. Many of them are still dressed traditionally, and I know from previous visits this is out of pride as much as necessity. I wonder if many of them reflect nostalgically about the way their city used to look.

When I was young I witnessed the transformation of the land in southern California where I was raised, and that change in the landscape of my youth was the single biggest influence catalyzing what became a lifelong passion for wild places. In grade school I lived on a one-acre plot surrounded by hundreds of acres of orange groves. I trapped gophers for the manager of one grove, earning one dollar a tail, and I hunted quail with my .22 single-shot in the Santa Ana riverbed. By the time I finished high school the river was contained in a concrete-lined channel, and the groves—every one of them—were replaced with tract houses. Even more than the houses themselves, I hated the hypocritical names the developers gave to their gridwork streets: Cottonwood Lane, Sycamore Court, Quail Road. Watching bulldozers rip out one grove of favored trees, I even considered sneaking in at night and filling the machine's gas tank with sugar. Instead, I started ditching school and driving my Honda 90 motorcycle to roadheads in the San Gabriel Mountains above the Los Angeles basin, where my first hikes to the tops of local peaks seeded what became a lifelong devotion to mountaineering, and at the midpoint of my years, a commitment to the preservation of the wildlands that in my youth offered me solace.

क

WE LEAVE LHASA and drive on the paved road to Shigatse, Tibet's second largest city, then continue on a gravel road until at sunset we stop for the night in a roadside inn where we share the dining hall with a group of German trekkers bound for the kora around Mount Kailas, the *axis mundi* for both Hindu and Buddhist pilgrims. Next morning they depart in a caravan of Land Cruisers, and although we don't realize it at the time, they are the last tourists—the last Westerners—we will see. We follow the same road out of town, passing the last villages with the last cultivated fields and then a row of poplars that are the last trees we will see for over a month. Soon we turn off the main track and head northwest on a less traveled route along the base of hills where, I tell the others, I saw on my previous visit a herd of thirty female blue sheep. Galen is excited and scans the hillsides, but today we see only two Tibetan gazelles, endearingly small animals that are common here but will become scarce as we continue north, toward the limit of their range. We climb a pass from where we can see ahead a wide lake whose turquoise hue suggests it is, like the majority of lakes in west Tibet, saline. As the folded hills continue to open there is a sense of entering a great, empty space.

"His holiness once told me that Tibetans are shaped as much by their landscape as by their religion," Galen says, referring to the time he spent with the Dalai Lama when they collaborated on a book called My Tibet: the Dalai Lama writing the text and Galen contributing the photographs. "He said that when you live in a place with few people and wide open spaces your vision gets mysterious and inconclusive."

"You agree with that?" I ask.

"Yes, and I think it's supported by science. When you live in a city, most of what you see you can be sure of because you have a richness of visual cues. There may be a dozen different things telling you something is ten feet or a hundred feet away, or that what you see is your wife walking toward you and not some other woman. But when you live in a landscape where visual cues are scarce, you become less certain about distance or color or form, and the landscape—everything around you—takes on an aura of the mysterious and also the auspicious."

As the floor of the plateau continues to rise, the surrounding hills continue to diminish, like archipelagos sinking below a rising sea. The sky widens until it becomes a dome so vast it seems to push down the encircling horizon. At last we are here, the great Chang Tang Plateau, the Big Open.[i]

क

IT WILL TAKE TWO DAYS to transit the southern half of the Chang Tang—the half that is occupied by the drokpa, the nomads of Tibet—and on this first day the gravel road climbs toward a pass over 18,000 feet in elevation. When we stop I can feel the thin air even when my only exertion is to walk a few feet to pee. It surprises some people when I tell them I am slow or average at best acclimatizing to high altitude; they assume, because I was an active Himalayan mountaineer in my twenties and thirties, that I must have unusually large lungs. My most significant ascent was in my late twenties when I reached the top of K2 on what then, in 1978, was only the third expedition ever to climb what is now regarded as the world's most difficult high-altitude peak. We also were the first to climb it without supplemental oxygen, but I managed that only because we spent nearly two months above 18,000 feet, and consequently I was superacclimatized. I know on this expedition I will be stronger once I am more used to the thin air, but at the moment I can't help recalling that day only a little over a week ago when we tested the rickshaws in the hills above Galen's house, and how hard it was to pull the carts, loaded with two hundred pounds, up even a gently sloping hill.

Just beyond the pass we see to our surprise a group of five male chiru, tawny in their summer pelage. (In fall, as they approach the winter rut, their fur lightens, their underbellies turn white, and they develop handsome black markings on their faces and the fronts of their legs.) It is uncommon to see chiru this far south, and as we stop so Galen and Jimmy can photograph and videotape them, they continue to graze with an indifference that is even more uncommon. On my previous visit every chiru we saw—males, females, and yearlings—ran away at full gallop as soon as they detected our vehicle. I tell the others that the confident ease of these five must mean the efforts of wildlife patrols to contain poaching has had some success, at least here in the more easily accessed southern margin of their range.

"And maybe those leaflets George passed out had some effect, too," Galen adds.

He is referring to a postcard-size handout that George Schaller distributed to nomads and suspected poachers he encountered during his wildlife surveys in the 1990s, when he crossed and recrossed the Chang Tang. One side of the card depicted Milarepa, the revered twelfth-century Tibetan poet and saint; the other side featured a quote, in Tibetan script, from the Buddha:

> All beings tremble at punishment,
> To all life is dear.
> Comparing others to oneself,
> One should neither kill nor cause to kill.

The cards were only one component of Schaller's efforts to save the chiru. After his initial visits, when he realized the "Chang Tang offers a last opportunity to study a high, cold steppe with its fauna still intact," he also realized that without a concurrent effort to conserve the wildlife against threats from poachers, and to promote policies that would allow wild animals to coexist with domestic flocks, then the Chang Tang "will ultimately be a desert where only howling winds break a deadly silence."[ii]

The Chang Tang was not the first place Schaller demonstrated his twin interests in science and conservation. This dual strategy has characterized his work most of his career.

"That's just what he was doing when I first met him in the Karakoram, in 1975," Galen says. At that time Galen was part of a team on its way to attempt K2, and Schaller was nearing the end of a survey of the megafauna of the Karakoram Mountains. Even then Schaller had a dual goal: adding information to his growing database of the natural history of the large mammals of the Himalaya, and at the same time assessing for the Pakistan government the region's suitability as a national park. Galen tells us what he remembers most about Schaller was how fit he appeared, and how focused he seemed on his work.

"Did you know he used to climb?" Galen asks.

"When I first met him he said he used to do some mountaineering," I reply. "But now with the demands of his work, he sticks just with the walking he does following animals. But I had the impression that's quite a bit of walking."

Galen tells us that when Schaller was a student in the early fifties at the University of Alaska, he had met an Austrian (Schaller himself was German, born in Berlin in 1933) about to leave for a climbing trip that Schaller volunteered to join. Heinrich Harrer—famous for his first ascent of the north face of the Eiger, and later for his adventures described in *Seven Years in Tibet*—and Schaller then made the first ascent of Mount Drum, a major peak in the Wrangell Mountains.

Galen shares another anecdote told to him by Terry Moore, an active climber in the 1930s and later, in the 1950s, president of the University of Alaska at the time Schaller was a student.[iii] "Terry said he had heard there was a young German biology student camped illegally on campus, so he went to investigate, and as he was approaching this tent he saw an arm come out the door and a raven land on it. So, you see, George has had a way with animals from the beginning."

Moore then invited Schaller to dinner, and later introduced him to a visiting scholar from Tibet. As a boy Schaller had read Sven Hedin's account of crossing the Chang Tang and remembered descriptions of vast herds of antelope, gazelles, and wild yak. Schaller told the Tibetan scholar he dreamed of visiting the Chang Tang himself, but it was an ambition that would have to wait nearly thirty years until the political climate thawed.

In the interim Schaller established his credentials as the most eminent field biologist studying large mammals in the world, as well as one of the best writers on the subject: gorillas in the African highland jungles (The Year of the Gorilla, 1964); tigers in India (The Deer and the Tiger, 1967); lions in Tanzania (The Serengeti Lion, 1972, a National Book Award winner); goats, sheep, and snow leopards in the Himalaya (Stones of Silence, 1980); giant pandas in China (The Last Panda, 1993).

Four years before our current expedition, when I was considering whether to make my own first trip to the Chang Tang, I had ordered a copy of Schaller's Tibet's Hidden Wilderness, and I had to read no further than the preface for my ambition to gel. "The Chang Tang," Schaller wrote, "is a wild and bleak land where humankind has barely intruded, and animals live as if becalmed in time and space."

As I planned that initial trip, I called Schaller and he invited me to meet him in his office in the Bronx Zoo. I took the subway out of New York in the early morning, and following his directions entered the zoo by the rear gate, where the guard had my name. I was excited to meet him, and pleasantly surprised he had offered to share some of his time, although I anticipated the visit would be short: I had the impression Schaller was a man who was direct and did not waste time on social niceties. My first knowledge of him had been years before when I read The Snow Leopard, Peter Matthiessen's account of his trek with Schaller into the Dolpo region of Nepal, where Schaller was studying blue sheep; Matthiessen had written that Schaller was "a stern pragmatist...single minded, not easy to know." Schaller himself, on a day in the Chang Tang when he was walking alone across the barren plain searching for migrating chiru, wrote that "I am most comfortable at the edge of existence in a remote place such as this; perhaps it suits my temperament, reflecting an inner landscape, a certain taciturn spirit, or perhaps it indicates a quest for something clear-cut and explicit."

It was a foggy morning before the zoo opened to the public, and the grounds were empty. I soon encountered the "Mountains of Asia" habitat, where a section of the Himalaya had been re-created. I paused to look through a glass window in the viewing area, where I saw a Temminck's tragopan pheasant scratching the dirt under a rhododendron. Then to the side my eye caught something moving, and turning I found myself looking into the smoke-blue gemlike eyes of a snow leopard.

I took that as a propitious prologue to my meeting. Schaller's secretary escorted me to a small work area, where I found a lean and fit-looking man who looked to be in his late fifties. When I expressed my gratitude for his time, he replied he was happy to help, then waved away my offer to make our meeting short. At first glance he didn't seem "single-minded" or "taciturn." I followed him to another room with a large table where we spread open the well-creased maps that had accompanied him on his several excursions to the Chang Tang. Schaller seemed in no hurry as we reviewed different routes I might take on my journey, except when he received a phone call and bounded away as sprightly as a gazelle. He returned in a few minutes and apologized, saying it was a call from China, where he planned to travel in two weeks to an area just east of the great gorge of the Tsangpo, one of the most significant geographical unknowns left on earth.

"There are several animals there I am interested in, including some monkeys that I believe have been misidentified. It's also the only place left in Tibet you can still find tigers."

Speaking with a residual German accent, he told me that the Aru was one of his favorite places in all of Tibet, and so my interest narrowed to that region, especially since it would give me the best chance of seeing chiru and wild yak. Schaller was also hopeful that in going there I could keep notes on what wildlife I saw, information he could compare with his earlier observations. After we had talked for nearly three hours, I said I had to leave to catch a flight, and he offered to drive me to the airport, a half hour away.

As we approached the terminal I thanked him for his hospitality and wished him good luck on his upcoming expedition; he wished me good luck on mine.

"You and I are very fortunate," he said, "because we get to spend time in the field. Of course I am a scientist first, and I can't go on climbs and long walks as much as I would like, as you can. But that's okay, isn't it."

"You look like you're still in great shape," I said. "How old are you?"

"I'm sixty-six," he answered with a smile. "I guess I'm doing okay, as long as I keep moving."

"I guess you are," I said.

We shook hands, and I stepped out of the car.

"That's the thing, isn't it?" he said as I was about to close the door. "You have to keep moving. Otherwise, you rust."

क

PULLING TWO-HUNDRED-AND-FIFTY-POUND rickshaws across nearly three hundred miles of uninhabited terrain promised a good antidote against rust, but we still have three, perhaps four more days of driving before we stop riding in our engine-powered vehicles and start pulling our muscle-powered carts. We continue from late afternoon into early evening toward Tzochen—one of a handful of towns that have developed along the remote gravel roads that frame the southern and central Chang Tang—but when we realize we won't make it before midnight, and that already it is too late to set up camp, we stop at the next mud hut we pass.

"The drokpa Hilton," I say as we pull up.

The shards of broken beer bottles that litter the ground around the hut sparkle in our headlights that a moment later illuminate two drokpa men, one perhaps in his twenties and the other in his forties, who step out of the hut to greet us. Even from a two car–length distance we can see they are drunk. Our vehicle stops, we get out and walk toward them, and when I shake hands with the first one I am hit with breath that is a volatile mix of expelled air and *bai jiu*, the potent distilled liquor favored across China. They invite us in their small room, and through the doorway the air inside, laden with the sweet smell of sour sweat, is so heavy I feel as though I have to press into it to make headway. There is a small stove in the center of the room, and one of the drokpa breaks a large cake of dried yak dung, opens the stove's door, and tosses it in. Conrad offers him a piece of hard candy, and with remnants of yak dung still on his hands that otherwise are dark with grease and dirt, he unwraps the candy and slowly places it in his mouth.

"I see what you mean," Jimmy says. "These guys are salty."

Galen then offers the other drokpa a banana from our stores purchased in Lhasa. The nomad holds it in his hand and stares perplexedly at it. Then, with a drunken grin, he looks from the banana to Galen.

"You eat it," Galen says as he motions how to peel the banana.

Galen then takes the banana, peels it, bites off the end and hands it back to the drokpa. The nomad then mashes the end of it in his mouth, frowns and hands it back to Galen.

"Anybody want a banana?" Galen asks.

MAY 29

IN THE MORNING I WAKE AT FIRST LIGHT, and my first thought is to breathe as shallowly as possible, because last night I was slow in staking out my sleeping platform here in the guest room of the drokpa Hilton, and I ended up farthest from the door, where the air is heaviest with the ammonia smell of our hosts' sour socks. I make as much noise as I can getting up, to wake the others as soon as possible, so we can make coffee as quickly as possible, and then get out of this place.

Soon we are in our vehicles, continuing on dirt roads tending north and west. Occasionally we pass a drokpa boy or girl herding the family sheep and goats, and every half hour or so we pass going the opposite direction another truck presumably en route to Lhasa or Shigatse. Other than that, there is only open steppe interrupted by occasional snow peaks. As remote as this feels, I know from my previous visit, however, that compared with where we are going, this corner of the Chang Tang is a wellhead of civilization.

Galen continues to sit in the front seat, as that allows him greater ability to exit quickly when he sees an interesting photograph, or to shoot from the window, steadying his long lens on a small sandbag he carries for that purpose. The sandbag, as well as other items of camera equipment Galen has with him—including the set of split-density filters and the camera bag itself—are things he has had manufactured to his specifications; some of them he markets through his photography company, Mountain Light. Located in an old bank building in Bishop, the company has on the first floor a gallery—handsomely designed by Galen's wife, Barbara—that sells his prints, and on the second floor offices for a staff that organizes his seminars and workshops, and helps distribute the seventeen books he has written on photography, travel, and adventure. Galen shows no sign of letting up this prodigious output. In fact, from my view, anyway, it seems the older he gets the harder he works.

When we divided the expedition's duties, and I asked Jimmy to shoot video, Galen volunteered, in addition to taking photographs, to share navigational tasks with Conrad, in particular to be in charge of acquiring positions from our handheld GPS. This is something Galen so far has been doing with an enthusiasm that reflects his fondness for electronic gadgets. It's an enthusiasm that also seems consistent with the professorial component of Galen's personality. He is a font of facts and figures seemingly about everything we see or talk about. Fitting the mold, he also is absentminded: He has somehow misplaced the field manual that accompanied the GPS, and today he discovered that the cable that allows him to recharge the battery for the satellite phone he has brought has somehow disappeared from the front seat. Guessing it fell out the door when we stopped to get a GPS reading, we backtracked and indeed found it lying in the middle of nowhere. The bad news was we apparently drove over it when we left, and it was crushed.

Bad news, that is, for Galen. It means use of the satellite phone will be limited to the three batteries we have with us that are still charged, a development that doesn't bother me in the least. I was reluctant to bring the phone in the first place, believing it would link us to the outside world in a way that would diminish the feeling of wildness out in the Chang Tang. Galen thought I was being senti-mental, and further, he argued, when it came time at the end of our trek to rendezvous on a preselected date with the vehicle that was to pick us up at a prearranged set of coordinates on the south margin of the huge Taklimakan desert (Taklimakan: Turkic for "you will enter and not come out") the phone could very well make the difference of whether or not we did indeed manage to "come out."

So we have with us the latest Motorola iridium satellite phone that, I admit, does relieve the pressure of adhering precisely to our itinerary: If we get behind we can phone the adventure travel agent in Kashgar who we have arranged to pick us up. But I also know that where we are going, the sat phone will be of little use if we get into serious trou-ble: Because there is no way anyone could come to our rescue, all we could do is phone home our last thoughts.

While figuring out how to get picked up at the end of the trek was a challenge, perhaps the hardest part was estimating the best date to begin it. When Schaller had tried to locate the calving grounds the previous year (by approaching from the north), he had arrived at what he suspected was the birthing site at about the same time as the first wave of migrating female chiru. He knew they might loiter in the area for two weeks before calving began, and, with his pack animals starving from lack of forage, he couldn't wait that long. I knew that if we arrived early we wouldn't be able to wait, either. Schaller had told us, however, that the female chiru travel in small groups that form a broken caravan that, from the first animals to the last, extends in a line that takes over two weeks to pass any given point on the migration route. The solution was to begin our trek following the last animals in the migration so they would lead us to the calving grounds, where we hoped to find the first animals that had already been there one or two weeks just beginning to calve. Timing had to be within a few days. If we were one week too late, there wouldn't be any animals to follow, and if we were one week too early we wouldn't have sufficient food to wait at the calving grounds for the birthing to begin.

Over the years he had spent in the Chang Tang studying chiru, Schaller had learned that the females of the western population—the one we were intending to follow—begin their migration in May when dozens of groups from across their winter range all head toward a glacial mountain that rises singularly above the steppeland, like a great beacon. Just south of this peak, Toze Kangri, the paths of these various groups converge into a single migration route that Schaller had assured us would be as easy to follow as hiking along a well-worn trail. He estimated the last of the migration would be passing Toze Kangri around the first week in June. Our plan is to arrive in our vehicles at Toze Kangri on June 1.

We are therefore on a fixed schedule, but I try to avoid letting that preoccupy me because I don't want it to distract from my enjoyment watching the landscape unfold. We pass a mountain with long glistening glaciers that our map indicates is 20,580 feet high. It is similar in shape and features to Mount Rainier—the peak that in the American Northwest is an icon—but here in the Chang Tang this is a mountain with no name. White clouds, in small cotton puffs, float across the sky with an even spacing that creates a pattern that extends to the horizon and, like clothing draped over a ghost, gives the sky form so that it appears to be a great dome enclosing the steppe. In the foreground a solitary nomad girl, wrapped in black homespun, shepherds her flock of goats and sheep. We wave, and she stops to watch us pass, but does not wave back, flummoxed perhaps by this apparition of strange visitors.

May 30

WE ARE FOLLOWING A ROUTE I have penciled on our TPC—"Tactical Piloting Chart"—that in turn I had traced off Schaller's maps when I visited him in the Bronx Zoo. Schaller's route is ten years old, but so far it has coincided with tracks of vehicles presumably belonging to nomads. Since Schaller's last visit many nomads have been able to purchase trucks with money earned illegally from selling chiru wool.

Soon we reach a point where the pencil line leads up a shallow drainage, and stopping to study the ground we can find no sign of tracks of any vehicle preceding us. With some reluctance we enter the canyon, and in less than an hour our new orange Dong Feng is mired in mud.

It is not possible to travel to the remote corners of the Chang Tang without digging vehicles out of mud. At 16,000 feet it is hard work, and we take turns with the three shovels we have brought. It takes an hour to free the truck, but then in another hundred yards its dual rear tires sink into another wallow, and again we start digging. I am reminded of my previous trip when, approaching the Aru Basin from the west, we dug for nearly a week to get our truck over a high pass. But, in an attempt to avoid fretting about falling behind schedule, I remind myself that this time we are approaching the Aru from the southeast, supposedly an easier route. I also remember Moliere's admonition that "men spend their lives worrying about things that never happen."

While the rest of us finish digging, Conrad walks ahead to scout a track between mud holes. When the truck is freed we continue, and scanning the rounded hills I can't see Conrad, but there is a dot that could be him, or it could be a rock: I realize I have no idea if this object is two feet high or six feet high. Then the object waves an arm and we head toward it, reminded of Galen's observation that in open landscapes you have few visual clues that allow you to distinguish small rocks from big people.

The shallow drainage we have followed ascends to a tableland dimpled with rounded hills. There are no tracks of vehicles, and we drive over the hardpan at thirty miles per hour. I know that somewhere nearby there has to be an established track into the Aru Basin, and clearly we are off that route; but as long as the surface remains firm we are making good time, and we are doing it with a free abandon that is fun.

We have now crossed the unmarked boundary that circumscribes the Chang Tang Nature Reserve. When Schaller first submitted a memorandum to the Chinese in the 1980s requesting permission to visit the Chang Tang, he also cited the need to protect a region that he told them was the last remaining alpine steppeland in the world still to have its native fauna intact. By 1990 the Chinese had agreed in principle to Schaller's proposal to create a reserve, but initially it was for a smaller area. Schaller then urged them to extend the border west to encompass the Aru Basin, explaining that it was one of the most vital strongholds of wildlife in the Chang Tang.[iv] Finally in 1993 Schaller received word that the legislation had been approved, and that the new reserve would include the Aru. The officially published size of the Chang Tang Nature Reserve is 109,000 square miles, but Schaller believes the area has never been measured accurately, and that the actual size is closer to 130,000 square miles. Either way, at roughly the same size as the combined country of Germany, it is second in the world in area only to a reserve in Greenland, and that is mostly icecap.

Through the day we pass small groups of gazelles and, occasionally, male chiru. Despite the fact we have entered the reserve, all wild animals are flighty and run at the sound of our approaching vehicles, suggesting they are still threatened by poachers. Creating a reserve is one thing, but policing such a vast area is another. The Chinese, by their own admission—and despite a concerted effort in the east part of the reserve—assume they are intercepting only a fraction of the poaching that continues to decimate the remaining herds of chiru.

We learn quickly, even at great distance, to distinguish chiru from gazelles. Gazelles are smaller and, in profile, almost rabbitlike. Chiru are taller and carry themselves erect in a manner that is distinct even when they are too distant for the male's horns to be seen. The chiru sometimes dip their heads as they run, in a manner reminiscent of the stotting behavior of some African antelope. Even though they have features and behavior similar to antelope, DNA analysis has confirmed chiru are genetically allied to sheep and goats. Schaller feels the chiru's similarity to antelope is related in smaller part perhaps to a common ancestor dating to the Miocene, some eight million years ago, and in larger part to the results of convergent evolution: During its long passage on the high alpine steppe, chiru have adopted antelope-like behavior and appearance. Chiru are the only representative of their genus, and Schaller feels the species is so distinct "that its loss would be far greater than just of a species with a number of close and similar relatives."[v]

In the next basin we see in the distance three black dots that, as we approach, form into the yak-hair tents of the drokpa. The dwellings, each tethered with a dozen guy-lines made of yak-hair rope, look like giant sea urchins that have attached to the floor of the steppe. Large flocks of goats and sheep graze the hillsides, and as the domestic animals have appeared, the wild animals have disappeared.

In midafternoon we drive into a broad basin with no sign of nomads, and soon in every direction there are herds of kiang, chiru, and gazelles, far more than in any place we have seen so far.

"This is what the early explorers saw!" Galen exclaims. "Sven Hedin, Rawling, Deasy, all of them, this is just what it was like."

In his many visits to Tibet, Galen has never ventured to the heart of the Chang Tang, and this is his first view of such a large swath of wild Tibet. His eyes dart from one herd to another. He calls the driver to stop and turn the engine off, and then he leaps from the vehicle, slaps his sandbag on the hood, positions his camera, and fires. He hops back inside the Toyota, and we race ahead, leaving our truck behind until all we see of it is a distant contrail of dust.

A single kiang runs alongside our Land Cruiser, and we pace it at thirty-eight miles per hour. Five chiru appear on our flank and cross in front of us, running like the wind. Then we are surrounded by kiang, most galloping parallel to our vehicle's path; making a careful count in front, to the side, behind, around to the other side, I tally two hundred forty-eight animals. We stop again and leap out. The driver turns off the engine, and as its artificial clatter is absorbed into the big open, we hear in its place the immutable drumbeat of the steppe: the pounding of hundreds of hooves.

क

AN HOUR LATER WE TRAVERSE ANOTHER BASIN occupied by drokpa, and again the domestic stocks displace the wild herds. Galen, still in the front seat, is turned as he shares with Jimmy tips he has learned from his long career as a photographer.

"The best way to shoot a rising full moon," Galen explains to Jimmy, "is to get the shot the day before the moon is actually full, when it's rising almost an hour earlier. That way it still looks full, but you have a lot more daylight for exposing the landscape."

"Wow, I never thought of that," Jimmy says.

Jimmy is also a talented photographer, and he is appreciative he is making this journey with Galen. Jimmy's interest in photography started when he made an ascent of El Capitan, in Yosemite, with a friend who was photographing the climb for an outdoor equipment company. Jimmy, who had never taken photographs, borrowed the camera and took one shot: It turned out to be the only one the company published.

A few months later he was planning his first overseas climbing adventure to Pakistan's Karakoram Mountains, and although he had no idea how to organize such an outing, he did know of one famous climber/photographer who had visited the region, and who presumably knew a great deal about expedition planning.

"Basically I showed up at Galen's office unannounced," Jimmy told me. "Galen had just returned from a long trip, and his staff told me he was slammed, but they encouraged me to wait because they said Galen loved to talk about climbing. That was on a Monday. By Tuesday afternoon he was still too busy, and I continued to wait in the lobby at his gallery. I waited Wednesday, then Thursday. About 4:00 p.m. on Friday, Galen came down the stairs and said, 'Okay, you've got my undivided attention for one hour, then I have to sign prints for another hour, but we can still talk while I do that.'"

Galen showed Jimmy his slides from one of his own expeditions to the Karakoram, and suggested a rock spire that Jimmy and his friends could attempt. Later, while Galen signed prints, he asked

Jimmy if he was a photographer, and Jimmy told him about the shot the outdoor equipment company was going to publish.

"They're paying me five hundred bucks," Jimmy told Galen, "so I thought I'd use it to buy a camera. Maybe you could suggest one I should get?"

Jimmy departed for the Karakoram, established a new route on the rock tower, photographed the climb, and was invited to present a slide show of the expedition at the annual meeting of the American Alpine Club. Galen and Barbara were sitting in the front row. When Jimmy finished, they came up and shook his hand.

"Those were beautiful photographs," Barbara said.

"They sure were," Galen agreed, patting Jimmy on the back. "You've got a good eye."

Even though on this expedition Jimmy has to apply that eye to the viewfinder of our video camera, he nevertheless has brought with him his still camera, but he also has told Galen, in his inimitably disarming way, that his focus will "definitely be shooting the video," a comment meant to include, on its flip side, the message that the protégé has no intention of intruding on the mentor's turf. Galen, who has a reputation of being protective of that turf, seems in turn appreciative of Jimmy's unprompted sensitivity as to how we have divided our media responsibilities.

By late afternoon we ascend a gradual slope toward a pass that we see on our map forms the southern margin of the Aru Basin. As we gain altitude there is, for the first time on our journey, snow on the ground. With two hours of daylight remaining, we crest the pass, stop our vehicle, and open the doors to get out and look into the basin. The cold air is a shock, like it is when you fly from a warm climate to a very cold one, and step out of the plane.

The prospect before us also feels different. To the left, shrouded in clouds suspended above the broad valley, are the Aru Mountains. The basin itself is white, other than the great lake that, reflecting gray clouds, is steel blue. As we gaze at this awesome expanse we remain silent, and I think I know why. We are now looking into a basin that appears arcticlike—as though we have been spirited suddenly to a cold frontier where human beings have dwelt only recently—and our reaction is complex. We are each of us feeling that involuntary forewarning you develop when you spend much of your life outdoors in places where the line that separates survival from oblivion is thin. At the same time, it is life spent walking that line that makes each of us feel most alive. We are silent because we are at that threshold, feeling that mix of caution and excitement before you cross into true wildness.

"Wow," Conrad says, breaking our silence. "Things have changed, really fast."

क

WHEN SCHALLER ENTERED THE ARU IN 1988 he was the first Westerner to see the place since the British explorer Captain C. G. Rawling transited the basin in 1903. "I breathed deeply," Schaller wrote of that visit. "Here was a place that spoke to the soul, a hidden sanctuary in the depth of the Chang Tang." On his second visit, two years later, Schaller often parked his vehicle and wandered on foot to a favorite place near the south end of Memar Co—one of two large lakes in the basin—where he sat on the concentric benches formed by ancient shorelines and watched wild animals. He noticed that nearly all the chiru were males. He described observing one group whose bodies were distorted through heat waves but whose horns were skylined above the steppe so that "the animals looked like one great spiny creature submerged just below the surface of the sea. Why did they stand there as if they worshiped light? I had noticed that the basin held almost exclusively males. Where were the females?"

It was a riddle that he started to solve on a later walk across the plains beyond the north end of Memar Co, when he saw in the distance what he described as a strange, tan, almost pinkish mass. "As my mind groped for a memory," he wrote, "it conjured a mirage of flamingoes on a lake in the Chilean Andes. But these were chiru, about two thousand of them, all females and young. The females had vanished from the region, probably to the north, to give birth, and now they were back. Over half the females had a young at heel."

Two days later, as the season closed, he had to leave the Aru, but now he was intrigued even more by the chiru, an animal he remembered from his childhood when he first read descriptions of the Chang Tang written by the early explorers. "Visions of chiru had floated in my mind for years," he wrote. But his observations of the chiru in Aru Basin had raised as many questions as they had answered. What was the migration route the females had followed? Where were their calving grounds? How many migratory populations were there in the Chang Tang? Learning more about the chiru became, in Schaller's words, "a distinct goal."

"Unhampered migrations are vanishing from this earth as humankind fences and plows the land and kills the animals," Schaller wrote at the end of his description of this early journey. "The chiru had long ago adapted to this realm, needing a certain space to roam and special places to give birth and spend the winter. My goal now was to make certain that they could retain their pact with solitude."

As we descend into the Aru, solitude is certainly the dominant overtone of the basin: There is no sign of any humans, and whatever vehicle tracks there may be have been covered with fresh snow. We camp at the base of a rock pinnacle some two hundred feet high that rises like a megalith out of the basin floor. When the tents are up and dinner started, the rest of us are content to rest in camp, but Galen spots near the top of the pinnacle the guano muting of a bird of prey, and he climbs the spire to investigate.

"There's a nest up here with three chicks," he calls down excitedly.

I climb up to have a look.

"It's a lammergeyer," Galen says when I arrive.

He is referring to a large vulture that occurs across Europe, Asia, and parts of Africa, sometimes called the bearded vulture after a distinctive feather tuft on its chin, and sometimes the lambs' vulture after its reputation for carrying away baby lambs ("lammer"—lamb and "geyer"—vulture).

"The mother flew off when I arrived, but the nest is right down there," Galen explains, pointing to a ledge about twenty feet down a near-vertical face of the pinnacle.

I start down, careful to move only one hand or foot at a time—that way maintaining three points of contact—and very aware I am wearing no rope. In rock climbing we call this "third-classing," easy when you are within the boundaries of your skill and climbing frequently so you are used to the height (what climbers call exposure), but requiring care when, like me, you've haven't been on rock in months. I lock my fingers around a secure hold, crane to see around a knob of rock, and there they are: three downy chicks staring at me. They look to be only days old. The nest is lined with wool, perhaps from a lamb or perhaps from a chiru carcass, and also bits of red rag, presumably from some fabric discarded by drokpa, a reminder of the seasonal nomads who venture here to take advantage of the summer pasture.

"They're too young to thermo-regulate," Galen calls down, "so we should let the mother come back pretty soon."

I climb back to Galen's position, and before we descend the more moderate south side of the pinnacle I pause to look across the basin—the lake, the rangelands now covered in snow, the mountains—and consider how birds of prey in the main site their nests in stunning positions: The noted falconer Dan O'Brien has written that the view from any peregrine's nest would make a salable postcard.

"I think I'll get back to camp," I say to Galen as I fold my hands around my arms covered only with long underwear. "I'm too old to thermo-regulate."

"I'm going to stay here a while longer, in case there's more good light," Galen replies. "Isn't this view incredible?"

"Yes it is," I tell him, leaving out that the steaming milk tea I know Norgay is preparing in camp might be even more impressive. As I climb down I consider how, in my opinion, anyway, the single biggest factor in Galen's success as a photographer is his unwavering discipline to wring out of every place he is in, every photographic frame it has to offer. When I first met Galen in Yosemite, in the early seventies, he was applying the same tenacity to rock climbing, where eventually—

counting both Yosemite and the Sierra backcountry—he accumulated over a hundred first ascents. Back then he was still in his hot rod stage, operating Rowell's Auto Care in the East Bay, which specialized in racing cars, an interest that went back to high school.

Galen grew up in Berkeley, where his father was a philosophy professor and his mother a cello instructor. His passion for the outdoors—both as a place to play and a place to protect—started as a young boy when he accompanied his parents, and sometimes their Sierra Club friends, to Yosemite and the High Sierra. One of the biggest influences in Galen's budding environmental awareness was his knowledge that David Brower, the president of the Sierra Club, lived just down the street. He was hesitant to approach such an eminence, but finally, when he was thirteen, Galen summoned courage to ask Brower if he could interview him for a school paper he was writing about the battle to save Utah's Dinosaur National Monument, in which the Sierra Club was involved. Brower agreed and Galen's paper was a success, but still he was reluctant to befriend Brower, thinking there was too great an age difference between them. His reluctance only increased when, a few years later, he learned that Mr. Brower didn't think too highly of his hot rod or of his penchant for burning rubber through the neighborhood.

"Once my mother called the cops on Galen," Ken Brower, David's son, told me. "My father grumbled [about Galen's hotrodding], but in moderation, mindful that he himself had a leaden foot. In the late 1930s, late at night, my father had set some ungodly record for the drive from Berkeley to Yosemite—just under two hours."

Ken reminded me that in addition to being a man described as the most important American environmental activist of the twentieth century, his father was also, in his day, one of the country's leading rock climbers. By the time Galen started rock climbing—and driving at every opportunity to the Sierra—he had also heard about David Brower's own fondness for fast driving, and of the record Brower held for the shortest elapsed time from Berkeley to Yosemite.

The parallel interests of the two men didn't end there. Galen's passion for photography grew from an initial attempt to record his rock climbs so he could share the images with his family and friends; Brower also had an interest in photography rooted in his friendship with Ansel Adams, and his desire to use the medium to share with as wide an audience as possible his passion for the Earth's wild places. "In the late fifties, Brower conceived, edited and produced the Exhibit Format Series of outsized photo books for the Sierra Club," Galen wrote in a memoir about his life as a photographer. "When [Brower] produced This Is The American Earth, I was the same age that he had been when he first met Ansel [Adams]...the media love to relate how one day in my thirties I walked away from my auto repair shop to embark on a career as a wilderness photographer. It wasn't that simple, and it wouldn't have happened without David Brower's influence."

Galen would eventually call David Brower his "phantom mentor." But as is common in relationships between mentor and student, the latter, at some point, tries to best the former. Galen, always competitive, never forgot who owned the record for the fastest elapsed time to Yosemite.

"My father was an old man and Galen middle-aged when the record finally fell," Ken Brower told me. "I was on hand to hear Galen gently break the news. My father accepted it gracefully, like some old ball player whose home-run record had finally been eclipsed."

MAY 31

AS THE RISING SUN RIM-LIGHTS the crest of the eastern ridge of the basin, the first ray of direct light hits the lammergeyer's nest, and I give this female vulture high marks for choosing a site that combines a good view with passive solar heating. The sunlight inches down the pinnacle, and in half an hour it hits our camp and suddenly both the angel's dust in the air and the downy snow on the ground sparkle in thousands of iridescent flashes. The air remains cold, however, and we hold our coffee mugs in both hands and later, as we take down our tents, we pause frequently to breathe on our fingers.

We depart in the vehicles, driving across a gravel alluvium sluiced from the Aru Range that frames the left side of our view; the sapphire Aru Co ("co"—Tibetan for "lake") is on our right. I recognize in the mountains the opening of a narrow canyon from which I gained the basin on my previous visit here in 1999—having approached on that expedition from the west—and I recall how a snowstorm had trapped our vehicles farther up this same canyon, and how while waiting for the snow to melt I had ventured into the basin on skies.

I was then with Asia Wright, my then nineteen-year-old adopted goddaughter, and later during that visit, walking the shoreline of Aru Co, we had spotted a Saker feeding on a kill. When we approached, the falcon flew up and landed a hundred feet away and watched us as we investigated the remains of a Tibetan snow finch it had apparently taken that morning. I bent down and recognized a small dot of red flesh as the finch's heart, and told Asia that normally that was one of the first things a falcon would eat. I reached down and carefully plucked the heart and held it between my fingers, and then—as though I were a shaman able to divine in the ordinary the extraordinary—I had the notion that in the fragile sacrifice of this small bird's tiny heart I was somehow holding the omniscient power of the wild heart of the Chang Tang. With that thought I stood and looked for the falcon, but it had disappeared.

Since we entered the Chang Tang four days ago, we have seen three of these knife-winged falcons, including one that, at the end of a stoop, had veered in front of our vehicle at a speed easily over fifty miles an hour. In the nearly fifteen years of his study of the wildlife of the Chang Tang, Schaller has recorded on these alpine steppes only thirty-seven species of birds, and other than the European kestrel, Sakers are the only species of falcon. These handsome birds occur across a wide swath of Asia—from northern India to southern Russia, from eastern Mongolia to western Ukraine—and although in this uninhabited northwest corner of the Chang Tang they are still frequent if not abundant, elsewhere in their range their numbers are diminishing, victims of both illegal and legal trapping.

Like all falcons, the Saker is an exquisite aerial predator, designed to overtake in midair the snow finches, larks, and ducks on which it preys. And like any wild creature whose success is built on a combination of power and speed, its subjugation by human beings seems all the more poignant. Nearly all the Sakers captured in the wild end up in the Middle East, where falconry is the favored sport of sheiks and wealthy businessmen. A newspaper in Abu Dhabi, citing local falcon experts, reported that over six thousand falcons a year are being smuggled into the region. During the Taliban regime, so many birds were secreted out of Afghanistan that falcons in that country are now nearly extirpated, and trappers have moved to China and Tibet, where they can still find birds.

The trade in Saker falcons is so lucrative that Mongolia has legalized it, and through the 1990s between eighty and one hundred fifty birds a year were exported. One Mongolian news source reported that in one shipment "80 falcons left the Mongolian steppes forever...on board a special charter flight...to the palaces of Arab sheikhs in Saudi Arabia and Kuwait, to the freedom of hunting an occasional desert fox. The price of their freedom was U.S. $3 million in credit for development projects pledged by the Saudi Arab Emirates and Kuwait."

I learned these facts about the plight of the Sakers, when following our trek, I did more research on chiru and chiru poaching. At the same time, I tangentially became more informed about what conservation biologists call "harvesting" of endangered species to satisfy not our basic needs but our superfluous desires. I encountered report after report of endangered species that are being trapped or killed to feed that mix of curiosity, arrogance, and conceit that seems to motivate our urge to keep rare animals as pets, to use their skins to make rugs, their various body parts to concoct medicines, their furs to make coats, their feathers to decorate hats, their skins to manufacture shoes and handbags.

I began to accumulate a larger understanding of what the statistics of "harvesting" meant not only in terms of the impact on wildlife populations, but also on individual animals, when I contacted TRAFFIC North America, a joint effort by the World Wildlife Fund and the World Conservation Fund (IUCN) to expose and control the illegal trade in wild plants and animals. They sent me a stack of past bulletins they had published, and a quick sampling revealed tidbits such as these:

INFAMOUS REPTILE SMUGGLER PLEADS GUILTY—
The U.S. Fish and Wildlife Service…revealed the unlawful impor-
tation and sale of more than 300 protected reptiles native to Asia
and Africa [including] the Komodo dragon (Varanus komod-
oensis) and the Madagascan spurred tortoise (Geochelone
yniphora), among the rarest of all tortoise species.

SHARK FIN FIASCO—*U.S. Coast Guard boarded the Honolulu-*
based fishing vessel King Diamond II and discovered 12 tons
of illegal shark fins.

JUMBO IVORY SEIZURE—*Two shipments containing 36 whole*
elephant ivory tusks and numerous other pieces of tusk were seized.

ONTARIO FAMILY CHARGED IN BEAR TRAFFICKING—
three family members in Ontario [were charged] for 84 offenses
involving the illegal possession, transport, export and trafficking
of 368 black bear gall bladders.

As disquieting as these reports were, I was astonished to discover the magnitude of the illegal trade in protected animals: Interpol estimates that worldwide it is worth $5 billion dollars a year. That makes it the second biggest illegal trade in the world, behind illegal drugs but ahead of illegal arms. To many criminals, however, it is more appealing than other pursuits because if they are caught the punishment is often only a small fine or a light jail sentence for a misdemeanor.

I also began to think differently about the word "harvest." It had always in the past carried with it pleasant associations of the bounty that nature has to share with our human species. But now, for me, it was increasingly freighted with the dark weight of our rapacious record of plundering what remains of the wild world, and I added it to that list of words, such as "resource," "management," and "multiple use," that are so often co-opted to promote the no-deposit-no-return agenda by which so many of us relate to our planet.

क

WE FLUSH A HERD OF SOME THIRTY MALE CHIRU, and mixed with them half a dozen yearlings that have stayed behind while the females are absent on migration. We stop so Galen and Jimmy can take photographs and video, and as the animals move away in a slow gallop—concerned but not yet panicked—the black horns atop each male evoke a cavalry of knights marching with their lances held upright.

We continue northward, and soon we spot a solitary wild yak that also spots us, and at a fast bovine trot it moves up a small river that braids across the alluvium, holding its head in a posture of aggressive defiance that is reminiscent of Africa's Cape buffalo. If we were near enough I suspect we could hear it snorting. I also suspect if we were on foot we could expect it to charge. We stop the vehicle but the animal disappears up the drainage before Galen can focus his camera.

I choose to take this animal's presence as a sign we will see more wild yak, although perhaps not here but farther north, once we are beyond the limit of the nomads' range. In 1990, on his second visit to the Aru, Schaller counted six hundred eighty-one wild yak, but by 2000 a Norwegian team, conducting a two-year survey of both the wild as well as the domestic animals in the Aru Basin, found only seventy wild yaks in the hills at the north end of the basin; last year, in the same area, they found none. Wild yak, hunted for their meat and hides, are even charier of humans than chiru, and their absence is evidence of the change that has come to this place in the fifteen years since Schaller's first visit, when he found the basin occupied only by a few nomads visiting briefly during the summer. "The Aru basin is one of the best wildlife areas in the entire 300,000 km² Chang Tang reserve," the Norwegian team wrote in their report. "Since the numbers of both nomads and livestock have increased substantially over recent decades, a clear conflict of interest regarding the use of the basin is apparent."

Then the yak emerges once more into our view, but having maintained its fast trot it is now hundreds of yards away, and once again Galen is stymied in his effort to get a photograph. Soon the animal disappears into the sanctum of the Aru Range, but like an illuminated image that leaves a ghostly imprint on your vision even after it is gone, I can still feel the venerable bearing this beast has left in its wake. Because of its irascible temper and wooly appearance, Schaller considers wild yak to embody the wildness of the Chang Tang, and even though the large herds have now moved out of the basin as the nomads have moved in, perhaps this one animal is a scout ready to signal to its brethren, who are waiting in the perimeter regions of the Chang Tang, when the time is right to reclaim the Aru.

We soon stop to examine the dried carcass of a male chiru, its black horns stark against white snow, its empty eye sockets fixed skyward in an eternal stare. Presumably it has died for reasons other than poaching, as its skin is still intact. I bend down and stroke the fine underwool on its belly, my first opportunity to touch a chiru. It is as thick and silky as any fur I have felt, and I can appreciate—or maybe a better word is understand—the appeal of the shawls made from this fur.

Shahtoosh shawls are so fine that once you've held one it is easy to tell them apart from a shawl of any other wool, even vicuna, considered one of the finest and most exotic wools in the world. Shahtoosh is a Persian word meaning "King of the Wools," and the shawls are sometimes called "toosh," and also "ring shawls" because a women's garment of average length and width—two to three feet wide, and five to six feet long—can be pulled through a ring of average diameter. Shahtoosh shawls come in three natural colors—white, beige, and ivory—and the color depends on the part of the animal from which the wool is plucked, with white fetching the highest prices. The shawls are made from the chiru's ultrafine underwool, or fleece, although some of the coarser outer hairs—the guard hairs—inevitably get mixed in. The luxurious feel of

shahtoosh is revealed in the statistics: A single fiber of the finest pashmina wool measures about 14 microns in diameter; vicuna is about 12
microns; and chiru comes in with an average diameter under 10 microns,
or about 1/7 the diameter of a human hair.

क

ALTHOUGH OUR LAND CRUISER leaves fresh tracks across yesterday's snow, we are nevertheless following a faint road because in a few
places we have been able to discern, where the snow is thin, the tread
marks of other vehicles, some of which appear to have passed this way
within the last few days. Then in the distance we make out a nomad's
tent, and as our small caravan approaches it, we decide to stop and visit.

"This will be your chance to savor a cup of Tibetan salt tea,"
I say to Jimmy.

"Salt tea?"

"The standard of hospitality among Tibetans, and usually in a
place this remote it's made the traditional way, with yak butter."

This nomad's tent is made of white cotton, favored for summer
travel (while they prefer for their winter dwellings tents made of
heavier and warmer yak-hair fabric). We park our vehicles, and as
we walk toward the tent we notice the guy lines are tied to chiru
horns staked into the hardpan. There are no dogs barking, and we
are commenting that this likely means no one is home when a
woman and her two small children peer out the entrance. They
hesitate to come out, and we take this as indication the man of the
household—along with their dogs—is tending their flocks. With a
disarming voice Norgay says *tashiy delay*—"hello"—and the woman,
perhaps in her late twenties and dressed in a homespun wrap,
cautiously steps out, her two children hiding behind her. Speaking
Tibetan, Norgay introduces us, and then the woman folds the
entrance flap open and invites us inside.

Although our hostess's skin, like that of nearly all nomads in Tibet,
is cracked and windburned, she is nevertheless beautiful: Her long
braided hair frames her high cheekbones, her dark eyes, her full lips.

Her two children, perhaps four and six years old, remain behind her skirt, peeking at us. She motions us to sit on a lambskin carpet that covers what elsewhere in the tent is a dirt floor littered with discarded bits of food. As she begins to plunge the handle of a butter churn that contains salted tea, the children venture into full view. When she finishes churning, she searches the tent but can find only three porcelain cups, which she then cleans with her fingers, fills with tea and hands to Galen, Conrad, and me. She then retrieves a jar at least three times as large as our cups and fills it.

"Uh-oh," Jimmy says, his apprehension confirmed when she hands him the jar.

"Bottoms up," I say mischievously.

I have found the maxim about your ability over time to develop tastes for odd foods to be generally true. I now enjoy tea flavored with salt and sometimes yak butter that is bordering on rancid, and I also remember how repugnant it tasted when I first tried it nearly thirty years ago—a memory that makes the pucker on Jimmy's face all the more amusing.

I finish my small cup, give a sigh of satisfaction, and then say to Jimmy, "It's really an insult if you don't finish all your tea."

He nods to me affirmatively, straightens his back and takes a big drink.

"Oh man," he says as he empties the jar.

He then lifts his eyebrows when he sees our hostess refilling our cups, and once more I hear him mutter, "Uh-oh." She turns to him and he holds his hand over the jar, but she keeps motioning she wants to refill it.

"Jha thung," she says. "Jha thung."

"What's that mean?" Jimmy asks Norgay.

"Drink tea."

"I'm in trouble," he says as he gives in and she refills the jar.

While we sip our second serving, Conrad asks Norgay to ask our hostess how long she and her husband have been coming to Aru.

"Ten years ago she starts coming here," Norgay says after he receives her reply.

"Are there many other families here?"

"Yes, now more families."

"Are there as many chiru that live here?" I ask.

"Yes, there are many still here. But the ladies have all gone now, to some other place where they have their babies."

We finish our tea, and Galen gives the woman a postcard of his famous photograph of the Potala at the end of a brilliant rainbow.[vi] The two nomad kids, now more confident, crowd around their mother as she shows them the card. She lightly touches it to her forehead, in the Buddhist manner of blessing sacred objects, then positions it on a small altar in the tent's corner alongside a half dozen votive butter lamps. We stand, clasp our hands and bow in sincere appreciation for her hospitality. Outside the tent I notice one of the children has a toy Dong Feng truck made of wood, with a pull rope tied to the front. I think about the closet full of toys my kids grew up with, and wonder if somehow my wife and I should have raised them so they each had just one toy that they valued above all else.

क

WE CONTINUE TO DRIVE OVER THE ALLUVIUM, and soon we are paralleling the shoreline of Memar Co, which like Aru Co, is nearly twenty miles in length. If these twin jewels were anyplace in North America or Europe, they would be national treasures. We pass a nomad tending a mixed flock of sheep and goats who returns our wave and who could be the husband of our tea-stop hostess. Seeing him with his animals in his summer pasture summons a notion that our journey has a fourth dimension that includes time, that since starting our drive our route has backtracked along a historical continuum that measures the cultural evolution of our species: On the first day we passed the urban denizens of Lhasa, walking through the city in the shadows of steel-and-glass towers; on the second day we drove through villages of mud hutments, waving to farmers standing in fields of barley; now on the fifth day we are passing nomads who have migrated with their flocks to seasonal pastures;

in one more day we will enter a high steppeland so wild it is as yet unoccupied by our species.[vii]

At the base of foothills demarking the northern end of Aru Basin we encounter an encampment of nomads who, it will turn out, are the last human beings we will see for one month. When we pull up, the headman is busy driving a stake in the ground, and when he turns toward us and sees we are foreigners—instead of Chinese, Tibetans, or other nomads—his jaw drops at the same moment his heavy hammer slips through his fingers and thumps on the ground. When he regains his composure, he cautiously walks to us, followed by three women, perhaps his wife and daughters.

When Norgay greets him he mumbles a reply while he continues to stare at us. After we shake hands Norgay asks him the best route north, and he explains how to navigate through the hills we can see in front of us. (Beyond that we will rely on a pencil line drawn on a satellite photo given us by a member of the Norwegian team.) The headman speaks to Norgay in Tibetan, who then, because his English is limited, translates to Jimmy in Chinese, who then gives us the translation in English.

"Has he seen any female chiru come through here?" I ask.

"He says they don't come through here, but they pass near here," Jimmy tells us. "He says they go north over a thousand kilometers to have their babies."

"That's a bit far," I say, "but it confirms that even the nomads don't know the location of the calving grounds. Ask him if there has been anybody hunting chiru in this area."

Jimmy asks Norgay, who passes the question to the nomad, who then is visibly agitated: He answers, but as he speaks he looks away from us, waving his arm in a gesture of dismissal.

"He's pretty adamant that no one hunts them anymore," Jimmy says. "He knows it's a high penalty activity."

"Clearly he wouldn't tell us if he was hunting them," I say. The nomad speaks again, and his disdain is palpable.

"He said he can't hunt them because the Chinese came through here and confiscated everyone's rifles."

We thank the nomad for giving us directions, climb in our vehicles and continue northward.

"Just from the kind of defensiveness in his voice," Jimmy says, "you know he used to be a chiru poacher."

"Or that he still is," I reply.

"But it's understandable," Conrad says, "when movie stars are paying fifteen grand a pop for the shawls, and you're trying to feed your family raising goats and sheep."

Conrad's point does require consideration: I have only to remember the woman and two girls standing next to the nomad, and then remember my own two girls and son, to empathize with his position. But then, too, I have only to remember the nomad's predicament is the same one told by the ivory hunters in Africa, the tiger poachers in India, the parrot trappers in the Amazon—I could go on—to know that these endangered animals must come first, for if they don't the poachers will hunt and trap them to extinction, spend the money, and then be in the same position of poverty they were in when they started, except in the cases of these nomads, they will in addition have trucks that need gas and rifles that need ammo.

This scenario is easy to imagine in a place like Aru Basin, where there were few if any people only fifteen years ago, and where sudden wealth from the equivalent of a gold rush has brought a population boom that has already reached numbers beyond the capacity of this area to maintain both the increasing numbers of domestic animals and the original populations of wild animals. More realistically the nomad population will reach equilibrium as the Aru becomes less attractive. Already the Norwegian survey has reported that with harsh winters and thin graze—combined with the ban on hunting (traditionally a subsidiary source of income)—three families said they were giving up and moving out. Even if there is a partial decrease in population, however, and even if the anti-poaching laws are enforced, the domestic stocks will likely still be in the majority, leaving room only for remnant populations of chiru, and even less for wild yaks, wolves, bears, and snow leopards.[viii]

क

WHEN THE NOMAD TOLD US that the migrating chiru had passed through an area some distance from his camp, his statement was consistent with Schaller's observations that the females follow various routes both west and east of Aru Basin. The Norwegian team had further observed that, once the migration gets under way in May, the pregnant animals from across their winter range head toward foothills on the west flank of Toze Kangri, at which point they converge into a single migration path. We have with us a report from the Norwegian team with the location of this point of convergence—a pass through the foothills that for our own common reference we have nicknamed "the funnel"—and our goal now is to get there following what the nomad headman has told us is the best route for our vehicles.

We ascend into rounded hills on the north end of the basin, and I am thankful—as I have been many times these last few days—we have a new truck: In low gear it maintains a steady crawl up the steeper grades. We stop every few minutes to look ahead and make sure our route avoids flats and bottoms where our vehicles might become mired in mud. We also take time to scan surrounding hills for any sign of migrating females, but so far we haven't seen anything more than the several groups of sedentary males and yearlings we spotted in the basin.

"What's that ahead?" Jimmy says, pointing. "A rock?"

"It's more like a sign or a marker."

It is a brown lump unnaturally out of place on an otherwise open hillside. Before I can focus my binoculars, the "lump" breaks into four parts each trotting in a different direction. When I have one of the "parts" in focus I say, "Wolves. Four of them." As we continue forward in our vehicles, the pack trots parallel to us for a half mile, then veers east and disappears.

"Where there are wolves, there are probably migrating chiru," Galen says.

We can only hope this is true. Then in a few more minutes Jimmy again has another sighting.

"There—four, no five, animals. I think they're chiru."

I glass them and indeed they are chiru, and they are females. They walk slowly, stop to browse, walk, browse. They are tending in a northerly direction, and they all appear pregnant.

"If there's five there has to be more," I say. "The Norwegian team said they sat on a hill above the funnel and watched them stream by, and that was a year ago almost to the day. So I think our timing's going to be perfect."

CHAPTER TWO

क

JUNE 1

"GOOD MORNING, EVERYBODY." It's Conrad's voice calling from the cook tent.

"Morning," I yell back.

"Coffee will be ready in a few minutes."

"Sounds good," Galen says from his sleeping bag spread parallel to mine. I stretch my arms, zip open my bag, and dress. Outside the tent, I find the sky partially clouded, but in a few minutes Galen will confirm the barometer has dropped only slightly and therefore we don't expect anything more than the light snowfall we seem to get every other day. I greet Conrad as I walk to the tracks where yesterday our vehicles had been trapped in mud, and stamp my boot on the ground.

"Hard as concrete," I report.

"We should get out of here soon," Conrad says. "Get in as many miles as we can before it turns to mud."

The evening before we had tried to drive the truck and Land Cruiser through the "funnel," but a wallow of mud a hundred yards long had stopped us. Knowing we wanted to start as early as possible, our truck driver woke during the night three times to start his vehicle to keep the engine from getting too cold. Now his vigilance pays off when the diesel fires on the third or fourth crank, but we lose a half hour trying to start the Land Cruiser, and the chauffeur of that vehicle shows no contrition that he chose to sleep through the night. His enthusiasm for this journey has been capricious, and more often than not he leaves the impression he would rather be home in Lhasa, where I imagine his ideal day is passed in a neighborhood café drinking beer and smoking cigarettes.

When finally we get under way, the ground is still hard, and we have no trouble crossing through the "funnel." The evening before, after we set up tents, we had walked to a hillside overlooking this col in the hope we would see the long lines of chiru the Norwegian team had reported observing in this same spot almost exactly a year earlier. We sat for an hour and didn't see a single animal. Now this morning we are hopeful to encounter what Schaller and the Norwegians have both told us should be a single migration route made of the various arms of female chiru converging from the south.

But so far we haven't seen anything other than a solitary hare that darted in front of our vehicle. We descend the opposite side of the pass to a lake that, although five miles in length and three miles in width, seems plebian compared with the noble sapphire waters of Aru and Memar. The surrounding hills descend to the lakeshore, forcing us to drive in the water, but fortunately the bottom is firm. We stop and survey the hills for chiru, but still we see nothing. We continue, and in a half hour Jimmy calls out from the backseat.

"Over there, on that hillside. It looks like animals."

We stop the vehicle, turn off the engine, and get out. Bracing his elbows on the hood, Galen focuses our single pair of high-quality binoculars on the hillside that is a half mile away.

"They're chiru," he says excitedly. "About fifty of them, and they're all females."

We pass around the binoculars and watch the animals as they walk in a loose group that stretches for perhaps a hundred yards. They stop to browse, walk, and again stop to browse. When it's my turn, I can see through the binoculars the bulging bellies of the pregnant animals, and I wonder if the older ones, who presumably have made this migration many times, feel any foreboding knowing in advance the distance they have to travel from here to the calving grounds.

I hand the binoculars to Conrad, and as I watch him watching the chiru, I have an image of poachers doing what we are doing: studying the movements of these creatures. But instead of wishing the chiru Godspeed on their journey, the poachers, in my imagination, are plotting which drainage to ascend to intercept the animals. In my mind's eye I see them return to their vehicle and then drive after the animals, chasing them onto the flats, and then leaning out their windows and firing their rifles; I see the animals dropping, and then the poachers disembarking from their SUV with their knives in hand; I see the skinned chiru scattered like slain victims on a battlefield, and next to the carcasses the stillborn fetuses, wet with natal fluid, steaming in the cold air.

क

"WEARING A SHAHTOOSH SHAWL," Schaller wrote, "is the same as wearing three to five dead chiru around your neck."

If the women who had bought shahtoosh shawls had known that fact, it seems probable that many of them would have paused before making their purchases. From the research I did both before and after our trek, I learned that at the beginning of the fashion trend everyone from the women purchasing the shawls to the retailers who distributed them to the craftsmen who wove them thought the wool was gathered from animals that shed it naturally, and that it was collected by nomads off bushes and rocks. From this same research I was never able to trace the beginning of the shahtoosh craze to any individual—to any movie star or celebrity who might have initially popularized the garments—but some women who bought the shawls early in the trend did state they thought there was a connection between the growing popularity of the shawls and the increasing public pressure against wearing coats made of spotted cat fur.

By the late eighties animal rights activists, especially those belonging to the notorious PETA group, had finally caused the haute couture set to grow tired of getting egged or sprayed with red paint when they wore their fur coats in public.[1] But if the animal rights advocates succeeded in getting spotted cat fur coats, hatbands, and purses to stay in the closets, their effort may have contributed to a shift in fashion trends that had an unexpected consequence for chiru. Bob Colacello, the author of the article in Vanity Fair on shahtoosh, described how one fashion might possibly have replaced another:

> Rich women who had grown accustomed to keeping warm in $50,000 sable coats during the Reagan years found that the lightweight but toasty shahtoosh was the perfect thing to wrap over the Republican cloth coat brought back into fashion by Barbara Bush. Understated, verging on the Bohemian, recognized as costly only by the cognoscenti, the shahtoosh might even be seen as a metaphor for the somewhat hypocritical 90's backlash against the supposedly greedier previous decade.

The high price of shahtoosh was no doubt part of its appeal. By the mid-1990s, as the trend was still in its ascendancy, an average woman's shahtoosh shawl was selling in New York for $2,000 to $3,000; later, after our trek, wildlife officers in Scotland Yard would show me an embroidered shawl they confiscated from a high-end shop in London that had a listed price of $18,900.

Before they became popular, the shawls for centuries had been favored in Europe by a small coterie who celebrated their virtues: Napoleon is said to have bought one for Josephine, and she was so impressed she ordered 200 more. The shawls had always been valued in India, where they were passed generation to generation as family heirlooms. Shahtoosh spreads were the preferred sleeping blankets of maharajas, and the shawls were a respected part of a bride's trousseau.

Because they had always been expensive, the demand, before the 1980s, had always been small. The origin of the wool that was used to make shahtoosh also remained myth. The story that the hair was from a Tibetan ibex, that the animal shed the wool naturally, and that nomadic children then gathered it off rocks and bushes was likely perpetrated by smugglers and wool traders to protect the real source of their wealth. Whether true or not, it was a story that had been in circulation for at least a hundred and fifty years, so that for the weavers in Kashmir myth had become fact, shielding them from knowing the real consequence of their craft, and also protecting the women in Hong Kong, Milan, Paris, London, and New York who bought the shawls from knowing the truth, allowing them instead to feel good about supporting the livelihoods of poor nomad kids in Tibet.

क

ANY DOUBT WHETHER we are on the migration route has dissolved with the sighting of these fifty or so chiru. After the animals disappear over the hillside, we continue around the lake, spotting another group of eighteen animals taking a route northward up a drainage too steep to follow in our vehicles; we continue westward but soon find a more moderate route north that then allows us to loop back to a position we guess will intercept the migration route. As we approach the north side of Toze Kangri, it is snowing lightly and the mountain is shrouded in clouds. Soon we encounter a wide bog, and driving along the front skirt of it one way and then the other, we find no place to cross.

"I think this is as far as the Norwegian team was able to get last year," I tell the others. "This could be the end of the line for us, too."

"Looks that way to me," Conrad concurs.

We know that ten years ago Schaller had been able to drive north of this point, getting as far as a large lake called Heishi Beihu, but we also know he was able to do so only by leaving behind his truck, and continuing, with as much gas as he could carry, in his Land Cruiser. Since we don't have that option—as we have to stick with our truck because it is carrying all our equipment, including our rickshaws— we never expected our convoy to make it past Toze Kangri, anyway.

"If this is as far as we get," Galen says, "then why don't we drive closer to the peak and find a place to camp that's sheltered?"

We all agree that's a good idea, and in little more than an hour we have the vehicles parked bumper to bumper, and our various shelters—cook tent, two camping tents, and community tent for the Tibetans to sleep in—set up in an arrangement that leaves open a common area large enough to assemble the rickshaws.

From the back of the truck Conrad and I hand down to Jimmy and Galen the six large cardboard boxes that contain the rickshaws. When we had tested the carts the day before we departed, we commented how the disk brakes, although case hardened, looked delicate; how the traces, although strong if used correctly, looked vulnerable; how the mountain bike wheels, although the most durable design commercially available, could perhaps be damaged in shipping. Now Jimmy and Galen watch apprehensively as Conrad and I cut the strapping tape on the first box: If the carts have been damaged we all know this expedition could be over before it begins.

"The moment of truth," Conrad says, "our precious eggs."

He tips his head and turns his hands up in his Inshallah gesture. I open the box lid and peer in.

"The first one looks good," I say as I lift out a wheel.

The other three wheels in the first box are in equally good shape. We open one of the larger boxes and lift out an aluminum cargo bin with the wheel frames and disassembled traces still secured firmly inside. All the components appear to be intact. Soon all the boxes are open; nothing is broken or damaged.

Each cart is in more than a dozen pieces, not including a large bag of nuts, bolts, and screws. We spread the components on the ground, and while Galen and Jimmy shoot the scene, Conrad and I assemble the first rickshaw.

"I feel like a kid again with his Erector set," Conrad says.

"Maturity is a bitter disappointment for which there is no known cure," Galen replies.

Even though nothing is visibly damaged, we all know it is still too early to celebrate. The tolerances of the carts are critical, and if any component has been bent, we might have trouble getting the wheel frames to bolt to the cargo bins, the axles to align through the frames and wheel hubs, the brake disks to spin without rubbing against the calipers. But all the pieces fit flawlessly, and in an hour we have the first cart assembled. While it is still turned turtle, Conrad spins the wheel and sights its edge relative to the frame.

"Straight and true."

With the wheel still spinning he squeezes the brake lever and the knobby tire instantly stops.

"Brakes feel good."

We turn the cart upright and move it back and forth: It glides effortlessly on the hard ground. Conrad threads the nylon webbing connecting the waist harness through its clips, then lifts the trace over his head and fastens the buckle.

"Norgay, you're the guinea pig. Come on and get in."

Norgay sits down in the cargo bin, and the other Tibetans cheer as Conrad, like a rickshaw driver from the China of old, pulls the grinning young cook around camp.

क

WHILE NORGAY PREPARES A CELEBRATORY DINNER, Conrad and I climb to the summit of a sharp hill behind camp. Southward a blanket of clouds has lowered over Toze Kangri, but northward we can see, across the hardpan plain, the first two to three stages of our trek.

"According to the map it's about twenty-five miles to that peak over there," Conrad says pointing to the base of an unnamed glacial mountain that rises from the plain like a gray wall of rock and snow supporting a gray ceiling of clouds.

"Twenty-five miles looks like a long way," I answer. "Not to mention that once we get there we'll still have maybe two hundred and fifty to go."

"We're in for an adventure, that's for sure," Conrad says, his grin framed by a blond bristle of whiskers that weights the bottom of his face in a way that gives it strength. Like so many people I know,

Conrad seems to live up to his last name (at least the eponymous equivalent in English), in that on trips like this he is an "anchor," a grounded force that, when conditions get tough, can keep an expedition from being dragged on the rocks. (I have wondered if, in some subliminal way, my last name—Ridgeway—was a reason I became interested as a young teenager in mountaineering. Once I landed a job as a climbing actor in a beer commercial, and an assistant producer asked me to complete a model release form. I signed it and gave it back to her, and she said, "No, I need your real name, not your stage name." "That is my real name," I replied. "Look, I don't have time to bullshit," she said. "Give me your real name.")

It has been two years since Conrad and I were last together on a journey, and I am looking forward to sharing this trek with him. I know it was hard for Jenny and him to make the decision to separate their new family for the two months it will take us to complete this expedition, but they both felt it important. Conrad has worked for The North Face for almost twenty years, and in addition to his position as a sponsored athlete, he recently was placed in charge of their environmental programs: He and Jenny saw this expedition as a way to participate in an adventure that also has an important conservation component.

I take from my pack a few sticks of jerky and some mixed nuts, and share the snack with Conrad. It brings to mind a midnight lunch on a day in Antarctica when Conrad and I, along with a few other friends that included his climbing partner Alex Lowe, were on a ski reconnaissance. We had finished climbing our main objective—an enormous overhanging granite wall—and with a few days before our plane was scheduled to arrive, we decided to investigate some of the lesser peaks in the region; with the weather solid, neither Conrad nor Alex could imagine sitting in camp when there were mountains in the neighborhood that had never been climbed.

It was my first expedition with Conrad and Alex, regarded then as perhaps the strongest alpine climbing team in the world. The adventure started in Cape Town, where we had waited over a week for the installation of an inertial navigation system in the C-130 that would fly us south. It was an unscheduled holiday: We surfed half the day and rock climbed the other half. When local climbers heard Conrad and Alex were in town, they showed up to escort us to the rock cliffs outside the city. They gathered at the base of the first climb to watch Alex lead. The crux was an overhanging roof that required the climber to pull up on wafer-thin finger holds. Alex grabbed the holds, cut his feet loose, and then by his fingertips hung in space. The locals began calling up, "Right heel hook!" "Swing up!" Alex pulled up, but then lowered down. "You can do it!" Once again he pulled up, lowered down, pulled up, lowered down, pulled up…. The locals became quiet, then one whispered to the other, "He's doing pull-ups." No doubt there was an element of showmanship in the exercise, but the truth was, Alex had been on a plane too long and needed a workout more than what the climb otherwise offered.

That's when I first observed that even though Conrad is one of the better climbers in the world, Alex Lowe was on a level all his own. There were six of us on that Antarctic climb, and for the seven weeks it lasted there was not a cross word between anyone. On Christmas, driven off the wall by a snowstorm, we welcomed the chance to lie in our tents at the base of the peak and rest. Except for Alex. He dug an eight-foot hole in the snow, positioned his skis over the shaft, crawled in and, grabbing two nylon loops he had tied around the skis, started doing more pull-ups. He did four hundred that day, not to impress us but because, like a shark that has to breathe, he had to keep moving.

When two years later in the Himalaya the avalanche swept Alex to his death, his oldest son, Max, was ten, his middle son, Sam, was eight, and his youngest, Isaac, was three. Max spent a lot of time by himself on the roof of their house in Bozeman, Montana. He would climb out his bedroom window and sit. Sam was less taciturn, and Isaac, perhaps too young to have a clear memory of his father, seemed least affected. Isaac, as it had turned out, is also the most like his father. Physically, he has the same wiry legs and lean muscles. Temperamentally, he can't sit still. He has the energy, effervescence, and drive of his father. Coupled with fearlessness, it is a combination that brings his mother to the edge of exasperation, and although it can challenge

Conrad in his role as father, he also realizes that Alex's spirit is still very much alive.

"I've seen it so many times," Conrad once told me. "Driving through Yellowstone, Isaac wanted to stop and throw rocks in the river, and I said, 'No, we've got to get home for dinner,' and he said, 'No, I want to throw rocks *now.*' It was Alex, and it was more than impatience because it was combined with exuberance and what you might call genetically driven determination."

JUNE 2

I WAKE IN THE DARK HOURS of early morning to the sound of snow graveling against the tent fly, relieved that, since we have decided to spend one more day in base camp packing food and preparing our camera and video gear, it doesn't matter if the weather is good or bad. Then I begin wondering if perhaps this is the harbinger of a longer storm, and if it is, whether it might slow us, and if we do travel slowly, whether the migration might pass us by, if it hasn't already. I lie in my sleeping bag wishing I could sleep, but instead find myself speculating whether the large herd of fifty chiru we saw yesterday might also be the last herd. If the animals travel twenty miles a day—as Schaller estimates they do— and if, as he says, the first females begin their migration about two weeks before the last, is it possible yesterday's group was bringing up the rear? There's no way to know, but nevertheless I wonder if I should have begun our journey a few days earlier.

Finally I fall asleep, then wake and see by the lightening of the tent fabric that it's morning. I zip open the door and look outside: four inches of new snow on the ground. I dress and go out to find the cook tent in shreds. Early in our drive a spare battery in the back of the truck spilled acid on the cook tent, and since then it has disintegrated day by day. Now there are wide gaps in the walls, one side has collapsed entirely, and the inside is blanketed in snow. I step through one of the holes, sit on a box, and start the stove to make coffee. Conrad walks over and peers through the hole.

"Hanging by a thread," he says.

He is referring to the remaining side of the tent, which is suspended literally by a single thread. Conrad sits down and soon Jimmy shows up.

"You guys are looking pretty drokpalike."

One of Conrad's sponsors is Peet's Coffee, and he has brought enough Major Dickason's Blend to last the trip. After coffee and the last fresh eggs we will eat for a month, we spend the day repacking our food, deciding to leave behind one bag that holds a three-day supply; it would be comforting if we could carry the extra food as contingency, but we decide we can't afford the weight.

"Should we take the wrist-rockets?" Conrad asks.

He is referring to two high-powered slingshots we have brought. We have tested them using marble-size rocks, and they seem powerful enough to bring down a marmot or a pika. Since we are in the Chang Tang Nature Reserve, however, and since we have a conservation objective, we all understand it would contravene our mission to kill an animal, and we would do so only if it were a matter of life or death.

"I think we should bring them," I suggest.

"They don't weigh that much," Galen agrees.

Even though we already have so much weight to pull, we know as a safety net we have to take a minimum of ten gallons of water: As Schaller told us, there might be fifty miles or more between streams. We divide the food, stove and stove fuel, water bladders and tents. Conrad volunteers to carry more than the rest of us, in part because he is the strongest, and in part because the weight includes several pounds of Major Dickason's Blend.

"How much do you think you have?" I ask him.

"Each cart weighs about fifty pounds, so I calculate total weight for each of you guys is about two hundred and fifty, and for me about two hundred and seventy-five pounds."

With the carts loaded we pull them around camp, then up a steep cutbank behind the tents. That effort requires one of us to pull while another pushes.

"I can't remember if assisted pulling is R-3 or R-4." Jimmy says.

He is referring to a system we developed one day during our drive to rate the difficulty of rickshaw travel. "R" is for "Rickshaw," and the corresponding number, on a scale of one to six, measures the degree of difficulty, similar to the system for rating aided rock climbs.

"I think we decided that was R-4," I reply, "but let me check in my journal."

I retrieve from my tent my hardbound journal and open it to the page where I recorded the conversation in which we developed the rating system.

"R-1 is flat, easy cruising over hard or frozen ground," I say, reading aloud. "R-2 is somewhat difficult pulling uphill or across rocky, sandy, or boggy ground. R-3 is very difficult solo pulling where you have to concentrate on secure foot placements. R-4 is when it's too steep or loose to pull the cart alone, and in places portaging may be necessary. R-5 is when portaging is essential, and without a rope belay there is risk of injury. R-6 is when the carts have to be abandoned because even with rope belays there is risk of death."

"Any bets whether we see R-5 or R-6?" Conrad asks.

"No way," I reply. "You want to hex us before we start?"

Even though we jest, the truth is that night we all go to sleep feeling a mix of excitement and unease. For me, even though I have been going on these adventures for thirty years, this one is requiring a level of commitment I have seldom experienced; it is not unlike what I imagine Sven Hedin, H. H. Deasy, C. G. Rawling—and the other handful of explorers who crossed the Chang Tang a hundred years ago—must have felt at the outset of their adventures.

JUNE 3

IN THE MORNING we have our final breakfast with our four Tibetan comrades, who so gamely have brought us to this juncture. They have their own apprehensions: Holding the map and compass we are leaving with them, Conrad reviews the route they must take to find their way back.

"We came this way," he says, pointing to the map as the two drivers huddle around, "so you go back this way. When you get to two roads, follow the bigger road, and always go south. Here is the compass."

Conrad hands them our spare compass. We give each of them a tight bear hug and with our mittened hands a thump on the back. The Tibetans climb two in the Land Cruiser and two in the truck, and waving from the windows, they depart. We stand next to our carts, waving back. It takes two or three minutes, but slowly the shifting roar of the truck's diesel fades to a murmur.

"It's getting awfully quiet out here," Galen says.

The Land Cruiser and truck round a bend and disappear.

"Boys," I say, "we just cut the cord."

With the rickshaws loaded and all traces of our base camp removed, we are ready to leave. Before we start, however, I suggest we record our thoughts on camera. Everyone agrees, so we take turns interviewing each other.

"How do I feel watching those trucks disappear?" Jimmy asks rhetorically when I point the camera at him. "A little nervous. This is definitely as far out as I've ever been."

"I'm scared," Conrad admits. "We're on our own, a thousand miles from Lhasa, a three-day walk from the nearest nomad camp, and we're about to leave in the opposite direction. Our gear? We've had two years to get it together. If we don't have it, we can't get it, and if we can't get it, we don't need it. Let the adventure begin."

With that, we buckle the harnesses around our waists and start pulling. The first hundred yards are easy, and then we encounter our first obstacle, a braided stream flowing off the north side of Toze Kangri. We unbuckle our waistbelts, Conrad jumps across on a series of rocks, I push the first cart as far as I can, and he grabs the handlebar at the end of the traces and pulls it the rest of the way. When all the carts are across, the rest of us jump the stream and we are again under way. We find a ramp that allows us to gain the bench above the stream bank, but each step feels like leg-pressing 250 pounds, except when the wheels hit even a small rock, and then it feels like 350 pounds. Once on the bench the carts are easier to pull, but at 16,500 feet we are all soon breathing deeply.

In two hours we angle our route 20 degrees east of true north so we can parallel the shoreline of Yue Ya Hu, a lake four miles in length that remains sheathed in ice. The snow has now melted and the ground is hard desert pavement, open save for evenly dispersed clumps of ceratoides, a stunted bush that here, in the northern half of the Chang Tang, is the principal forage for chiru. Other than two males we see grazing near the lakeshore, however, there are no chiru. We are precisely on the migration path that Schaller observed when he visited this area in 1992, but so far we have seen no sign of the long lines of animals he told us we could expect to find at just this location.

This isn't living up to the name "Antelope Plain" given this place in 1897 by the first European to see it, Captain H. H. Deasy of the 16th Queen's Lancers. The next visitor, Captain C. G. Rawling, arrived in 1903, and then the redoubtable Sven Hedin, in 1906. After those three, no other Westerner passed this way until George Schaller traversed the plain in 1992, hoping to find the elusive calving grounds of the chiru.

It was the expedition accounts of Deasy and Rawling that in part had led Schaller to suspect the Antelope Plain might safeguard the calving grounds. Despite the weight, I have packed in my rickshaw a copy of Schaller's *Wildlife of the Tibetan Steppe*, and in it is a quote from Captain Rawling's *The Great Plateau* that is analogous to Lewis and Clark's journal of the American Plains two hundred years ago. Rawling wrote:

> Almost from my feet away to the north and east, as far as the eye could reach, were thousands upon thousands of doe antelope with their young. The mothers were mostly feeding, while the young ones were either lying down and resting, or being urged on by their mothers. All had their heads turned toward the west, and were traveling slowly in that direction, presumably in search of the fresh young grass springing up in the higher western tablelands.
>
> Everyone in camp turned out to see this beautiful sight, and tried, with varying results, to estimate the number of

animals in view. This was found very difficult, however,
more particularly as we could see in the extreme distance
a continuous stream of fresh herds steadily approaching;
there could not have been less than 15,000 or 20,000 visible at one time.

Based on reports such as this, Schaller estimated that a hundred years
ago the chiru population in Tibet was well over a million. When he first
arrived on the Antelope Plain, however, he found nothing but a vast
alpine tableland that stretched like a gray void under a leaden sky.

"We had seen little wildlife so far," Schaller wrote, describing the
first half of his 1992 expedition. "The great steppe was to the south.
This was desert, a bleak high ground, most of it 16,500 feet and higher,
where grasses and sedges grow only in patches and where large tracts
were devoid of vegetation except for occasional gray-leafed Ceratoides shrubs partially buried in silt...[the Antelope Plain] was
empty...absolutely still except for a few stray chiru which seemed
absorbed by the immense landscape. Where were the great herds?"

Schaller described the following ten days as memorable mostly
for their misery. With his wife, Kay, and several Chinese and Tibetan
scientists and camp personnel, they explored the plain west to east,
but saw few chiru. Then when they moved camp to Yue Ya Hu, the
same lake that we are now paralleling with our carts in tow, their fortune suddenly changed.

"About 350 chiru females passed us, intently heading northeast,"
Schaller wrote. "Here was the migration route! The herds funneled
out of one valley, passed the western spurs of Toze Kangri, crossed a
flat, and then vanished high among the foothills of an unnamed glacier
peak. At least two thousand females hurried past camp in four days."

क

I HAD BEEN DILIGENT PLANNING both the route and the timing of
our foot traverse, and if I had it to do over again I still would have no
additional information to suggest doing anything different than what

we are at the moment doing. Did the migration start earlier this year? Were those animals we spotted two days ago the tail of the migration? And if they were, does that mean there will be too few animals to guide us to the calving grounds?

Reminding myself that negative thoughts only drain you, I decide instead to consider how well, at least on the first half of this first day, the rickshaws are performing. When the ground is hard and flat, as it is now, the carts are easy to pull. Occasionally we hit patches of ceratoides where the foot-high bushes are spaced closer than the width of our wheels and we have no choice but to muscle the carts over them. This requires a firm placement of your feet, and then a hard tug against the waist harness while, at the same time, you either push on the handlebar or grab and pull the two traces. I am already thankful the rickshaw designers have added a foam-lined plastic plate on the front of our waistbelts that distributes the load, as I can tell already a detail like this, after a week or two of pulling, could easily make the difference between discomfort and agony.

Two hours later, however, good design notwithstanding, my 250-pound rickshaw is starting to feel like—well, like it weighs 250 pounds. The exercise seems to demand most from muscles on my lower back and buttocks, and I realize those places are likely soon to be very sore. I'm guessing it will take a week or two before my body adjusts, and even then chances are I will have to dig deep to keep up with the others, including Galen who, despite being the oldest, seems indefatigable.

"How you feeling?" I ask Galen when he pulls alongside.

"Great. How are you doing?"

"Great," I answer.

"I figure we get a couple of Tibetan friends," Galen continues, "and we convince the Olympic Committee that this is an ancient Tibetan way of crossing the Chang Tang, and we get carting entered in the next Olympics."

"Sign me up," I say, keeping my reply short because of my quick breathing. I am starting to wonder how long I can keep this pace when, out of the corner of my eye, I see something scurry over the gravelly hardpan. It's a small lizard, and I am both relieved and thankful for an excuse to stop.

"Hold up, you guys," I say. "Over here, it's a Chang Tang lizard."

The others unbuckle and we all four huddle around a three-inch lizard with a pug face and two rows of dots that run down its back and continue down its tail.

"It doesn't really have a common name," I say. "Only its scientific name. But it's the only reptile found out here."

"Amazing," Galen replies as he lowers his camera to ground level, twisting his head to see through the viewfinder. "A cold-blooded animal in this place: I wonder how it survives the winter."

Galen shoots a full roll of film, and we continue. Two hours later, I am relieved when Conrad suggests camping in a shallow, dry drainage that offers some protection from wind. We have pulled the carts eight hours, and I am beat. We're a few hundred yards from the north end of Yue Ya Hu, and I choose not to dwell on the fact we haven't even passed this first physical feature on our map. Galen takes out the GPS, and when he has a satellite fix he reads our coordinates to Conrad, who plots them on our U.S. aeronautical chart.

"How many miles did we go?" I ask.

"Six," Conrad replies. "But it's just the first day."

"Don't remind me," I reply.

We pitch our two tents, Galen and me in one and Conrad and Jimmy in the other. I am carrying our small stove, and once I have it assembled I hand it to Conrad, who sets it on a small flat stone in the middle of his tent. Because their tent is larger than ours, we decide we will use it for cooking and eating, and because each evening I will be busy transcribing my tape recordings, Galen busy organizing his camera notes, and Jimmy busy servicing his video gear, Conrad has volunteered to do the cooking. Once Galen and I have our sleeping pads inflated, sleeping bags fluffed, and other gear organized, we go to the other tent, where Conrad is preparing spaghetti with marinara sauce. Because the noodles take so long to cook, however, this is the first and last time we'll have this dinner. But we will each evening be enjoying a small portion from a length of salami and a wheel of

Parmesan we have brought, and while Galen and I work on our day's notes, Jimmy portions with his pocket knife these meager but welcome hors d'oeuvres.

"Ooowww," he calls out. I look up from my journal and see he's holding his hand over this index finger.

"Cut yourself?" I ask.

"Yeah."

"Is it bad?" Galen asks.

"It might be."

He lifts his hand away and his fingers and palm are smeared with blood. The cut is deep, and no one needs to voice what we are all thinking: Out here any injury could be serious. Conrad goes outside to his cart to get the first aid kit. We wash the wound, then establish that, because he has no feeling in the finger but can still move it, the nerves are cut but the tendons are intact. We treat the wound with disinfectant and antibiotic ointment, and bandage it. As long as it doesn't get infected it will be okay. I can tell the cut is deep enough the finger will probably have a numb area that may last the rest of his life, and also it is likely to scar, but we all have scars from previous trips so Jimmy's just starting his own collection of expedition souvenirs. Still, it's a reminder that out here we are on our own.

I offer to finish cutting the cheese, but Jimmy insists on completing the job. He wipes the blood off the Parmesan, cuts the wedge into four precisely equal squares and hands them out. He then skewers the rind with the knife, roasts it on our small stove, cuts it into four equal pieces, dips each in a bottle cap of olive oil and offers them to us. Conrad learned this trick in Patagonia when he shared a campsite with an Italian climber. When the spaghetti is finished we pass the pot, scraping it clean and licking the spoon. After dinner we have hot chocolate, and Conrad asks Galen if he wants to rinse his cup first, to clean the spaghetti sauce, and Galen says no, the chocolate will do a good job of that.

"Whoa," Jimmy says, "only the first day on the trail and we're starting to adapt, just like the drokpas."

"Maybe we should award points for whoever does the grubbiest things," Conrad suggests.

"Drokpa points, on a one-to-five scale," I offer, meaning no disrespect for the drokpas, but rather a fraternal recognition of how, in adapting to such a harsh climate with little more than the clothes and shelter they make from their animals' furs and hides, they can live without the comforts so many of us assume are essential.

"Sounds good," Conrad answers. "One is like you're still on an outing in the Sierras, and five is like you've adapted completely to the Chang Tang."

"So what do I get for a dirty cup?" Galen asks.

"Only one point," Conrad replies. "All you did was mix spaghetti with hot chocolate."

JUNE 4

IN THE MORNING Jimmy inspects his wound. It's what in mountaineering we call a "flapper"—when the cut is deep enough the sides flap—and there is exposed bone at the base. He changes the bandage covering his wound, then wraps his finger and palm in athletic tape so he can more easily pull his rickshaw. It will be painful, but he has no choice. For breakfast we have oatmeal mixed with dried fruit and a spoonful of powered milk. Conrad purchased the oatmeal from a health food store in Bozeman and it tastes great; I could eat another helping. I sense that in two or three weeks fantasies of food will likely be monopolizing our thoughts as well as our conversations. From the food bag Conrad hands each of us our lunches, then we step outside the tent, break camp, and pack the rickshaws.

Getting a running start, we pull the carts up the bank of the dry wash where we have camped and get a look at the day's challenge: the expansive northern half of the Antelope Plain. A light snow fell during the night, and a dawn wind has brushed the tops of the endless corrugations, leaving across the landscape a zebra pattern of white and dark bands: snow, soil, snow, soil.

"This looks like classic Chang Tang," Galen says.

We haul our rickshaws toward the terminus of a distant butte as though it were a buoy marking our course. I can feel the altitude— about 17,000 feet—and I try to keep a rhythm: step, breathe, step, breathe. I have learned that if with each step I make a slight push on my handlebar, I can even out what otherwise is a jerk on the waist-belt, that way reducing the strain on my hips. That's important, because on a long trip like this a raw spot on my waist could be as debilitating as blisters on my feet. On that point, the new trekking boots I purchased for this trip seem to fit well, and the others have also reported no blisters or even hot spots on their feet.

The ground is hard, pulling is easy, and as the morning unfolds we walk silently, the others probably daydreaming as I am. I consider how the desolate emptiness of this place seems to evoke a feeling similar to the one I have had in the interior of Antarctica— of being on a planet other than Earth—although I convince myself that here it is more interesting because of the wildlife and the subtle but nevertheless rich colors in the landscape.

In two hours we reach the butte, park our carts, and climb to the top, where we find a three-foot cairn. The rocks could have been stacked by someone from Schaller's party (we all doubt George would build something like this, as he doesn't seem the type compelled to mark his presence), or perhaps from someone of the Chinese geological survey that the Norwegian team reported visited this area two years ago. Through binoculars Galen spots vehicle tracks in the distance; but again, they could be two years old or ten years old.

"No chiru," he says.

He hands the binoculars to me, and I scan the steppe while he lifts rocks off the summit cairn to see if anyone has left a register. He doesn't find anything, and neither do I. We see a lammergeyer coming from the west, and it passes close enough to distinguish the beard of feathers under its chin. It eyes us but does not diverge from its flight, continuing eastward as though nothing on this barren plain, including us, is worth investigating.

We return to our carts and continue. For the next hour I stay in front setting the pace; then Conrad pulls up and asks if he can lead.

A half hour later, as I try to keep up, I find myself approaching my aerobic limit, and it doesn't help when I remember that Conrad is pulling twenty-five pounds more than the rest of us. We cross a shallow wash that is dry save for patches of snow accumulated in the bottom that are now melting into slush.

"Should we stop and top off our water bladders?" Conrad asks.

"Great idea," I reply, thankful for an excuse to rest. I unbuckle the waistbelt, lift the trace over my head, and lie on my back, crossing one leg over the other, to stretch my muscles. There is an audible but welcome crack in my back.

"How do you feel?" Jimmy asks.

"By the time this is over," I answer as I push down on my other crossed knee, "I'll either be in killer shape, or I'll be dead."

After there's another crack in my back I stand and retrieve the bladders from my cart. Jimmy is filming me dipping our plastic cooking spoon into a shallow pool of brown water when suddenly he lowers the camera and exclaims, "Look, it's a chiru—no, it's a wolf!" I turn and see a lone wolf standing about a hundred feet behind me. It continues to eye us for a minute or two, then turns and trots northward, then stops again. We tie the bladders to our rickshaws and continue, and for the next hour the wolf paces us, maintaining a distance between a hundred and two hundred yards. Then it disappears.

In addition to wolves, the other predators I am hopeful to see during our trek include foxes, lynxes, and brown bears. There are also snow leopards, but they are so elusive it is unlikely we will see one. The numbers of Tibetan brown bears in the northern Chang Tang is also declining, but when I was in the Aru in 1999 I saw four, including a mother and cub I encountered while hiking by myself in the mountains. Fortunately I was downwind and able to retrace my steps without the mother bear sensing my presence. From reading Schaller's books and from talking to him, I knew these brown bears—related to North America's grizzlies—could be potentially dangerous. In 1992, on the flanks of an unnamed glacial peak we will pass on our trek, two of George's assistants had gone for a walk and been charged by two bears. On another occasion Kay Schaller, while driving in a Land

Cruiser with others from her team, had encountered a female bear with two cubs that charged their vehicle. They drove ahead and the bear stopped, but when they stopped the bear resumed her charge.

"I have never, ever, seen such an angry animal," Kay commented.

When planning my previous trip I had asked George Schaller what to do if we encountered a hostile bear while on foot.

"Oh, you'll learn very quickly the biggest tree in the Chang Tang is a stunted dwarf about twelve inches high," he had told me.

Recalling his bemused grin, I suggested to my teammates that on our rickshaw trek we bring with us canned bear spray, and they agreed. We have two cans with us, and Conrad and I each have one in our panniers, the zippered pouches we have suspended between our carts' traces to store small items we want to keep handy.

Each of us also has tied a silk kata to our front handlebar, and now the sacred scarves flutter in the wind. In another hour the previous night's snow is melted, and under a clouded sky the steppe is an expanse of dull pewter. The only sound is our footsteps and a squeak that has developed in one of Galen's wheels. Conrad slightly shifts the angle of his cart and pulls away from the rest of us, then slowly merges back.

"This is like being lost at sea," he says as he nears me.

"And those mountains are like unknown islands," I reply, referring to singular peaks that rise above the far horizon.

At a place marked by nothing other than our watches indicating it is noon, we stop for lunch: a small packet of mixed nuts, dried fruit, jerky, and an energy bar. We leave an hour later, stopping every hour or so to rest for a few minutes. At six thirty we reach a small tarn at the base of foothills surrounding the 20,000-foot glaciated peak with no name.

"This would make a good campsite," Conrad suggests.

"I like the idea of having something at my back," Galen agrees, pointing to a small but steep hill above the tarn that creates a windbreak. While Jimmy and I pitch the tents, Conrad and Galen hike a half mile to a higher hill in the hope that from the vantage on its summit they will be able to spot on the plains the long lines of migrating chiru that so far have eluded us. We are just finished pitching my tent when Jimmy looks up and says, "Oh my God!" I turn and once more there is the wolf, standing less than fifty feet from us. Its coat, thick and tawny, ruffles in the wind. It sniffs the air, lowers its snout to the ground, then looks up and sniffs again.

"Should we be afraid?" Jimmy asks quietly.

"I've never seen a wolf come this close," I reply. "We better put our food inside our tents tonight."

Jimmy gets his camera and videotapes the wolf as it walks cautiously around us, maintaining the same close distance. Then it climbs the hill behind our camp. On the ridge, in silhouette against the indigo sky, it raises its head and howls, and the wind carries its wild call across the Antelope Plain.

क

WHILE CONRAD AND GALEN REPORT that they saw no sign of chiru, Conrad did find an old bamboo tent pole, with brass ferrules weathered dark verdigris. We guess that it likely belonged to the Deasy expedition that passed through here in 1897. Even though it weighs several pounds, and even though he will have to carry it some two hundred more miles, Conrad decides to strap the pole to his cart.

"This is just too cool to leave behind," he says. "It'll go in the living room, next to an oxygen cylinder from the '75 Chinese Everest expedition and Alex's first ice axe."

We set up the other tent, and over dinner we agree that the wolf must be an indication that prey animals are in the area, and that the most likely prey are chiru.

"What but the wolf's tooth whittled so fine," Galen says, quoting Robinson Jeffers, "the fleet limbs of the antelope."

After dinner I stand outside the tents, and in the dull half-light I make out at the frozen edge of the tarn, huddled against the cold wind, a pair of diminutive Mongolian plovers; I can't help but wonder if they feel as miserable as they look; and I wonder if that wolf approached us more out of hunger than out of curiosity; and I wonder about those fifty chiru we saw just before we set up base camp, if at this moment they are bedded down with their backs to the wind, like this pair of plovers, preparing to wait for dawn, when once more they will stand, shake off the cold, and begin the day's march.

Why do the female chiru migrate? Why walk two hundred miles and more through this barren country where there is so little to eat, and then walk all the way back with newborn calves that are nursing? I had asked George Schaller, but he didn't have a definitive answer. "You can argue they go to calving grounds to escape predation," he said, "but that doesn't explain it, because the fact is they all have their babies within two weeks, and in two weeks wolves can only eat so much. And to say it's because they are looking for high protein ceratoides doesn't hold up because there is ceratoides in the south.

"All you can do is guess, but my way out is to call it historical. The present migration probably dates to the last glaciations, eighteen thousand years ago. Since then all the lakes have shrunk and even dis-appeared, and for the last five thousand years the amount of habitat has increased. Judging by pollen profiles, it was certainly more lush five thousand years ago, so maybe the migration is tied to a time when it was more nutritionally adaptive for the females to move north."

He then paused and looked off, as though in his mind's eye he were watching the chiru migrate across the alpine steppe.

"Whatever happened in the past there are probably still enough advantages over disadvantages that they keep doing it. But if the poaching continues," he concluded, "the migration will die. There will simply be too few animals to transmit the culture."

क

BY THE TIME SCHALLER WAS CROSSING the Antelope Plain—pass-ing close to where we now camp, and also like us, trying to locate the calving grounds—he had already been to the Chang Tang on five pre-vious expeditions, and he was beginning to see evidence that chiru were being shot for their wool. Eight months earlier he had been in the central Chang Tang to observe the winter rut of the male chiru when he encountered three nomads in a lone tent who had traveled by yak caravan to their remote location. They were hunting chiru, and bloody carcasses were "stacked like cordwood" next to the tent, and the animals' skins were inside, folded neatly. Then, in the town of Gertze, a trading center in the southern Chang Tang, Schaller saw in a courtyard several Tibetans plucking wool from chiru skins. He took a photograph, and when he showed the pictures to other nomads, he was told the wool was sold to middlemen who were taking it to Nepal and selling it to other middlemen who were then taking it to India. In another town he saw dozens of hides spread out to dry, and he was told they belonged to a chiru wool dealer. Then he learned that a local official was using vehicles to organize hunts with modern weapons in which at least a thousand chiru a year were being shot.

Six years earlier, in October 1985—on his first expedition to the Chang Tang—Schaller had witnessed an unseasonably brutal snowstorm that had killed thousands of chiru. When he returned the following year the hills were covered with the dehydrated carcasses of the dead animals, but all their skins were still on them. If at that time there had been a strong market for the wool, the nomads would have gathered the hides—it would have been as easy as picking money off the ground. So it was clear that in the short interim something significant had changed. Schaller didn't know what it was, but he did know, if it were to continue unchecked, what its effect would be: After observing the devastating impact the 1985 storm had on the chiru population, Schaller realized that apart from human intrusion the survival of these animals in such a harsh climate was always tenuous; and with the addition of uncontrolled and extensive poaching, he also knew he would likely be devoting his studies to an animal heading toward extinction.

CHAPTER THREE

क

JUNE 5

THE SKY IS OVERCAST and we are thankful the morning remains cold, as the ground stays frozen. We are pulling the carts up a series of shallow drainages, and while still hard work, we realize this section would probably have taken all day if the ground were soft. By eleven a.m. we gain the crest of a tableland that frames the east side of the unnamed glaciated mountain that, from its altitude on our map, we call "Peak 20,041."

We stop to rest. Galen turns on the GPS and then gets a fix on our position. "We just crossed the thirty-five-degree latitude mark," he says, "and we're heading east quite a ways, almost to eighty-two degrees, twenty-four minutes."

Conrad plots our position on a Russian map we have brought. In addition to our TPC map—from the 1:500,000 series of "Tactical Piloting Charts" printed in the United States that cover the globe—a friend who travels extensively in remote places in Asia gave me a tip to a small company that sells Russian-made 1:200,000 maps covering all of Central Asia, even this remote NW corner of the Chang Tang. They were expensive—over $500 just for the panels that cover our trek—but they also appear to be very accurate. They are dated 1942, and we guess they were made in the war years when the political alignment of Mongolia, Xinjiang, and Tibet was in question.

"Awesome pull this morning," Conrad says after he plots our position.

"We gained two hundred and seventy feet in an hour and a half," Galen adds, continuing to punch buttons on the GPS. "So elevation gain is pretty slow in these parts: Most of us could do twenty-five hundred or three thousand in that time, walking without a load."

I'm happy with two hundred seventy feet, but I'm not so content with the fact that, on this third day of our walk, we still haven't seen any chiru. We continue another hour and stop for lunch, each of us sitting on the ground, leaning against our carts and using as backrests the balloon tires strapped to the cargo bins. Before we continue, I decide to have another look through my binoculars, and I ask Jimmy to videotape me, to make sure we have coverage of the increasingly worrisome fact we can't find the migration.

"I don't know," I say for the camera as I scan hills in the mid-distance. "We're right on the migration route George drew on the map. But there's not an animal to be seen. I don't get it, unless we're late, or the migration has passed us, or the animals have taken another route—no, wait. Wait. I've got—yes, I've got three females against that hill, one, two, three, no there's more, and they're going the right direction."

I lower the binoculars, look back to the others and then realize they think I am acting this out for the camera. "Come here, Conrad, come here. This isn't bullshit."

Conrad, who is closest to me, walks over.

"This ain't the real world?" he says, apparently still thinking I'm trying to act out some scene for our film.

"It is the real world," I say, handing him the binoculars. "Look, against that hill, just this side of it."

He squats to brace his elbows on his knees, and I bend over him, pointing my finger toward the chiru.

"See them?" I ask.

"Yep, I've got them," he replies. "For real."

"I counted four."

"Four is what I've got, too."

I am excited as I continue to watch the animals slowly move north, until I remind myself that four animals is not enough to conclude we have found the migration route. The chiru disappear behind a hill, and I continue to scan the plain both north and south of their position. But once more the steppe is empty. I replace the binoculars in my pannier, zip it shut, lift the handlebar of my rickshaw over my head and step inside the traces, fasten the buckle on my waist belt, and resume pulling my rickshaw. The others follow. In the half hour we have paused to eat our lunch, the surface of the steppe has softened, and now I have to push with my feet to advance each step. I continue to scan the horizon, and the steppe continues to be barren of anything but scattered clumps of ceratoides.

The tempered excitement I felt seeing the chiru is displaced by vague melancholy, and the image of the four animals that disappeared behind the hill toward which I now pull my cart becomes emblematic, as though somehow they have become the last of their kind, the lone repository of genes that have taken eight million years or more to evolve into a code that has created creatures perfectly tuned to survive on this stark steppe. In my imaginings they become the final individuals, the last chiru making their last walk down a dark corridor leading to oblivion.

ॐ

As THE BUMPER STICKER SAYS, Extinction Is Forever. The first time in my life I had a sense of what this means, I was eleven years old, reading for homework an article in *Weekly Reader* about Martha, the last passenger pigeon on Earth, which lived out her life in a cage in the Cincinnati Zoo. I remember at the time wondering what people must have felt when they stood in front of the enclosure, looking through the wire at Martha. I suspect some of them, anyway, felt the same melancholy—the same loneliness that seems as deep as evolutionary time—that I have watching what in my imagination are the last chiru.

When Martha (named after Martha Washington) died, she was sent to the Smithsonian, where she was stuffed and then displayed with a plaque that read:

MARTHA
Last of her species, died at 1 p.m.,
1 September 1914, age 29, in the
Cincinnati Zoological Garden.
EXTINCT

What did the zookeeper feel when he entered the cage and found the pigeon dead? When he picked her up and held her in his hand? In his mind's eye, did he see the flocks that only fifty years before had darkened the noonday sun, flocks that took not hours but days to pass as the birds, flying at up to sixty miles an hour, migrated from their nesting areas around the Great Lakes to their wintering grounds in the Southeast? When the flocks would land for the night in the mixed hardwood forests, so many in a tree that branches would frequently break?

The rarest songbird in the United States, the Bachman's warbler, is now almost certainly extinct. This diminutive bird with a yellow breast and olive-green back once wintered in Cuba, then each spring crossed the Gulf of Mexico and fanned out across the southeastern United States, occupying a specific habitat of evergreen forest in winter and southern hardwood forest in summer, both of which, in the years following World War II, were increasingly cleared for agriculture. In May 1954 the eminent ornithologist and Harvard professor John Terborgh, then eighteen years old, learned that a Bachman's warbler had been sighted on a tributary of the Potomac, near Washington.

The next morning I was on the road by four-thirty, driving through the darkness with fears that my quarry might vanish with first light.... By the time I reached Pohick Creek, the sun was shining brightly, and the birds were singing everywhere.... To my astonishment, I walked up to the place that had been described to me and heard it! I had no trouble seeing the bird. A full-plumaged male, it sat on an open branch about 20 feet up and gave me a perfect view while it sang. It hardly stopped singing during the two hours I spent there. Reluctantly, I pulled myself away, wondering whether this was an experience I would ever repeat.[i]

The male warbler returned to the same place for the next two years. Each year he arrived on the bank of Pohick Creek, and each year he continued to sing through the day for a female that never came. After that, the bird was never seen again. The last verified sighting of a Bachman's warbler was in South Carolina, in 1962.

The plants and animals on our Earth have, of course, been on a continuous evolutionary progression of emergence and extinction, beginning with the first single-cell species that evolved in the Precambrian soup. E. O. Wilson, in his seminal work The Diversity of Life, estimates that fewer than one percent of all the species from one evolutionary epoch ever survive into the next. Using fossil records, scientists have determined that in the geological past there have been five periods when cataclysmic events have suddenly overwhelmed the biodiversity of our Earth and extinguished sometimes as many as ninety percent of all species that existed at that time. Most of us know about the great dinosaur kill-off sixty-five million years ago, caused perhaps by the collision of a meteor that spewed smoke and dust around the globe so thickly there was a noonday darkness that broke the existing food chains, causing entire ecosystems to collapse. There were earlier mass extinctions as well, two of them close together two hundred forty-five million and then again two hundred ten million years ago that were also most likely related to cataclysmic events, perhaps meteors, perhaps periods of extreme volcanic eruptions.

Our planet is now entering the sixth major spasm of extinction, and it is important to understand that it has been under way now for many thousands of years. It started about forty thousand years ago when most of the marsupial and large avian species in Australia suddenly died out in a short period of time that happened to coincide with the arrival on that continent of the species Homo sapiens. It gained momentum about ten thousand years when in North America about eighty percent of the megafaunal species suddenly went extinct, coinciding once again with the arrival of our species. In the past one thousand years, and especially in the past two hundred years, as our species' population has increased at the rate Malthus foretold two hundred years ago, the rate of extinction has continued to increase. In the rainforests, for example, species are now disappearing somewhere between one thousand to ten thousand times above what E. O. Wilson calls "the normal background extinction rate."

So we are in the middle of the first great period of extinction triggered not by natural cataclysm, but by us. To understand both intellectually and emotionally the degree to which we have already altered the environs of this planet, you need to be able to imagine landscapes as they used to be. Imagine them not as they were in some frontier era, but as they used to be before humans arrived. You must learn not only to see them in your mind, but also to hear them and to smell them.

The only way I know to do that is to travel to places that are still somewhat wild. When you see the savannas of East Africa, for example (especially in those parklands where there are few people), when you lie at night in your tent and hear the faint background cropping of tens of thousands of wildebeest grazing on the grasslands, and when you smell the fecund earthiness of the soil rise into the air as a rain squall passes, then you can imagine, with what might be proximate accuracy, the Los Angeles basin eleven thousand years ago when it was a grassland savanna with lions that looked just like African lions, with horses that had stripes just like zebras, with three species of elephants, herds of camels and bison and giant tree sloths and bears and wolves, with a sky that still held eleven species of vultures.

क

MUCH OF THE PREVIOUS EVENING'S SNOWFALL has melted, and the landscape is a patchwork of white and brown. The meltwater, trapped by permafrost, turns hardpan to soft mud that soon sticks to our tires and clogs our brakes. Each step is a struggle, and I ask myself whether it makes more sense to stop and wait until morning when the ground is frozen. Before I ask the others, however, I answer the question: With over eight hours of daylight left, we have to keep going, even if now we are expending more calories per mile.

We stop to get a bearing using the compass function on Conrad's wristwatch. "We want northeast by east," I tell him. "Fifty or fifty-five degrees."

"That hill there is fifty-five," he replies

"Perfect."

Conrad takes the lead, heading toward the hill. Although I don't need it at the moment, I now have a small compass mounted on the handlebar of my trace, thanks to Conrad. Earlier in the day I had admired the compass, which then was on Conrad's cart, and despite my protestations he cut it off his handlebar and mounted it on mine. "I don't need two compasses," he had said, referring to his wristwatch. He has left the ends of the two lock ties he used to secure the compass uncut, so they now stand in an upright V-shape that mimics the horns of a male chiru. Each time I check the compass it triggers a reminder of Conrad's generosity, and that's a thought that I find pleasant.

Which is good, because pulling the carts through this increasingly soft mud is not so pleasant. We stop at three p.m. to rest, and cleaning the mud off his wheels Galen discovers the setscrew that keeps his axle in place is missing. Conrad gets another from our bag of parts, but cautions that it is our only spare, and that we must all get in the habit of checking through the day that the fasteners on our carts are tight. It's a reminder that in this uninhabited vastness even a small thing like a lost screw could be serious.

The ground continues to soften, and the carts become even more difficult to pull. We designed the rickshaws to accommodate the balloon tires we have tied to the back of each cart in case we encountered soft soil or snow, but as it takes over an hour to change the tires on each cart we decide it is not worth it: By the time we had the balloon tires on it would also be time to camp, and in the morning the ground will be frozen, making the mountain bike tires again the most efficient choice. Instead we decide to deflate the mountain bike tires, lowering the pressure to about ten pounds per square inch.

That makes the carts easier to pull, but the effort is still arduous. There is a dull ache from my shoulder blades to the small of my back, and I would like nothing more than to stop and stretch, but I discipline myself to keep making one step and then another. Finally at four p.m. we make the twin decision to camp early and also to wake early so in the morning we can cover more miles while the ground is frozen. When we have the tents pitched, Galen and I walk a mile or so to the edge of the tableland, where we sit on top of a cutbank that allows us a view north and east for twenty miles in both directions.

"Two hundred square miles, and not a single animal," Galen says as he scans the wide steppe with our binoculars.

"I guess it's just those four chiru we saw this morning," I reply.

At least our reconnaissance has revealed the easiest way off the tableland. Looking north, we can see that tomorrow we will cross an open steppe perhaps five miles wide, and on the far side, even though we again have to enter foothills, the ascent looks gradual. On the way back to the tents I notice the ground is covered in thin, round plants that look like fungal growths on the skin of the steppe.

"Arenarias," Galen says. "They grow at 17,000 feet and even higher, in barren places like this."

At camp the sun sets through a narrow open in the striated clouds, and the slanting rays bathe our tents in gold light. As we stand sipping cocoa, an iridescent band—blue-green-yellow-red—forms above the northeast horizon.

"A circum-horizontal rainbow," Galen says excitedly. "It's in ice crystals, not in water vapor, the way you have in regular rainbows that are in arcs. It's quite a rare phenomenon that you see in high mountains and polar areas every once in a while, and we're lucky to see it now."

We're also lucky to have our own professor of the outdoors on our team. Since his boyhood growing up in the Berkeley Hills, Galen has been an avid amateur student of the natural sciences—especially geology—and I know Conrad and Jimmy appreciate, as I do, his amplifications on the things we are seeing. We watch the rainbow until it fades along with the sun, then we crawl into our tents. Propped on my sleeping bag, I plug in my miniature earphones to the small tape recorder I carry, and transcribe into my journal the notes I have made during the day. Galen completes his camera notes and then asks, as he has every evening, if I am reading Schaller's *Wildlife of the Tibetan Steppe*. I tell him, as I have every evening, that he is welcome to borrow it. I give him the book, and while I finish my notes he begins where he left off, reading aloud the end of the chapter on chiru:

> So far even the location of the calving grounds of the migratory populations remains unknown. This chapter offers a baseline of information about chiru, but it also represents a call for action, for the pressing need to study the species while it still roams the Chang Tang in moderate numbers.

"So I guess we're answering the call to action," I say.

"It's just too bad George isn't here with us."

"He didn't think he'd be strong enough to pull a cart," I reply.

"He probably could have done it," Galen says. "He's not even seventy yet."

There is no irony in the tone of Galen's comment, so I know he regards it as matter-of-fact. I consider how the comment is also a window into how Galen imagines the arc of his own life, and of the physical strength he expects to own when he is seventy.

"'How old would you be,'" I say, quoting the baseball great Satchel Paige, "'if you didn't know how old you was?'"

Galen laughs, telling me he's going to remember that one. [ii]

JUNE 6

WE WAKE AT FIVE THIRTY A.M., when the star-studded sky is black and the coming day only a vague glow in the east; we leave camp at seven, when the sky is a deep blue that graduates to deep orange that becomes in the east a bright yellow. Save for a few clouds in the west, the sky is clear, and as we jump with our carts across the braids of a stream a hundred feet from where we camped, the water reflects the single beam of intense light that breaks above the long, flat horizon.

We follow the edge of the tableland that surrounds the east flank of Peak 20,041, and to our right our view sweeps across the Antelope Plain to Toze Kangri, thirty miles away. An hour out of camp we descend a cutbank that leads to the shallow basin Galen and I observed the evening before. We have inflated our tires to full pressure, and now the rickshaws glide almost without effort over the frozen desert pavement. We cross what in the afternoon will be a thin flow of water but now is a veneer of ice, and the wheels of our heavy carts break through as though they were fracturing panes of glass.

An hour later to the west we see, toward the base of Peak 20,041, two groups of female chiru: sixteen animals still bedded down, their tawny coats inconspicuous against the dun floor of the steppe, and five other females beginning the day's start-stop-start migration. Through Galen's long lens—with a viewfinder on the rear element converting it to spotting scope—we watch the animals browse for a minute or two, walk a few yards, and then stop again to browse.

"That means they've been to the west of us all this time," I say.

"That's what I've always thought, from what George said," Galen replies.

He is referring to the migration track Schaller observed in 1992 that we have copied to our map. For the last twenty miles that line has been to our west, but since it crosses foothills much more difficult to traverse than the flat plains to the east—and as there seems to be as much browse in one place as in the other—I have intuited that the chiru have more likely been to our east, following the path of least resistance.

"East or west, I don't care," I say. "As long as this is the migration route."

But we know that even these two groups of chiru are not enough to match the description of the migration route told to us by Schaller. In another hour we enter rounded hills, and as we pull the carts up a gradual slope we pass a small lake where I identify, by their black heads and pintails, two Tufted ducks. By noon the sun is stronger than on any previous day.

"The mud is starting to happen," Jimmy says.

We discuss switching to the balloon tires, but once again we decide the trade-off of time it would take to make the switch isn't worth it. In the deeper wallows each step takes extra effort to pull our boots free of the mud, and when they do release they make a sucking sound. We stop for lunch and notice on the softening surface, like the fossil record of the passage of some ancient creature, the barely perceptible tracks of a vehicle that somehow made it to this remote place, presumably on a day when the ground was much firmer than it is now.

"They look old," Conrad notes.

"They're probably Schaller's," I say. "Given the terrain, this would have been the only place he could have got his vehicle through these hills."

"This is classic," Galen says. "One of the wildest places I've ever been, and still I'm following the tracks of George Schaller."

क

FROM READING SCHALLER'S ACCOUNT of his expeditions to the Chang Tang, and also from my interviews with him before leaving on our trek, we know he had been able to drive another twenty-odd miles north from where we are currently stopped to have lunch. Then he encountered a rising ridge of black lava that was too steep to cross in his Land Cruiser. He set up camp, and next day he and his Tibetan driver continued on foot in the distant hope that the calving grounds might be on the other side of the ridge.

Schaller wrote a description of that walk, and when I read it while planning our expedition, it had whetted my desire to see what is one of the most remote and little-known places on our planet:

> Below was a huge basin divided into two arms. Giant peaks of the Kunlun Shan bordered the arm most distant from us and sent glaciers down to the basin floor. Across from us and dividing the arms were three massive volca-noes, their tops blown off and covered with snow and ice. In the basin were two lakes connected by a stream; a small lake sheathed in ice and a much larger lake extending

toward the northeast. At least five small volcanic cones and lava fields were along the eastern margin of the large lake, which Chinese maps aptly call Heishi Beihu, Blackrock Northlake. I viewed the topography with special interest. The chiru had vanished here, and, to my knowledge, no other Westerner had ever viewed this imposing scene, one of the most remote and untrodden spots on earth. Deasy, Rawlings, Wellby, and Hedin had all bypassed this basin.

For the next three hours Schaller and his Tibetan companion continued to walk north, following chiru tracks, but they saw only six animals. Schaller concluded that the migration had already passed, and that the calving grounds were still farther north. Through binoculars he could see, beyond the basin, a range of low foothills that he concluded must offer for the chiru a route to Xinjiang, where he assumed they go "toward their traditional and mysterious goal, too far for us to follow with our limited gasoline supply."

He turned and walked back to his camp where the Tibetan co-leader of his expedition, who had also accompanied him on his exploration of the Aru Basin two years earlier, said that perhaps they were fated not to discover where the chiru go to have their babies. Schaller then quoted a Tibetan proverb that said, "The goal will not be reached if the right distance is not traveled."

By then his frustration was propelled by more than simply a scientist's desire to fill the gaps in the knowledge of the chiru's natural history. He had also seen the nomad women plucking wool from chiru hides, and he had heard the stories of corrupt officials organizing hunts in which thousands of chiru were being killed. He knew that if chiru were to be saved from extinction something was going to have to be done about the poaching, but it was difficult to know where to start when he didn't even know what the market was for the wool. Then unexpectedly he received a letter from a businessman who had a trading company that purchased rare wools—including cashmere, camel wool, and yak—in Mongolia and Tibet.

His name was Michael Sautman, and what he had to say in the letter was, for Schaller, revelatory.

"I am writing in regard to some research I am doing on a wool product called Shahtoosh," Sautman stated. "As you may know, Shahtoosh is found mainly in Tibet where we believe it is derived from an animal called Capra ibex…. The animal molts its winter coat in the spring by rubbing its body on rocks and bushes after which passing nomads collect the wool. It is brought into Nepal and Ladakh where it is bought by Kashmiri weavers who produce the famous shahtoosh shawls."

Sautman explained that he had a client who was interested in obtaining this wool, but that he was writing Schaller first because he wanted to learn more about the origin of shahtoosh, just to make sure harvesting the wool was indeed a benign benefit to the local economy, as he had been told, and not, as had happened with vicuna wool in South America, killing the source animal.

"Is it in fact from C. ibex or is it derived from some other animal?" Sautman asked. "Where in Tibet are the animals found? What is the precise chain of supply? What is the condition of the herds?"

Schaller had never heard of shahtoosh, which isn't surprising as he is in the business of tracking wild animals, not fashion trends. But he did know there were no ibex in Tibet, and he had never seen any nomads plucking wool off rocks or bushes. But he had seen them in that courtyard plucking wool off the hides of chiru. Seemingly out of nowhere the missing piece of a puzzle had come in over the transom and landed on his desk.

He wrote back to Sautman explaining that since there are no ibex in Tibet, this shahtoosh wool had to be from Tibetan antelope. "You cannot gather (Tibetan) antelope wool like you can pick up muskox, yak and camel wool," Schaller wrote back to Sautman. "You have to kill the antelope. I just returned from Tibet, where I witnessed such killing. A herdsman can sell an antelope hide to a dealer for the equivalent of $30, a considerable incentive to kill."

Schaller knew the next step was to learn more about the smuggling of the wool and the manufacture of the shawls. Knowing he was fortunate to have encountered a businessman interested in more than simply making money, he asked Sautman if he could supply more information about shahtoosh.

"What I can tell you about the shahtoosh trade in Nepal," Sautman wrote back, "is that it is mainly conducted by wool traders from Darchula, in the northwest of the country. They barter and buy from the Tibetans and then smuggle the wool into India to sell it in Delhi to Kashmiris or bring it directly to Srinagar."

Sautman had been to Kashmir many times, and even on his first trip, in 1976, he had heard the story told by the weavers that shahtoosh was the hair of the ibex, and that it was shed naturally and plucked off rocks and bushes. Because it appeared that everyone believed this story, Sautman suspected it had been in circulation a long time. This suspicion was confirmed when, after doing more research, he found in a book by William Moorcroft—a trade officer of the British East India Company who had traveled to Kashmir and Tibet to investigate, among other things, the shahtoosh trade—the same story. Moorcroft's book was published in 1839.

With the picture connecting the slaughter of chiru with the growing popularity of shahtoosh shawls coming into focus, Schaller's next step was to explain to Chinese officials in the Forestry Department—the agency charged with administering the lands that encompassed most of the chiru's habitat—why the animals were being poached.

"They quite astonished me," Schaller said when he recounted this part of the story of the effort to contain the poaching of chiru. "In effect they told me, 'You have to let this be known internationally because we can't handle it just ourselves.' The Chinese often try to hide a problem, but here they were encouraging me to move on it."

With characteristic alacrity, Schaller promptly did just that.

क

AFTER OUR LUNCH BREAK, we ascend another long slope. A wind has picked up and, with sun that shines through a mostly open sky, the combined effect is beginning to dry the ground, and pulling the rickshaws is easier, although "easier" only compared with the exhausting work required to advance the carts through even softer mud. At the top of the slope we find an arcticlike meadow covered with tussocks of hearty alpine grass. The gently rounded hummocks, each about two feet across, give me an idea, and unbuckling my cart I lie down on one and roll on my back side to side.

"Wow, how does that feel?" Jimmy asks.

"It's a kind of self-administered Swedish massage," I answer.

Jimmy joins me, and soon we are both sighing in pleasure as we roll on our backs. Pulling the heavy carts seems to strain my back even more than my legs, and as I roll around, the top of the hummock kneads my sore muscles like the palm of a masseuse. Galen and Conrad are standing next to their carts, and when I finish my massage I remain on my back, looking at the sky. No one is talking, the wind has died, and the silence is so pervasive it seems to have weight.

"We better get going," Galen says.

"Get going to what?" I ask, impatient with Galen's impatience.

"You want to stay here?"

"It would make a good campsite."

"But we still have at least four hours of daylight. Maybe five."

We continue, but I sense Jimmy and Conrad had wanted to camp at the col as well. I cart alongside Conrad and ask, "Do I need to be a leader here?" and he nods. I step up my pace so I can catch Galen, who is in the lead.

"Galen, Conrad and Jimmy say they're ready to camp, too."

"Well, I think we should still get in another mile at least."

"But we need to pace ourselves. It's like Amundsen beating Scott to the South Pole. I can't remember what it was, but he set a moderate pace going the same number of miles each day."

"Eight miles a day," Galen says.

"Yeah, eight miles."

"I agree we need to pace, but I'd like to find a better campsite."

"Okay," I reply, deciding it's better to accommodate Galen, as I suspect Conrad and Jimmy are flexible—for now.

We keep going, descending into a new drainage that tends west. In a half hour I see just above the incipient creek an attractive flat large enough for our two tents, with a hill behind it that would offer at least partial protection from wind.

"How about that bench over there," I call to Galen.

"It looks pretty good," he replies. "Okay, let's camp there."

There is no frustration in his voice, and there is none in mine, either. We park our carts, and as we unpack I realize that Galen is pushing to go as far as we can because he pushes himself to go as far as he can in whatever he does. For him, it's a daily ritual; for the rest of us it's a trait of personality that I suspect we can all easily accommodate, as it also has the potential to be an attribute that could very well prove valuable before this is over. After dinner we all agree to wake an hour earlier than we have been, so that we can leave even before first light and that way cart a mile or two farther before, as Jimmy likes to put it, the mud starts to happen.

JUNE 7

TWO HOURS BEFORE DAWN I wake to a sound like a blowtorch: Conrad, in the neighboring tent, starting the stove. I zip open the door on my side of the tent and peer out: the cone-beam from my headlamp illuminates six inches of snow fallen during the night. Galen is also awake, and I give him the weather report. So much for our early start so we could take advantage of frozen ground. Pulling through snow will be just as difficult as mud.

Galen and I zip open our warm sleeping bags and begin what in only five days has become a ritual. First, I maneuver into my cold pants, sit up and pull on my fleece jacket. I stuff my sleeping bag, roll up my inflatable pad, then position everything I've brought into the tent near the door so I can reach it easily once I start the task of loading the rickshaw. With boots on Galen and I crawl out of our tent and cross to Conrad and Jimmy's tent for our brief breakfast.

"Top of the morning," Conrad says as I crawl in.

Like families do at the dinner table, we each have claimed our favorite corners of the tent. Conrad is sitting legs crossed in the corner that is at the head of his sleeping bag and Jimmy, who is most mornings still asleep when Conrad wakes, is propped up in his sleeping bag. I always take the same corner near the tent's entrance, and Jimmy always reaches under his bag to retrieve his folding backrest that doubles as a sleeping pad, and gives it to me so I have a comfortable seat. Then Galen zips open the tent, hands me his cup, bowl and spoon, crawls in and takes off his boots, and zips closed the tent. We are now ready for a fine cup of Major Dickason's Blend.

"If this was a climb," Conrad says, pouring the coffee, "today would be a chillin' day."

"But we're not going up," I answer, "we're going across, which means there's no such thing as a weather day."

"If we can't have fun," Conrad replies, "at least we can suffer."

We finish our coffee and eat our small but very equal portion of granola mixed with powdered milk to which we have added water. Jimmy hands out lunch: an energy bar, a small packet of dried fruit, small packet of nuts, and a couple of sticks of jerky. Same thing we had yesterday, same thing we'll have tomorrow.

"Should we have a second cup of coffee?" Conrad asks.

No one replies. With reluctance I say what I know we are all thinking.

"We should probably get ready to go."

By the time we are under way a vague light illuminates the gray hills. There is no wind, and dawn reveals a sky of patchy clouds. The wheels of our carts leave deep furrows in the snow, and as the day brightens I listen to a snow finch sound a morning chirp that carries a springlike cheer incongruous in this arcticlike landscape. The half-light reflects off the stream and makes the virgin snow, expansive in smooth, shallow dimples, sparkle with iridescent flashes. If the night's snowfall has dashed hopes for a morning of easy pulling, it has awarded us a dawn of wintry spectacle: To the east the slanting sun feathers through a reef of clouds; to the west alpenglow paints the snow-blanketed hills pink; to the north a luminescent band of purple, green, yellow, and red hovers above the horizon.

Then the sun breaks above the clouds and our figures cast long shadows over the fresh snow. I take the lead, and looking up I see a mile ahead a lake that becomes my goal. I keep a steady pace, pushing with each step against my waistband in order to pull the cart through the snow: It's like making very high reps on a leg press machine.

"R-2?" I ask.

"R-2," Conrad replies.

As we follow the stream toward the lake, the hills open to a broad steppe now covered in snow, and I suggest bearing left to stay on our rhomb-line.

"First let's top off the bladders," Conrad suggests.

It's odd in this snow to be concerned about water, but we all know that by afternoon it will likely have melted, and we could be crossing an arid steppe where water could be scarce or even absent. With our water bladders full we are about to leave when Conrad suggests we all coat our faces with sunscreen: The clouds are dissipating, and it promises to be a cloudless day. We continue, and as we descend to the plain the central range of the Kunlun Mountains comes into view. These mountains—surely one of the most remote ranges on Earth—are from my dreams; after all these years of reading Sven Hedin, of hearing that magic name "Kun Lun," they are in my view.

As the snow softens it sticks to our tires, building on the rims and spokes—as a snowball builds when it's rolled along—until finally the accumulation breaks away. Then the cycle starts over.

"Why don't I be the guinea pig and try switching out to the Roleez," I tell the others, referring to the brand name of the balloon tires tied to the backs of our carts.

"You think it's worth it?" Galen asks.

"When the snow melts it's going to turn to mud. I don't know, it'll take maybe an hour per cart?"

"Maybe less," Conrad says.

"Let's see how it goes," Galen agrees. "It'll be a good test."

I unload my cart, and we turn it on its side, remove the mountain bike tire and rim, then unbolt the wheel frame, as it needs to be repositioned on the cargo bin so the cart has sufficient clearance once the smaller balloon tires are installed. While I hold the balloon tire in position, Conrad inserts the new axle and spacer-bushings, and then inserts a drift pin to line up the hole for the bolt that holds the axle in alignment.

As Conrad estimated, it takes just under an hour to complete the switch. I reload the cart and pull it a few yards to try it.

"So are we going to be jealous?" Galen asks.

"You might be for the next few hours, but then it's going to freeze and your tires will be better. Who knows?"

For the next hour we take turns pulling my cart, and while everyone agrees that in the snow it is easier, we also agree it isn't worth the nearly three hours it would take to change the other three carts. As the snow continues to melt we stop for lunch on the first exposed ground we encounter. Even though we rest for less than an hour, by the time we start again there are only a few patches of snow remaining on the steppe. Perhaps because the sky is clear and the air drier, much of the snow seems to be sublimating, so there isn't as much mud as the day before, and pulling is relatively easy.

I've noticed that we each have developed our own favored method of holding the traces or the crossbar as we pull our carts. While each method allows the cart driver to vary the force of the pull between the traces and the waistbelt, Galen holds his traces on the side, with his elbows bent, and further, he has rigged a string to the traces that loops over his neck and keeps the two aluminum pull-poles at the correct level. Jimmy also holds the sides of his traces but with his elbows locked and his hands slightly aft of where Galen positions his. Conrad, on the other hand, instead of holding the traces, grabs the front crossbar at eye level, pushing sometimes with two hands and other times with only one hand while the other dangles. I also tend to favor holding the crossbar, but with both hands and lower, as though I'm pushing a shopping cart.

We go for nearly an hour without talking. The snow melts, and we pull the carts through a section of ceratoides spaced too closely to avoid, and we have no choice but to muscle the carts over the procumbent shrubs. To our left, the Kunluns—in this part of the range a series of volcanoes whose tops in some epochal past have blown—frame one side of our view. To our right a distant rainsquall moves across the plain like a curtain across a stage, while in front the horizon shimmers under heat waves as though the sky were melting into the earth.

"Look, animals," Jimmy exclaims, pointing ahead. "Hundreds of them!"

We stop and squint toward the liquid horizon, and sure enough, through the heat waves, we can make out dozens of dark bumps. I loosen my waistbelt so I can turn and pull my binoculars from my pannier, but when I bring the animals into focus I see instead dozens of rocks shimmering as though they were alive.

"It's like a mirage of water in the desert," Jimmy says when I give him the report, "but instead of dying of thirst, we're dying to see chiru."

क

TWO HOURS LATER we reach a thirty-foot cutbank with a small stream nearby and, with no other shelter from wind visible for miles, we decide to set up the tents.

"This is Camp Five," Conrad says.

"Maybe we should name them," I suggest. "With some kind of mnemonic, to make it easier to remember."

"Any suggestions for this one?"

I look around at the flat steppe extending in all directions.

"How about Kansas?" I offer.

"Perfect," Galen agrees.

"And we'll call last night's camp Arctic Camp," Conrad adds.

The sky is without a single cloud, and using our GPS Galen confirms that the barometer is rising. It is unlikely it will snow tonight, and since the clear sky also suggests the night will be cold—and by morning the ground deeply frozen—I ask Conrad to help me switch my cart back to the mountain bike tires. We have just finished the job when I hear a gull-like cry, and looking up I see a Saker falcon fly close enough over camp I can make out the distinctive malar stripe below its eye. It veers downwind at high speed, its knife-wings cutting the air.

When all the tents are pitched, the four of us climb the cutbank and, hands in pockets, walk along its edge. As the sun approaches the horizon to the west, the Kunluns, though thirty miles away, are so vivid they appear to be half that distance; to the north we see the black hills that we know from our map surround Heishi Beihu; to the east the smaller ranges of the Chang Tang diminish until only their tips appear above the horizon; to the south the glacial massif of Toze Kangri and the Aru Mountains rise like white islands out of a sere sea.

I leave the others, continuing along the edge of the bank, and for the first time on our journey I regret a decision I made in Lhasa to leave my camera. This for me was unusual, as I have over the years made a portion of my living taking photographs, but on this journey I didn't want to intrude on Galen's turf, and further, I was attracted to the idea of relying only on my eyes and pen to record the expedition. Even though at the moment I have a desire to take a self-portrait of my long shadow casting across this landscape, I console myself with the reminder I am walking the bank free of the weight of a camera around my neck, as well as with the knowledge the image will remain imprinted in my memory.

I return to camp, where Conrad has started dinner, and in a few minutes I hear him call, "Soup's up." Galen and I crawl in Conrad and Jimmy's tent and sit in our habitual corners. Using a plastic serving spoon with a folding handle, I apportion the soup, a thin broth made from two cubes of beef bouillon, two tablespoons of olive oil, and a dash from a bottle of Chinese hot sauce we picked up at a roadside restaurant during our drive from Lhasa to the roadhead. Meanwhile Conrad is finishing the main course, which is always one of three menus: rehydrated and fried falafel mix, three-bean stew, or TSP, "textured soy product," a bland powder that cooks into chewy pellets that by perverse optimism we call, only because of their shape and color, baby clams.

At the same time Jimmy cuts (with great care) our daily portion of Parmesan, and also our daily slice of salami that he then, with a surgeon's precision, quarters. The Parmesan breaks into uneven pieces that he arranges on the pot lid into four equal piles, adding to each a small wedge of salami. Then he takes the rind from the Parmesan, skewers it on his pocketknife, leans down on one elbow—so he can hold the knife under the cooking pot on our stove—and roasts the rind. When the rind turns brown and bubbles, dripping cheese fat, Jimmy cuts it into quarters and hands each of us what we have come to call "roasties." Conrad pours a thimble of olive oil into the container's cap, and we each dip our piece of roastie into oil that out here seems as precious as gold.

Jimmy moans as he eats his tidbit, saying it's as good as the best hors d'oeuvre in the most expensive restaurant. Conrad eats his with a smile while Galen pops his in his mouth and swallows it quickly.

"Have either of you guys ever been on a trip like this one, focused on wildlife?" Galen asks Jimmy and Conrad.

"This is my first one," Conrad answers, and Jimmy says the same thing.

"It's what we're designed to do," Galen says. "To stalk animals. That's why it's so much fun."

"We're also designed to kill and eat them," I add.

"I think wildlife photography is just channeling our basic instincts," Galen replies.

"Anybody ready for TSP?" Conrad asks.

"Sure," Galen says, passing his bowl.

"I agree about basic instincts," I say. "In fact, I've done some thinking about that following a long trek I made a few years back across the Tsavo, that desert bushland area in Kenya that's still pretty wild. After that trip I started to wonder whether or not humans as a species have a predilection not just for hunting, but for hunting out the animals around us. I studied East Africa and other places of the world, then had a look at the prehistoric record, how we apparently killed off most of the megafauna in Australia when we first showed up, and then did the same in North America. So I've come to the conclusion that whenever given the opportunity combined with the capability, we'll more often than not hunt them to extinction. That's not to say there weren't some cases where native peoples were good stewards—some of the tribes in the Northwest regulated their salmon fishing—but I think if somehow the Plains Indians had managed to get four-wheel-drive vehicles and semiautomatic weapons instead of horses and rifles, they would have taken out the buffalo before we did."

"Just like some of the drokpa are taking out the chiru," Conrad says. "Even though they're Buddhists."[iii]

"Which some people, for a while anyway, refused to believe," Galen adds. "Schaller was once supposed to speak at a conference on Tibet about wildlife, and some of the people advocating Tibet's freedom wanted to blackball him because he was claiming the drokpa were involved in the poaching, and they refused to believe that because the drokpa are Buddhists."

"The Buddha also admonished his disciples to see things as they are," I say. "And if you really try to do that, then you also realize we're smart enough to overcome whatever basic instincts or imperatives we've inherited to hunt animals out. Like you say, Galen, we can channel it into things like wildlife photography. That's exactly what Denys Finch-Hatton did, the character Redford played in Out of Africa. In the 1930s Finch-Hatton was one of the leading big-game hunting guides in east Africa, but as he started seeing things like hunters bagging dozens of lions in a single trip he started advocating photography safaris in place of shooting safaris. He was way ahead of his time in seeing how adventure tourism could be an economic justification for establishing wildlife reserves."

"Then the next step is to include people like the drokpa in those economic benefits, so they also see the value in protecting the wildlife," Galen says.

"I've talked to George about that," I reply. "He's not sure that model would work in the Chang Tang. It's just not the kind of place that's going to pull in lots of tourists."

"You mean they're not going to line up to pull two-hundred-and-fifty-pound rickshaws through mud for a month?" Jimmy says with a grin.

JUNE 8

WE WAKE NEARLY THREE HOURS before dawn, determined to log as many miles as possible across the hardpan before it thaws. By headlamp I pack my cart: foodbags in the bottom (because they are heaviest), fuel bottles at the back, duffel on top, tent behind the duffel, water bladders behind the tent to add weight to the back of the cart, because that seems to make it easier to pull. When I have everything packed, I turn off my headlamp and pause for a moment to enjoy the night-sky, familiar at this latitude: the Big Dipper pointing to Arcturus, then to Scorpio and Sagittarius; then the Little Dipper pointing to Polaris. There is only a small band of clouds to the northeast, and the light of the stars illuminates in ghostly outline the Kunlun Mountains.

Once the others are ready, we leave. To conserve batteries, every-one but Conrad turns off their headlamps. In the east a fingernail moon glows through a reef of clouds. When Conrad's light exposes marmot or pika holes—some as wide as our boots—we fix their posi-tions in our minds so we can step over them in the dark. The ground is frozen, and we move fast so that in only ten minutes I am sweating, and I have to call a quick stop to peel off my jacket. We are traveling at a compass bearing of thirty degrees, and I assume that Conrad, like me, is using the stars in the sky to maintain our course.

We arrive at a stream flowing across the hardpan whose shallow edges are coated in ice. It is too broad to jump, and the only alter-native to walking in wet boots is to cross barefoot. Like standing at the edge of a cold swimming pool trying to summon courage to dive in—when you know hesitation is only going to make it worse— I decide the best strategy is not to think about it, but just cross the stream as quickly as possible. As I pack my boots and socks under the bungee cords strapped over my cart, the ground stings the soles of my bare feet like cold steel. I refasten my waist belt and step onto a sheet of ice that is like a wide pane of glass. I'm struggling to get traction to pull the cart when the ice cracks and my feet plunge into water. I pull the rickshaw as quickly as I can into the open stream, and halfway my exposed calves disappear underwater. On the oppo-site side I have to dig footholds with my toes into the rubblework bank, and once I have my feet on top I then pull with all the force I can muster to get the cart up the undercut.

"How was it?" Conrad calls out in the dark.

"About like it looked," I reply.

While the others cross I sit on the back of my cart and use the upper part of my socks to dry my feet. Jimmy is the last, and once across he borrows Conrad's camp towel to dry off.

"I finally got to wash my feet," he says.

Under way again, our feet warm quickly, and we cross the frozen hardpan at a pace close to a jog. As dawn brightens, from all directions across the plains come the cheering chirps of the snow finches. Because the carts pull so easily across the frozen ground, we try unfastening our waistbelts and propel the carts either by pushing on the crossbar or by grabbing the traces and pulling; Conrad calls this technique "trad rickshaw style." These alternatives offer welcome relief to our sore hips, until we hit a "ceratoides forest" and have no choice but to buckle our waistbelts. Then it takes a few minutes until the sore spots around my waist once more go numb.

"Full-contact carting," Conrad calls it. "Like playing rugby where you're getting beat up."

"R-2?" I ask.

"R-2," he replies.

At eight a.m. we stop to fix our position. Galen, reading the GPS, calls out the figures to Conrad, who plots them on our Russian map. The sky is cloudless, there is no wind, and Galen reports the barometer is still high. Then a Saker flies over—perhaps the same falcon I saw yesterday—and its single-note call is absorbed by the vast steppe.

क

WE STOP FOR AN EARLY LUNCH at the base of a ridge that on our map we see leads to Heishi Beihu. We can also see it will be a long pull. The ridge appears to be a basaltic flow originating from a series of cinder cones to the west, and the ground is covered with black pumice. Beyond the cinder cones, farther west in the

Kunlun range, is a snow- and glacier-covered caldera that is all that remains of what appears once to have been a huge volcano whose top in the geological past must have blown off; indeed, tracing the angle of what remains of the cone into the sky, the vestigial peak was probably above eight thousand meters, and I wonder if we are looking at a mountain that prehistorically was higher than Everest.[iv]

We begin the climb up the ridge, each step a strain to advance the heavy carts. We are heading toward what I pray is the pass when we see eight migrating chiru. Does this mean we are approaching the main migration route? Or are these animals, perhaps like those we saw two days ago, solitary groups traveling apart from the main migration? The animals disappear behind the ridge above us, and when finally we reach this "pass," we see on the other side that instead of a descending slope there is another long pull uphill to another "pass." Just as disappointing, there is no sign of the eight chiru, and no sign of a migration trail.

For the last hour I have been developing a cough, and now my eyes are watering. I'm not sure if it's the beginning of a cold, flu, or perhaps just allergies, but I feel enervated. It's hard enough pulling these two hundred and fifty pound carts up a grade at seventeen thousand feet when you're feeling good, but now it's a struggle to make each step. I don't want to fall behind, so I try to match the pace of the others, but slowly the gap between us increases. Then I have to stop to catch my breath, and they pull away even farther.

When they reach the second "pass" I am relieved to see they stop to wait for me. I lower my head and focus on the hope that the three of them at the moment are gazing into an inviting basin with a gently declining slope that will allow the rickshaws to roll effortlessly to our next campsite. I keep my head down, feeling with each step the muscles in my legs and back tense. I try to breathe evenly, but then I cough and have to gasp to get enough oxygen. I force myself at each stride not to look up in case the distance I have to cover is still substantial. Then in the top of my vision I see my comrades. I take ten more steps and I am there. Slowly I raise my eyes. There is Conrad...then Galen...then Jimmy...then another long uphill pull to another "pass."

"You doing okay?" Conrad asks.

"Just a little slow," I reply, struggling between coughs to catch my breath.

He nods and leaves, and the others follow. I don't want to fall behind, but I have to rest for at least a minute or two before I can start. Searching in my pannier, I am relieved to find I have one remaining cough drop. By the time I catch my breath and start again, the others are already partway up the next hill. I can feel a pain developing in the top of my left lung, and now I fear that instead of an allergy maybe this cough is the beginning of pneumonia.

Once again I stare at the ground, following their tire tracks. Now in addition to my cough I am starting to feel dizzy, indicating I am also hypoxic. I force myself not to dwell on these negative thoughts, but instead to focus on making each step. I refuse to look up until finally I see my companions in the top of my vision, maybe thirty feet away. I keep walking toward them, eyes to the ground. I am only ten feet away when I steel myself and raise my eyes and there beyond Jimmy, Conrad, and Galen is...a gentle downhill slope that goes for several hundred yards to a small pond surrounded by a wide ring of cracked mudcake.

"What if we camp next to that tarn?" Conrad says.

I am thankful for his suggestion, and we descend to the pond to have a closer look. When we arrive, however, we find the area barren. There is not a single ceratoides bush, and any ground that is flat is also muddy. We taste the water, and it is brackish. It's an ugly campsite, but still I am searching for any rationale to stop and set up the tents.

"We have enough water in the bladders to make it until tomorrow," I offer.

Conrad and Jimmy agree with my desire to camp, but Galen wants to keep going to see if we can find a location that might offer a better view, and with it, the hope of seeing chiru.

"I'll run down there and see what it looks like," Galen offers, pointing down the drainage we have been following. He unbuckles his waistbelt and I watch as he runs at a fast pace downhill and disappears around a bend. In a half hour I spot him jogging back. I check my watch. It's four p.m. We have been pulling our rickshaws for ten hours. For the last four hours we have been trudging uphill at an elevation above seventeen thousand feet. Galen is sixty-two years old. How does he do it?

"I got down to the bottom," he reports when he reaches us, "and could see the beginning of a valley where there were about a dozen chiru grazing."

"You think there might be more?" Conrad asks.

"There's a good chance. There was stipa grass in the valley, and we haven't seen any of that since we left Toze Kangri. It's a perfect place to camp."

Conrad looks at me, shrugs his shoulders, and says, "I'm okay camping here or there."

"Same with me," Jimmy says.

Once again I am in the position of having to be the expedition leader. At the moment it is a role I wish I could pass to one of the others. My left lung hurts when I cough, which is frequently, and my hips and back ache. This tarn is more mud hole than pond, and there are no chiru. But I would love nothing more than to set up my tent and crawl in it.

"Okay. Let's keep going," I tell the others.

Conrad takes the lead, moving downhill at a pace that even Galen can't match. He is perhaps a quarter mile ahead of me when I see him stop, park his cart, and hike up a sandy ramp on the side of the hill that borders the lateral drainage we are descending. By the time we reach his cart he is coming down.

"We'd have to double-team our carts, but if we can get them up this ramp, there's a gorgeous campsite at the top of this ridge that's hidden from the valley. If there are any more chiru in the area, they wouldn't be able to see us."

"That's a great idea," Galen says. "That would increase our chances of getting some photographs."

While one pulls and two push—and the fourth alternates shooting either photographs or video—we work the carts one at a time up the ramp. Once more I feel dizzy, indicating I am again hypoxic, and I struggle to keep my mouth closed as I cough, so I don't make any unnecessary noise. When finally all four carts are at the top I look around to see a small bench nestled in a ridge of black basalt interspersed with pockets of soil supporting patches of golden grass tipped with feathery awns.

"This really is beautiful," I say, forgetting for the moment, in my exuberance seeing this beautiful nestlike clearing, our need for stealth.

"Keep your voice down," Galen whispers.

When the fourth cart has been pulled and pushed up the ramp, we sit and catch our breath. Looking around we can see above our campsite what appears to be the crest of the ridge and, presumably, a view beyond to the valley of which Galen, when he made his scout, saw only the beginning. After we've had a drink of water Galen suggests we have a look, but first he and Jimmy mount their long lenses on their cameras.

"Be very quiet, and keep your heads low," Galen cautions.

We follow Galen's lead, crouching as we approach the crest, and then crab-crawling the last twenty feet. I peer over the edge. The valley runs north to south, and it is small, no more than a half mile in length. But it is breathtakingly beautiful. A small lake in one end remains frozen. Elsewhere the floor of the valley as well as the opposite hillside is covered in a soft bristle of stipa grass that in the afternoon sun is tinged gold. Beginning on the south end of the valley, and moving my eye slowly north, I count just over seventy female chiru. They all appear pregnant, and they all are ambling northward, stopping to browse for a minute or two, then continuing. I watch as twenty or so animals disappear around a bend at the north end of the valley, and a minute later, on the crest of a ridge that defines the south end of this small Eden, about thirty chiru appear. Conrad has his arm over my shoulder, and Jimmy is patting Galen on his back, taking care not to make any unnecessary noise.

"We've found it," I whisper. "The migration route."

PART TWO

THE BIRTHING GROUNDS

CHAPTER FOUR

क

JUNE 9

LYING IN MY SLEEPING BAG, I see by the faint glow through the tent's fabric that it is already dawn, and as my mind clears of the night's dreams I remember that the evening before we had decided to take it easy this morning; we had even discussed the possibility, on this seventh day of our trek, of taking the day off, but then realized that in spite of the biblical dictum that would not be a wise decision: We can't spare the food to take a day off. Now I rise on my elbow and find along the side wall of the tent the plastic bag that holds my small roll of toilet tissue. Careful to use only one panel, I clear my sinuses

"How are you feeling?" Galen asks.

"A little better, I think. It's still early to tell."

In Conrad and Jimmy's tent we decide after breakfast to have a second cup of coffee, a luxury we couldn't afford if Conrad, the evening before, hadn't walked two hours round-trip to find water. After the first hour of his absence I had started to worry, remembering my encounter with that mother bear and cub three years before in the mountains above Aru Basin.

"I think we should have two new camp rules," I now tell the others as we enjoy our second mug of coffee. "First, keep the foodbags inside the tents at night, in case there are wolves around, and second, take the bear spray whenever we walk very far from camp."

Everyone agrees. We disassemble the tents, pack our carts and leave this camp that we have agreed to name, after the area's similarity to the basalt outcrops in southern Idaho, "Craters of the Moon." We drop to the frozen lake in the small Eden where the previous afternoon we saw the migrating chiru, and now we see a herd of twenty animals grazing on the hillside. In the floor of the valley we encounter no defined migration trail, but then we didn't expect one: Because the hillsides are covered with grass, the animals have spread out to graze as they slowly migrate.

Soon a sandstone cliff frames one side of the valley that, combined with the basalt and the yellow feather grass, leads Jimmy to say, "This place does look like southern Idaho, or maybe Utah." A moment later, crossing a mud pan, I look down at the footprint of a large wolf and say, "Not quite like Utah." It was my suggestion to call last night's camp Craters of the Moon, but even then I try to avoid comparing one place to another, preferring instead to look for what makes one place different from another. In this case, in addition to the wolf print, there is the Tibetan woolly hare we flush, a line of fifteen migrating chiru skylighted on the ridge above us, mutings on the sandstone cliff that, when examined through binoculars, signpost a nesting Saker falcon, and two Ruddy shelducks on a tarn that reflects on its mirror surface the snowcapped volcano with the blown top that perhaps in some mythical epoch was higher than Everest.

The ground is reasonably flat as well as firm, and at least compared with yesterday it is easy pulling our cart. Conrad calls it R-1, and it's a welcome relief from the strain of yesterday's long uphill pull. I still have my cough, and my nose still runs, but on this comparatively flat terrain my breathing is less labored, and there is no longer the pain in my left lung. As the valley opens and the grass thins, I am heartened, as are the others, to encounter several parallel and deeply worn tracks of migrating chiru. At last we have a "highway" that is as easy to follow as the John Muir Trail in the High Sierra. I cart alongside Galen, and to our right, walking on a ridgeline parallel to us, is a group of seventeen female chiru. We stop while Galen fastens a 1000-mm lens to his camera, mounts it on his tripod and then, holding his breath, shoots several frames.

"Not as easy as the Serengeti," I say, "where you can just lean out the window."

"Yes, but I've always preferred photographing on foot as opposed to being in a vehicle," Galen answers. "It's a lot harder, but this way you're a lot closer to the animals emotionally."

"If only some of the people wearing those shawls could experience this," I say. "Maybe even the weavers in Kashmir. You could get more converts to saving them."

"That's what I hope the photographs do," Galen replies.

We expect to reach Heishi Beihu by evening, but we also expect the lake—like the majority of lakes in the landlocked Chang Tang—to be saline. Given the distance Conrad had to walk yesterday to find water, we are hopeful today that at some point we will cross a stream, but when that doesn't happen we stop at a small patch of snow dusted with windblown dirt. We unroll two foam rubber sleeping pads, spread them on the sloping bank, and position a water bottle under one and a cooking pot under the other. We then sprinkle some of the snow on the pads, and in a few minutes, under the noonday sun, there is steady drip-drip-drip of tea-colored water into the containers.

We have followed the migration trail of the chiru into a shallow but closed canyon where the animals have fanned out, and none of their tracks seem to lead to any obvious exit. While we wait for the water containers to fill, we study through binoculars a few scattered groups of females. They are all grazing, and none of them move in any direction that reveals where they go from here. While I stay behind to mind our meltwater catchment, Conrad, Galen, and Jimmy leave to scout the end of the canyon to find a possible exit hidden from our view. I am continuing to watch the chiru when I see at the end of the valley a solitary animal start up a ramp, reach the crest, and disappear down the opposite side. In the next half hour I see two more do the same thing, and when the others return I report my observations.

"It looks a little steep, but I bet we could follow them," Galen says, studying the ramp with our binoculars.

"I bet we could too," Conrad says. "But I wouldn't mind camping at the base and doing it in the morning, when we're fresh."

"Except there's no water there," Galen replies, "and on the other side we'll probably have better photography."

"But we agreed to make it an easy day," Conrad counters. "Yesterday was hard, we're all tired, and Rick still has his cough."

"Yes, but we also have several more hours of daylight," Galen points out imploringly.

We buckle our harnesses and continue. Galen pulls into the lead, and when he arrives at the ramp he begins in a series of switchbacks to pull his cart up it. Conrad is behind me, but turning around I can see he is overtaking me at a furious speed that I must guess is his way of venting anger. When he passes he says, "Let's just pull the carts right over the highest peaks." There is no way, even propelled by anger, I could match his power and speed, and I watch him go by with a combination of amazement at his strength and foreboding that he might start an argument with Galen. At the second switchback his pace slows, but he still overtakes Galen before they reach the crest. His anger seems to have dissipated, however, and even though I can't hear what they say to each other, it seems from a distance to be cordial.

We reach the crest, and any residual discontent is forgotten as we behold the scene before us. In the foreground, crossing the open slope, is a herd of forty female chiru migrating northward. In the midground, the gem-blue surface of Heishi Beihu, a lake that is ten miles long and four miles wide, is patterned with ice breaking up in the beginning of the season's thaw. In the background, the peaks of the Kun Lun, rising to an altitude of twenty-three thousand feet, are stark against the sky. Sere hills, sapphire lake, white mountains, azure sky: In any place in North America or Europe, it would be a treasured national park; in nearly any other place on Earth, it would be a World Heritage site; in the northwest Chang Tang, it is all but unknown.

We take photographs and video, and then we turn to the descent. The hill in front of us is steeper than anything we have yet negotiated, and to get down safely we agree to lower the carts one at a time. Our plan is to tie the two ends of our climbing rope to each side of a cart, and while one of us holds the rickshaw by the handlebar and lowers it backward—as though we were descending holding a shopping cart—two will belay from either side, leaving the fourth free to take photographs or video. We spend another half hour turning the brake handles 180 degrees on the front handlebars, so we can still squeeze them while holding the rickshaw in front of us.

The strategy works. It takes an hour but we get down safely and find above the lake an attractive campsite next to a small stream. Above us, coming off the crest of the ridge we just descended, like a torsade of interwoven paths, is the migration trail; Jimmy observes that to be worn that deeply into the hillside the paths could be thousands of years old. We pitch our tents, cook and eat dinner, then step outside to admire the last light of day. Below us, Heishi Beihu glows like a blue jewel with what appears to be an inner luminosity, a wonder of the world in a place no one in the world knows. Above us, a herd of 130 female chiru, their pelage gold in the low light of day's end, amble over the ridge and continue, in a slow, browsing contour, to traverse the hillside above our tents. We watch as they continue north into the same hills where, ten years earlier to the month, George Schaller also watched them disappear, when he was the first Westerner—and until we had arrived the only Westerner—ever to behold this majestic scene.

There are few places, if any, left on Earth where at the beginning of the twenty-first century you can say with confidence you are only the second group of Westerners to see it. With helicopters, snowmobiles, and Twin Otter aircraft, scientists and adventurers have peered into every valley and plateau, and seen every peak, in Antarctica. The same is true for Greenland and Baffin Island. I have heard there are one or two narrow tributaries in the upper Amazon, and perhaps a small subrange of hills in the jungles east of the Andes, that are as yet unvisited, and the same may be true for a few pockets in the Congo, and also the hill forests and jungles of the remote area where China, Myanmar, and the Arunachal Pradesh state of India join.

Even then, if I were to organize an expedition to any of those places, I wouldn't be surprised if, at the most distant village of the most remote tribe, I arrived only to learn that a backpacking hippie had been there the year before.

Schaller's task plotting the previous exploration of the Chang Tang was, by comparison, straightforward. All the explorers between the first in 1891 and the last in 1908 wrote books describing their adventurers, and most of the volumes came with maps showing the authors' routes. From the beginning of World War I through World War II and afterward, only a few outsiders crossed the Chang Tang, including Heinrich Harrer and Peter Aufschnaiter, who traversed the southern margin on their way to Lhasa after escaping from a POW camp in India, and Douglas Mackiernan and Frank Bessac, two Americans fleeing out of Xinjiang in 1949 as the Communists were moving in, who crossed the eastern margin of the Chang Tang on a long walk to Lhasa.[i] After the Communists closed Tibet there were few outside visitors until it opened to tourists in 1980, and even then no Westerner was allowed into the northwest quadrant of the Chang Tang until Schaller was given permission to travel to the Aru in 1988.

So Schaller could say with a scientist's discipline for accuracy that in 1992 he was the first Westerner ever to see this place. A hundred years ago, at a typical meeting of the Royal Geographical Society in London, you could have encountered any number of people who had been the first outsider to see some remote corner or other of the planet. Today, the number of people who have had that privilege is dwindling fast.

क

THE SUMMER OF 1992—when Schaller was the first Westerner to look down on Heishi Beihu—was only a few months after he had alerted the Chinese and Tibetan authorities of the link between chiru and shahtoosh, and in turn they had encouraged him to seek help internationally. Schaller decided to do just that, and his first move was to contact Ashok Kumar, director of TRAFFIC India, part of a cooperative effort of the World Wildlife Fund and the IUCN to contain the international trade in endangered species.

"Ashok is very determined and energetic," Schaller told me when he recounted this phase of what would eventually become an international campaign against shahtoosh whose impetus, in large part, would come from the work of Ashok Kumar. "I sent him the information and he immediately got on it."

In the early nineties Ashok Kumar was rising quickly as one of India's foremost environmental activists. Early in his career he had been a business executive for Tata Steel, then the largest corporation in India. While posted in the eastern part of the country, he happened upon a jungle habitat home to a population of wild elephants that was threatened by ongoing development. He had been fond of wild animals since his boyhood, and he persuaded Tata to support a program to protect the elephant habitat as a wildlife reserve. Later he was transferred to Dubai, where there was no organized interest in wildlife, so he filled the gap, founding the Dubai Natural History Club and conscripting dozens to join his frequent birdwatching and wildlife viewing excursions into the Arabian deserts. Back in India he was invited to be the founding director of the India office of TRAFFIC, the position he held when Schaller's fax arrived explaining the connection between chiru poaching and shahtoosh weaving.

"Of course we all knew who George Schaller was, having read his book on tigers," Ashok told me in his office in Delhi when, as I was writing this book in the months following our trek, I traveled to China, India, and Europe to talk firsthand to people like him involved in the anti-poaching and anti-shahtoosh campaigns. "Before that we didn't know anything about tigers [from a scientist's viewpoint]," he continued. "No one in India knew how much meat a tiger requires per year, and therefore what the relation is between predator and prey. To me it was totally fascinating. Until then, most of the work in India about tigers was more conversation than conservation."

With that Ashok chuckled, his twinkling eyes squeezing in what, over the next few days, I would realize is a near-endless capacity for amusement over his own as well as his countrymen's foibles. I would also realize he is mischievous and greatly enjoys his role as arguably India's foremost environmental gadfly. In his sixties, he is of medium height and build, and his partially bald head, round face, and frequent grin give him a teddy bear appearance that would make him anyone's favorite uncle. He is energetic—in the way people are who are genetically proactive—and I had the impression he will be leading the environmental charge in India for many years to come.

"So in this fax," Ashok continued, "George says, 'This is what I have discovered, that the wool from the Tibetan antelope is coming to India and made into these shawls that you people wear. So you need to find out about this.' That was easy because on my mother's side I am Kashmiri. So I went to my aunts and cousins, and they all said, 'No, no, this is totally untrue. Everyone knows that the wool is picked from bushes,' and 'No, no, Kashmiris are very nice people and we would never kill any animals.' Then I went to some shops in Delhi. I took my secretary from the office and said we were interested in some shawls, and they got them out and went through the drama of pulling them through a ring and all of that. I said, 'Oh, they are very pretty,' and I looked at my secretary and said, 'Let me get a photo of you with the shawl,' and that way we had the first pictures of shahtoosh. But the shop owners all told me the same story about the wool being collected off rocks and bushes from an animal that lives in the mountains. So I wrote back to George and I said, 'Look, this is what everybody is saying, that no animal is killed,' and George wrote back a very short note and said, 'Do more research.'"

With that last anecdote, Ashok's face squeezed in delight, and he paused while he chuckled, as though in his mind's eye he were seeing that side of George Schaller that Peter Matthiessen had once called the "stern pragmatist."

"By then George had given me the Latin name for the Tibetan antelope, *Pantholops hodgsonii*—I can remember Latin names of animals but I can never remember people's names [another chuckle]—so with my associates in TRAFFIC, especially Vivek Menon, who is a wildlife biologist, we did some research and found out that the chiru did have the highest level of protection [Schedule I] in India's own Wildlife

Protection Act and the CITES agreement [Convention on International Trade in Endangered Species], to which India is a signatory. So we wrote to the wildlife section of the Indian government and said we are in violation of India's own law by permitting this trade. They were in total disbelief. 'How do you know this wool is from this animal?' they asked us."

Ashok and Vivek had no way—at least at that time—to prove scientifically that the wool in the shahtoosh shawls was the wool from the dead chiru Ashok had seen in the photographs Schaller had sent him. In addition to the photographs, by then Schaller was preparing his article for NATIONAL GEOGRAPHIC about his work in the Chang Tang (the same article that had inspired me to organize our rickshaw trek). Using both the slides and the preparatory materials for the magazine story, Ashok and Vivek put together a presentation on the shahtoosh issue that Ashok made to government officials. The secretary of the handicraft association that represented the shahtoosh agents and weavers in Kashmir was present at the meeting, and he countered their argument, claiming the whole thing was an American conspiracy to close the trade, that the Chinese wanted the market for themselves, and that this George Schaller was probably a CIA agent.

Ashok and Vivek knew then they had a battle on their hands, and from the twinkle in Ashok's eye, and the relish with which he told me the story, I suspected they also welcomed the challenge.

JUNE 10

IN THE PREDAWN THERE IS NO WIND, and the steppe is cold and silent. The million stars in the rarefied night now melt into the sky, and their light, absorbed by the deep black, turn it to deep blue. The great waters of the lake mirror the heavens, and the mountains are a black band separating water and sky. In ghostly silhouette, like four couriers emerging from the netherworld, we descend toward the lake, and when we reach its shore we halt.

"This is just too beautiful," I call to the others. "Even if it takes time, we have to get some photos and video."

"I was hoping someone would say that," Jimmy replies. "This is like unbelievably awesome."

With Heishi Beihu as backdrop, Jimmy and Galen set their camera positions, and Conrad and I then pull our rickshaws across their views. We continue, and soon from the middle of the lake there is a cracking sound. We stop and turn, and across the water we see a tsunamic swirl—as though made by the stirring of some creature from the deep—and the inexorable current carries the pancake ice in the center toward a long parapet of broken plates that line the shore. As the surge approaches there is a growing sound of bumping plates, then a cacophony of grinding and shearing as the new ice collides into the old and the parapet, like a long line of giant shards of broken porcelain, buckles and surges upward, gaining another two feet in height. We applaud, and when our cheering quiets, and when the plates of ice settle into their new positions, once again all is still, and the lake is calm and cold, as though it were frozen in time.

"This fits Mark Twain's description of Mono Lake," Galen says, "'This solemn, silent, salient sea.'"[ii]

Conrad unbuckles and walks to a small lagoon framed by the parapet of ice. He squats, reaches with a cupped hand, scoops the water, and samples it.

"Phew!" he says as he spits it out. "This is the most saline lake yet. Yuck!"

An hour later he complains the briny taste still lingers in his mouth. By now we have reached the north end of the lake, and following the trodden paths of chiru, our route gradually bends westward. We pull our carts diagonally up and down the corrugations of ancient shorelines, dating perhaps, as Schaller has told us, to a time five thousand and more years ago when the Chang Tang was more lush. In the distance the peaks diminish in thinning shades of blue-gray, the way they do in the mountain ranges of Central Asia. Indeed, our map indicates we have crossed the political border, leaving Tibet and entering Xinjiang; at the same time, we have left the boundary of the Chang Tang Nature Reserve, and we now enter territory that is under no protection.

We are also beginning to cross a section of the planet never before seen by Westerners. As we ascend in a northwesterly direction up a broad alluvium, we follow the dozen-odd grooves worn into the hardpan that, weaving and crossing, define the migration trail. In the distance we see chiru, and we follow them toward a distant col at the end of the range of snow-covered volcanoes that parallel the west shore of the lake. We stop to rest, and Galen, consulting the GPS, tells us we are at 17,000 feet. We continue up a long but moderate slope, and I find myself playing over and over in my mind Ravel's Bolero. The Germans have a word for this—ohrwurm, or "earworm"—a song or tune that is stuck in your head. But this is one worm that isn't bothering me: Bolero seems perfect music for pulling rickshaws across unexplored expanses of Central Asia.

क

WHEN WE REACH THE TOP of the long alluvial slope we realize that what we thought was a col is instead a bend in the valley. Now we have a choice: to continue up the main valley or to take a route up a lateral valley that at least on the map appears more attractive because it leads more directly to another basin. We decide to stop for lunch and at the same time watch for chiru, to see which route they take. It has required three hours to pull the carts up the alluvium, and as I still have my cough, I am tired. But the sun is shining, and the air feels warm. I lean against my cart, and while I am slowly eating an energy bar, I fall asleep. My head tips forward and I jerk awake, straining a muscle in my neck. It's a minor annoyance, but it adds to my torpor.

In a few minutes we spot a group of a dozen chiru, and watching through binoculars we follow them as they turn and ascend the lateral valley. Another small group approaches and takes the same route, so we decide to follow. Soon we are pulling our carts up an increasingly steep trail, and as the lateral valley narrows, it compresses the various migration trails into a single track so heavily used by the chiru that our footsteps release from the mud the ammonia smell of their urine. To our right, we spot a group of eight chiru, but the pleasure of their company is offset by the strain of pulling the carts. My left lung again hurts, and again I fear I may be getting pneumonia, but then I convince myself that, because I have no fever, it is only a high-altitude cough.

Ahead we see what appears to be the top of the gully, but the slope steepens even more, and we have to double-team the carts, one pulling and one pushing. The altitude is approaching seventeen thousand five hundred feet, and when at last we have all the carts to the top, I sit on top of my rickshaw and try to recover from a fit of coughing. Jimmy walks over, points the video camera in front of me, and says, "Wow, look at this face."

"This is what separates us from the animals," I say, shaking my head and trying to smile. "They would never do something this stupid."

JUNE 11

NEITHER CONRAD NOR JIMMY wakes when their wristwatch alarms beep—not because their ears are bad but because their bodies are tired—and consequently we don't get up until 5:30, an hour later than planned. It takes another two hours to breakfast, break camp, pack our carts, and also inflate our tires that we deflated the previous afternoon when the ground had softened. It is colder than it has been the previous few days, and with the bare steppe as hard as ice, we pump the tires to 30 PSI. Following the rule I had suggested two days ago, the evening before we brought into our tents the food bundles we each carry, and also our water bladders and bottles, to prevent them from freezing. But I missed one plastic water bottle, and unless it warms enough today to melt it, it will lie useless in my cart, as cold and as heavy as concrete.

"I can definitely feel I'm getting thinner," I announce to the others as I buckle my waistbelt.

"We should patent rickshaw pulling as a new weight-loss program," Conrad says.

"It's like a martial arts practice called Shaolin," Jimmy adds. "It conditions you by putting heavier and heavier weights around your ankles and arms. Only we've got two-hunded-fifty-pound carts strapped to our asses."

"But I bet in Shaolin they eat better than we do," I reply.

We depart, following chiru tracks toward a gun sight between two volcanic cinder cones topped with snow that rise above the featureless hardpan like two perfectly shaped breasts, although my mind does not dwell on the metaphor. As I predicted at the outset of our trek, at this stage our conversations as well as our thoughts all seem eventually to morph into fantasies of food. As François Villon said, "There is no care but hunger." Soon we see ahead of us five chiru walking at the same slow pace, and Galen says they have tacked to their asses signs that read, "Follow-me." As we near the gun sight, the multiple tracks again compress into a single trail textured by prints of hundreds of hoofs, and as the ground is still frozen, the wheels of our carts bounce over the castings.

By noon we are crossing a bare gravel pan miles wide in all directions. Here and there cinder cones, with remnants of snow near their crater summits, rise out of the expanse. Once more I note the air has a haze that leaves the volcanoes and ranges receding from light blue to light gray as they distance toward the far horizon. We pull our carts toward another col at the base of a snow peak we have nicknamed, because of its similar shape, Mount Cook, and Jimmy spots a bird that until now we haven't seen. I have brought, bound in a folder, photocopied pages selected from Birds of China—a field guide that weighed too much to carry—and luckily I have copied the correct page.

"A Rufous-necked snow finch," I tell Jimmy. "They're associated more with the high deserts and steppes of Xinjiang, so that's why we haven't seen one before."

"That's cool," he says. "Let me have a look."

I hand him the binoculars, then he takes the folder and reads the description. It's fun to infect Jimmy with my enthusiasm for watching birds, and also to consider how this journey could have a major influence on the direction he takes in his life. It has also been fun, for example, to coach him how to cover a scene with the video camera so the editors will have the pieces they need, and he has commented several times he might try in the future to land filmmaking jobs as well as photography assignments. Whether he does or not, the more valuable lessons learned from an experience like this are more likely to be subtle. Take this rufous-necked snow finch. Before this trip I'm not sure Jimmy would have noted it was a bird we hadn't seen before: It is very closely related to the other snow finches we have seen, and different from them only by a few distinguishing marks. Now, however, he seems to have adopted the habit, perhaps from watching me watch birds, of paying attention to such details, and this will serve him whether he follows photography or filmmaking or some other path. It reminds me of when I was a young writer, reading a biography of Antoine de Saint-Exupéry—one of my literary heroes—in which he was asked the secret of good writing. "The secret is not to learn how to write," he replied. "It is to learn how to see."

क

TWO HUNDRED YARDS BELOW THE COL we notice water beginning to percolate between rocks, and soon we are pulling our carts alongside a small stream. The drainage opens onto another broad basin, and we are pleased when the chiru tracks continue to follow the stream because in a desert there is always comfort, rooted perhaps to an instinctual sense of safety, when you are close to water. By midafternoon the stream flows directly toward a small hill that rises singularly out of the hardpan, like a nunatak of the desert. An hour later, when we arrive at the hill, we take a break and discuss whether we should camp.

"We've got water as well as a place to hide our tents," Galen says, referring to the possibility of using the hill as a blind to conceal our camp from approaching chiru.

"I like the idea," Conrad says, and Jimmy and I agree as well. We walk behind the hill to search for a place to pitch our tents, but to hide them we would need to be close to the base, where, unfortunately, there is no flat ground. Then I notice that on the backside of the hill, just below the summit, there is a small but flat bench. I hike up to investigate, and the others follow.

"Plenty of room for the tents," Conrad says.

"Killer view," Jimmy adds.

"If the chiru don't look up they might not even see us as they pass," I point out.

"And I love the camera angle," Galen confirms.

We look at each other, smile, and nod at the illogical impracticality, or perhaps call it the Sisyphean absurdity, of the idea. But it's too good a spot to pass up. This time instead of double or triple teaming, we each pull our own cart up the hill, each man carefully placing each foothold, straining and grunting with each step. It takes fifteen minutes of focused work, but then we are at the bench setting up the tents.

An hour later, perched on my elbows, my head cradled in my hands, I lie atop my sleeping bag and from my tent door watch female chiru migrate past our hilltop camp. Although none of them fail to notice us, most usually take a minute or more once they come into our view before one of them happens to look up. Then invariably they stop, stare for ten to fifteen seconds as if they didn't believe their own eyes—as if in chiru-talk they were saying to each other "what in the hell?"—then take off at a trot or run, stopping to look back to see if we are in pursuit. After a short while they resume at a slow amble their northward migration.

JUNE 12

WITH OUR DISK BRAKES SQUEAKING and our headlamps illuminating the way, we abandon what we have agreed with fondness to call Aerie Camp. Once on the flats we turn off the headlamps, and in a few minutes the sky begins to lighten.

"I love this time of day," Jimmy says as we pull our carts side by side.

In front of us the snow on top of a nearby volcanic cone begins to glow. The air is cold, and as Conrad has enjoined—following advice from the training coach of the Russian Olympic cross-country ski team—we have dressed light and started cold "because soon enough you'll be warm." I wear on my torso only my two thin inner layers, and soon enough I am indeed comfortable. Two hours later the sun rises behind the volcano, and through thin clouds soft light reflects in silver strands off a stream descending the alluvium at the base of the cone. From a brief flurry during the night, snow has packed against the windward sides of the stunted ceratoides, and the gravel hardpan appears as though it were decorated with thousands of cotton balls.

This is the third day we have been traversing country never before seen by anyone from the Western world, and once more I have the thought that our expedition is a rare opportunity to experience exploration as it must have felt to adventurers a hundred years ago. That brings to mind a passage from Sven Hedin, describing his own crossing of the Chang Tang:

> It was a no man's land; rivers, lakes, and mountains were all nameless; their shores, banks and snow fields had never been seen by any traveller's eyes but mine; they were mine own kingdom of a day. It was delightful—it was a great thing to cruise, like a vessel that leaves no track behind her, amongst those upwellings of the world's "high sea." To make our way over those gigantic mountain waves. Only the waves which roll across the Tibetan highlands are petrified; and all distances and dimensions are cast on such a gigantic scale, that you may march for weeks at a time and still find the situation unchanged.

We continue to follow the stream, now large enough to call a small desert river. Beyond the opposite bank we see herds of chiru waking up and beginning to browse. We pass a grouping of about a dozen wallows cleared in the gravel surface, each a couple of feet across and each marking the place where one of the animals has made its bed. From behind a cloud above the cone peak heraldic rays beam into the heavens, and when we stop for a short rest I unbuckle from my harness and walk alone across the hardpan, my feet crunching gravel.

I walk perhaps fifty yards, and with each step I feel more deeply the openness of this place, the last great expanse of Central Asia still without any humans in any direction, other than my companions, who now grow small. I stop and turn one way and then the other. It is absolutely quiet, as though this expanse possesses a gravitational pull that has absorbed all sound. I have the thought that if I were somehow on this journey alone, making a solo traverse, I would at this moment feel as though I were the only person on Earth. With that, I walk back toward my companions, thankful in advance for what I know will be my greeting: Jimmy's perennial smile, Conrad's playful shrug, Galen's affirming nod.

क

AT MIDMORNING the river we have followed for three days turns west while two groups of female chiru we see ahead of us appear to be veering north, into a wide basin framed in the distance by low hills. We decide to take an early lunch. Parking our carts, and each putting in our pocket the plastic bag that contains our small but precious midday meal, we cross the river and climb the flank of a hill to study with binoculars the animals' movements.

"It's hard to tell where they're going," Galen says. "They seem to be all over the place."

"I see five or six on a ridge just to the right of that low point over there," I say, "and at least fifteen or twenty on the flats to the north. But none to the west."

"We've seen they generally take the path of least resistance," Conrad adds. "Although they're not averse to a well-thought-out shortcut."

"Kind of like us," Galen replies.

"Everything suggests they're heading toward those low hills in the distance," I offer. "I hate to leave the river, but I would hate even more to lose track of these guys."

We have noticed that in general the chiru seem to spend more time browsing in the mornings and more time walking in the afternoons. The animals we see now all seem to be grazing, but we can't wait until afternoon to see what direction they head. We have finished lunch—our browse is gone—and Jimmy comments that the air seems to be getting colder.

"And the high-altitude cirrus are moving in," I add, pointing to the sky.

"Feels like snow is coming," Conrad says.

We pick what appears to be the lowest point in the hills to the north, and steer our carts that direction. We flush two chiru who then walk a quarter mile ahead of us, and despite having lost completely the deep-cut trails we have enjoyed following since we first encountered the migration at Heishi Beihu, we convince ourselves we are still going the right direction, and that these two animals are our guides. When we arrive at the hills, however, there are only the scattered tracks of a few animals. We choose a route through the hills that appears to have the most moderate gradient and scare up a Tibetan woolly hare that runs away, darting through the ceratoides one way, then the other.

A few seconds later Galen, in the lead, calls out, "It's a nest! Look!"

We gather in a huddle around three small bunnies nestled together in a shallow scoop that the mother hare has scratched from the ground. Galen gets down on his knees to photograph them, and the rest of us stand in a semicircle around the nest.

"They look pretty good—I mean pretty cute," I say.

"Oh, I think I'm having the same thought," Jimmy says in a confessional tone.

"I don't know," Conrad replies skeptically. "They're three of them, and I also have three kids."

"We should leave soon," Galen says as he gets up, apparently not paying attention to our conversation as he concentrated on his photographs. "So the mother can come back before they get cold."

"Good idea," I reply, knowing it would be grounds for divorce if word got back to my wife that her husband had harmed—much less devoured—three cuddly little bunny rabbits.

Even though I didn't plan the food on this expedition, I know, as the main organizer, when word gets out that on this trip we were hungry, it will add to a growing reputation I have in outdoor circles of leading expeditions that tend to starve the participants. This started in 1977 when I organized an expedition to the upper Orinoco to climb a remote rock spire rising out of the jungle. We ran out of food, but fortunately, because we were in a restricted area, we had an army sergeant assigned to us, and he used his rifle to shoot a monkey. As it roasted over the fire, the flames singed the hair to expose a blackened, naked body that looked disconcertingly humanlike. We ate it anyway.

Fifteen years later I returned to the same area to climb another spire, and again we ran out of food. We sent a Yanomami, working for us as a porter, into the jungle to forage, and at day's end the Indian returned with a basketful of grapelike fruit. By then we were half-starved, and one of the climbers, Paul Piana, and I sat on a log in the dark eating the fruit, relishing every bite. I turned on my headlamp and directed the light beam into the basket, revealing dozens of white worms wriggling in and out of the fruit. We were both quiet for a moment, then Paul slowly said, "Turn out the light," and we both resumed eating.

Another of the climbers on that trip, Todd Skinner, would go on to become one of the world's top rock climbers, and to make his living as an inspirational speaker to sales groups and corporate managers. I later heard through the climbers' grapevine that Todd started his presentation with a full-screen image of me. "See this face," Todd would tell his audiences. "If he ever invites you on one of his trips, say, 'No!'"

On both those expeditions, at least we were in the Amazon, where it was comparatively easy to hunt and forage. Here in the Chang Tang, our wrist rockets notwithstanding, we all realize that if anything serious were to happen that slowed or stopped us for any significant amount of time, we could easily run out of food. Still, it's a risk that is proportionate to the other types of risks we take climbing mountains, running rivers, and skiing icecaps. And in some ways the specter of running out of food in this uninhabited corner of the world is offset by the fact that the goal of our trip is to try to preserve the area, even if, to survive, we are eventually forced to eat some of its inhabitants.

क

AFTER WE LEAVE THE THREE SMALL BUNNIES, we continue pulling our carts up the low hill, hopeful at every turn we will encounter the worn trail that for so many days has made our effort to follow the migration as simple as driving an automobile on a paved road. Instead, all we encounter are a few scattered tracks. Adding to our gloom, there is a circular rainbow around the sun that Galen identifies as a solar parhelion.

"It's twenty-two degrees from the sun," he explains. "It looks impressive, but it also portends bad weather."

We reach a saddle in the low hills and see a scattered group of seven chiru, but no single migration, and no definitive trail. We glass the terrain in all directions. It is after three p.m., and we decide to camp nearby. We find a bench on the side of a hill that will give us a vantage across a small basin where, if we are lucky, we might spot a few chiru and observe the direction they are taking.

We set up the tents, and Galen and I position our rickshaws next to our tent's twin front doors and unload our gear: sleeping pad first, then sleeping bag. Then we unload the stuff sacks with the gear we'll need for the evening alongside the tent wall: toilet kit, eyeglasses, mess kit, pee bottle, journal, and tape recorder for me, film and notes for Galen. Before getting in my tent I take the stove and fuel bottle and hand it to Conrad, who assembles it and sets it on a flat fieldstone that he has picked up and placed inside his tent. Then I take off my boots and jacket, crawl in my tent, and, sitting on top of my sleeping bag, plug in my earphones and begin transcribing into my journal that day's entries from my pocket tape recorder.

In a half hour Conrad calls out that dinner is ready, and Galen and I cross to the other tent. Conrad serves our evening meal of "baby clams" into the one-pint food storage containers he brought for us to use as bowls. ("They're small," he said when he gave them to us at the beginning of the trip, "but we don't have much to put in them, anyway.") When we finish dinner Conrad starts the stove again and heats water for hot chocolate, and when that is served he puts on his black-rimmed eyeglasses and plots our position on our map.

"Eighty-two degrees, fifty-five point two minutes east," Galen says as Conrad notes the coordinates. "Thirty-five degrees, fifty-five point six minutes north."

Conrad marks with a pen the position on our map, then using the ruler on the side of his Rite in the Rain pocket notebook, calculates our day's travel.

"Eleven point five miles today," he says. "That puts us only fifteen miles as the crow flies from the other side of these hills, and the possible location of the calving grounds. But there are a lot of contours between here and there."

We take turns studying the map.

"This drainage here looks like the easiest way through the hills," Jimmy suggests.

"It's tempting," Galen agrees.

"I still think we need to find out where the chiru are heading," I say, "and follow them."

Everyone recognizes this should be our strategy, but everyone also recognizes the chiru from here seem to be spreading out, and it is possible they are taking multiple routes to the calving grounds.

"Maybe we should take tomorrow off," I suggest, "and scout this area. One could go west, one north and one east. We'll try and quantify how many animals we see going where. Then if they are dispersing in myriad routes, well, that will be useful information for the scientists, and we'll just follow what seems to be the most traveled route."

"It's pushing the envelope using another day of food," Conrad says, "but we can do it."

We all agree, and with the plan a holiday mood suddenly spreads in the tent, and we decide to celebrate with a second cup of chocolate. Then, as it always does these last few days, our conversation shifts to food.

"Too bad we didn't bring that extra bag," Conrad says, referring to the decision when we packed our carts at the base of Toze Kangri to leave behind our contingent bag of food.

"We just couldn't carry the weight," Galen reminds everyone.

"I was thinking today," I add, "that if you graph the line of how many calories we use against how much weight we can carry, they intersect at a trip that is four, maybe five weeks long. The only way to extend it would be to trade camera gear for more food."

"Or to live off the land," Conrad says, "But we decided not to do that."

"We might not be able to do that, whether we decide to or not," Galen observes.

"I'm still having fantasies," I confess to the others. "Today I was looking at those two chiru walking in front of us all morning, and in my mind they turned into these barbecued hammock-looking things with four legs."

"I've been having those same kinds of hallucinations," Jimmy says.

"I guess you've entered new territory," I reply, "when as a pretend wildlife biologist the animals you are studying are starting to look pretty tempting."

JUNE 13

ACCUSTOMED TO OUR EARLY STARTS, I wake at four forty-five a.m. and it takes a moment before I remember that today I don't have to pull the rickshaw. Even though I have no idea of the day of the week, it feels like Sunday morning as I stretch in my warm bag, curl back up, and fall asleep. I wake again at seven, fall asleep again, and wake once more at nine when I hear Conrad start the stove. Although it's not a day off, the lazy start nevertheless feels wonderful. At breakfast we make our plan: Conrad will walk west along a frozen salt lake near our camp, Jimmy will climb the ridge we crossed yesterday to scan the basin for animals, and Galen and I will scout north and then west, following the direction of the majority of chiru tracks we have seen in the area.

A storm moved in during the night, and an inch or two of wind-swept snow covers the ground. Galen and I head north, following tracks of a small group of five chiru. Soon their spoor merges with a swath of tracks some fifty feet wide, all going northwest.

"They're heading towards that saddle in the hills," I tell Galen, feeling as though I were a wildlife detective.

We follow what is now a total of about fifty tracks, and when we reach the saddle Galen continues westward, along the crest of the hills, while I walk a transit of the col one side to the other, and count one hundred nineteen hoof prints. I note the observation on my tape recorder to pass to Conrad, who is keeping the log of our chiru sightings to pass to Schaller. Then I follow the ridgeline and find Galen on a promontory overlooking the northern arm of the lake that lies just west of our camp. As he examines the far shore through our binoculars, I squat next to him and study our map.

"The map doesn't even show this arm of the lake existing," I tell Galen.

"How big do you think the whole thing is?" he asks.

"Transposing it on the map, I'd say maybe four miles long and two miles wide."

He lowers the binoculars and scans the water, then looks north where the arm of the lake disappears in a narrowing bend of the surrounding hills.

"This is real exploring, isn't it," he says, raising the binoculars again.

"Well, we're the first outsiders ever to see this lake, with a huge arm that doesn't even exist on our map, which is the best one we could get. So yeah, I guess this is real exploring."

"There's some chiru," he says. "Five, six, seven, all heading north."

He points to the animals, then hands me the binoculars. In a minute I notice another group of five that seem to be following the first seven.

"So that's twelve that we can see here," Galen says.

"And I got a hundred and nineteen prints back at that col, but that was over who knows how many days."

"They're taking multiple routes, for sure," Galen replies. "It'll be interesting to see what Conrad and Jimmy find."

"Earlier this morning," I tell him, lowering the binoculars, "when we were following those tracks to the col, I had the thought that all of this is like detective work. It's like trying to find the clues to the migration."

"That's because it is detective work," Galen replies. "That's what George has been doing out here all those years. Tracking, observing, making notes, trying to fit the pieces of the puzzle together. Outdoor detective work."

क

DETECTIVE WORK of a more traditional sort was also what Ashok Kumar and his associates started to do in India when, posing as shoppers interested in purchasing shahtoosh, they began entering high-end tourist stores and fashion boutiques. When they did find a shop selling the shawls, they then worked with authorities to organize raids. At the same time the wool merchant Michael Sautman was also doing some of his own detective work, and it was about to lead to a connection that no one at the beginning of the international effort to save the chiru could ever have imagined, much less foretold.

By using informants to make discreet inquires in the border area between Nepal and India, Sautman was investigating the trade route the smugglers used to transport chiru wool from Tibet to Kashmir when he received information that more than just shahtoosh was being smuggled. His informants told him they had learned some Tibetan exiles were acquiring tiger bones in India and bringing them to the border, where the illegal body parts were then bartered for illegal shahtoosh wool. The wool was then smuggled into Kashmir, and the bones were smuggled into China.

Shortly after learning this startling news, Sautman traveled to India, where he met with another environmental activist, Belinda Wright. Belinda had recently started an environmental organization called the Wildlife Protection Society of India (WPSI), and Ashok had recently left TRAFFIC to join the new group as a founding board member. Ashok had known Belinda since she was a teenager. Both Belinda's maternal and paternal grandfathers worked for the British colonial government in India, and her parents lived in Calcutta on an acre-and-a-half property where they kept horses, deer, cranes, a bear, a tiger, a lion; as a little girl Belinda even had a leopard that had the habit of sleeping in her bed. In her twenties she became a wildlife photographer and later a filmmaker for National Geographic, winning two Emmys for a television special on tigers. In 1994 she left filmmaking to move to Delhi, first to work as an investigator for TRAFFIC International, helping to organize raids to seize tiger products, and then to launch WPSI, with the intention of doing more work on tiger protection. Even then, Michael Sautman's revelation about the international barter in tiger bones was for her a shocking surprise.

"Before we had never had any trade in tiger body parts here in India," she told me when I interviewed her in New Delhi. "Well, skins a little bit, but it wasn't big. We didn't know there was a market for tiger bones and tiger body parts in China—we didn't know about tiger wine, aphrodisiacs, things for epilepsy, for toothaches, all the different medicines—so nobody at first could believe Chinese tiger bone traders could infiltrate India and have middlemen and contacts."

We were sitting on the roof of the Wildlife Protection Society's office in a tree-lined residential district in Delhi. It was late afternoon, and a cooling breeze rustled the leaves in the tops of the trees. Belinda's light-brown hair was cut medium length, and she was dressed, like a typical middle-age, upper-middle-class Indian woman, in a print-pattern shalwar kameez. When an assistant came up the stairs to ask her a question, Belinda replied in fluent Hindi that included a native's hand and head gestures. She was leaving in an hour to catch a train to central India, where the next day she was scheduled to teach a conservation workshop. I told her I was appreciative she had made time for our interview, and she replied she welcomed the chance to sit on the roof with a cup of tea and take a break.

Belinda explained that apparently there had long been a trade between India and Tibet based on barter rather than money because neither side could use the other's currency.

"For a while Chinese pistols were in demand," she said, "but then India started making pistols. Enamel plates, then we started making plates. Electronics, then we made electronics. The traders were running out of barter items, and then we heard this story that tiger bones were being bartered for this wool that was said to be like gold."

She sipped her tea, gazed out at the tops of the trees lining the street, and then said, "You must understand, tigers have always been my obsession. I was brought up with them, and they are everything, every-thing, everything to me. So I became shahtoosh-obsessed because if we didn't contain the shahtoosh trade, then the tigers were finished."

"This is all happening shortly after you started your new organization?" I asked her.

She said it was, so I then asked her why she had left behind a successful career as a photographer and filmmaker.

"It was such an idyllic life," she replied. "You can't imagine. I had a home in central India, in the jungle. I was living on my own, my companions were the local tribals, and I had a good, happy, rich life. I was fulfilled and content, but then things changed. First I began to hear, mostly from my tribal friends, about a sudden upsurge in tiger poaching. That's when I decided I had to become involved in enforcement, but then the more I learned about what was really happening, the more I found myself becoming more and more discontent. Life was no longer so idyllic. When I went in the jungle I couldn't sit still as I used to. I could no longer walk along a forest path and look at the light and the dew on the leaves and hear the deer scurry away and see the leopard tracks, and just absorb it and feel good. I still felt it, but I felt it while in a state of panic because I was becoming increasingly aware it was disappearing, and that it could be gone in a minute. It upset me more than words can express."

"In the U.S.," I told her, "there are now psychologists and therapists who specialize in treating environmentalists who get in a funk when they realize how bad the problems really are."

"I don't need therapy," Belinda replied. "I am very comfortable with who I am and what I am doing. I simply have to accept I can't go in the forest anymore with the same calm I used to, and that now I have to dedicate my time to saving it."

She paused and sipped her tea, and then, looking across the tree-tops, said, "Because to me, a world without tigers is incomprehensible."

क

WHEN WE ARE ALL RETURNED TO CAMP, Conrad reports he saw about a hundred chiru at the west end the lake. Jimmy reports he saw only scattered small groups. Galen and I share our evidence that the animals are crossing several small passes over foothills to the north. We conclude that indeed the animals are dispersing, taking multiple routes over the hills that separate our position from Shor Kul, a huge basin to the north where we expect to find the calving grounds. Now we must decide which of those routes we ourselves will follow.

Once more we study the maps. The contours of our smaller-scale Russian map are fifty meters apart, and with that detail we have some confidence we can judge the terrain that lies ahead. If the animals Conrad saw were heading westward toward what looks on the map to be a gradual climb up a narrowing alluvium, they could also be going down what looks to be another drainage that turns and descends gradually into the big basin north of us.

"If that's the route at least some of them are taking," Conrad says, "it could also be the best way to get the carts across these hills."

"Based on the information we have, I'd say that's our best bet," Galen agrees, nodding his head positively.

"I would, too," I add. "Although it's still a bet, isn't it? But then that's the trade-off when you're in a place no outsider has ever seen."

JUNE 14

WITH MY INTERNAL CLOCK APPARENTLY set to the schedule we've kept this past week, I wake once more at four thirty a.m., and it takes me only a moment to remember that this morning I do not have the luxury of falling back asleep. I had a hard night, finally getting up and going to Conrad's tent to ask for a Benadryl out of the first aid kit, in the hope that it would reduce the drainage in my throat that seems to exacerbate my coughing. I finally fell asleep, although Conrad said I then snored so loudly it kept him awake in the next tent. Galen, who also is at that age where he snores, said he slept fine, and this morning he seems to have as much energy as he did the day we started trekking.

We head off at first light, leaving what we have named "Dispersion Camp." The sun breaks above the horizon as we gain the edge of a meadow where Conrad tells us he sat yesterday and watched about a hundred chiru grazing peacefully. Even though I am physically weak, I feel invigorated as I view the scene before us. Watered by a spring, the meadow has the highest density of stipa we have seen since we left the "small Eden" near Heishi Beihu where we first encountered the migration. Now the canted light brushes the tops of the grass's feathery awns, creating a gold carpet where twenty-five chiru graze in this Chang Tang equivalent of an oasis.

We continue, and for the first time our morning shadows are in front of us, indicating that the direction of our trek has veered west. We all four pull our carts side by side, like cowboys in some Western film trotting across the badlands, and our conversation veers to other wild regions we have visited. Galen says there are places in Eastern Europe, especially in the Carpathian Mountains, where people live nearly as they did in the Middle Ages, and even in Austria he once encountered in a remote farm two brothers who shared the same wife.

"I heard polyandry is common among the drokpa," Conrad says.

"The Sherpas sometimes practice it, too," Galen replies.

"I guess you could say that's what I'm doing as well," Conrad says. "I'm married to my best friend's wife."

No one responds to that, and we pull our carts a few more feet, then Conrad continues, telling us that he would bet if you were to ask a drokpa or a Sherpa about it, he would tell you it feels like the natural thing to do.

"And if we asked you?" I ask, even though I know the answer.

"I'd say the same thing," Conrad says, nodding his head.

At the west end of the salt lake we cross a mud flat a mile wide, like a tidal estuary in a place with no tides. Even though it is morning our tires sink a half inch into the spongy surface, and we are all thankful we are not crossing in the afternoon when it is probably a bog. We jump a small river at a point just above its entrance into the salt lake, and even though the bottom is soft, the water that runs under sheet ice covering the ten-foot-wide channel is clear. Consulting our map, we realize it is the same river we picked up four days ago when it had started as a few small pools emerging between rocks just below the col where Jimmy spotted the rufous-necked snow finch. We stop to fill our water bladders, and I retrieve from my cart my plastic insulated drinking mug to use as a scoop, with my nom de guerre, "Rick Shaw," written on the side in indelible ink. While I scoop the clear water Jimmy videotapes me.

"Every chance we get we have to stock up on fresh water," I tell the camera, as I pour water from my cup into the bladder. "This is some of the best fresh water of the trip—it's delicious. Plus I find satisfaction that it is the river we have followed from its source several days ago when it was just a tiny flow off the side of a cone-shaped peak we had called Mount Cook. Now we've come around a corner and encountered the same river just as it ends its life in the salt lake over there. There is a kind of poignancy in that, because out here you come to appreciate a small river like this, here in this high alpine desert steppe where water is precious and something that you do not take for granted."

We leave the river, cross the mud flat, and then enter an area of spongy loam that seems to have puffed like rising bread into loaves and buns of odd shapes. As we pull our carts around these curious humps Galen speculates the soil may have high concentrations of various salts that prevent it from freezing. In places the bicycle wheels sink in an inch or more, and pulling the carts is laborious. The loam gives way once more to gravel hardpan, and we begin a long ascent toward what on our Russian map appears to be a pass through this range of small peaks. Each step requires a pull or push on the rickshaw traces, and we keep as steady a pace as we can, stopping every hour or two to rest a few minutes. My cough today is as bad as it has been, and Conrad has given me from our day's food bag a double ration of menthol cough drops.

At our lunch stop I sit against the balloon tires of my cart next to Galen who also, despite his energized start earlier this morning, leans against his cart exhausted, and as he falls asleep his head jerks up. In a minute he nods off again and repeats the cycle. I look in the other direction, to a small stream flowing down this long alluvium we are ascending.

"Look, Conrad has the right idea," I say, seeing him with his shirt off, washing his face. "Let's take a bath."

Galen opens his eyes, and his head slowly turns toward the stream. "Good idea," he agrees.

"It'll wake us up," I offer as I start toward Conrad, who is now returning slowly to his cart, shirt in hand. As we pass he nods in what I take as acknowledgment I don't need to expend the energy required to exchange greetings. At the stream I pull down the suspenders of my insulated polyester pants, take off my moisture-wicking top, bend down and splash ice water over my head and shoulders. The goal is achieved: I wake up.

Under way again, we pull the carts, slow step by slow step, for two hours. The incline of the slope eases gradually, and even though I realize this indicates we are nearing the pass, I don't want to dwell on it, but rather I try to achieve a trancelike state where I am thinking of nothing. This is hard to do, as my mind tends always to conjure some scenario or daydream, so instead I try to be aware only of the sound of my footsteps on the gravel surface. This seems to work, for when I next look up, uncertain how many minutes have passed since I previously raised my head, I can see the ground around me has leveled, and ahead, where the alluvium constricts between hills, there is a kind of horizon line that must mark the beginning of the descent. It's three p.m., and, after pulling the rickshaws for nine hours, we have reached the col. We descend the opposite side of the pass for another hour until a small stream that began to flow a short distance below the pass joins a larger one flowing in from the south. We erect our tents at what we call "Confluence Camp." Galen retrieves our coordinates, and after Conrad plots them he announces we have traveled eighteen miles.

"Pretty good," he says, "considering it was almost all uphill."

"And all at nearly seventeen thousand feet," I add.

We are pleased with the achievement, and we would be satisfied, other than the fact that since leaving the shore of the salt lake this morning we haven't seen a single chiru. Through the day we found a few prints here and there, but nothing like a migration trail. We know that from Dispersion Camp many of the animals took routes north instead of west, but we had also assumed the animals we saw in the grass oasis this morning were taking the same route we have followed. Now we begin to doubt that assumption.

"We have to keep looking," I write in my journal, the last line I enter before I fall into a deep sleep.

JUNE 15

THROUGH THE GRAY GAUZE of falling snow I can see fifty yards ahead Conrad and Jimmy in the lead, their parkas, one red and one yellow, like small tints of color hand-painted on a black-and-white photograph. The snow started to fall about three in the morning, and after breaking camp and packing our rickshaws we had to wait fifteen minutes until there was sufficient light to see where we were going.

"It's a Mars-scape this morning," Conrad had said.

Even through the falling snow there is now enough light I can see that steep hills border both sides of the drainage we are following. The floor of the valley is a hundred yards wide, and although the surface is rockier than the alluvium we ascended yesterday, the extra resistance against our wheels is neutralized by the fact we are going downhill, and we are still making good time. Last night, while studying the map, we all realized that if carting conditions were even moderately favorable, we could by day's end reach the Shor Kul basin, and if that happened, by the next day arrive at the suspected location of the calving grounds.

The only thing missing is chiru. None of us have an explanation why we haven't seen any animals; this route we are taking seems, at least on our map, the path of least resistance through these hills and the logical direction, at least from our perspective, for the chiru to take. The canyon begins to turn, and on the outside of the first bend the stream flows against the bordering hillside, forcing us to jump across. It's only about six feet wide, and we manage to make the leap without unbuckling from the carts. Soon it bends again, and now we find a mud bar around which the stream divides, allowing us once more to jump while remaining strapped to our carts, a minor convenience but one that saves what otherwise is the extra time required to unbuckle and push the carts across.

"Look, chiru tracks," Jimmy says.

Across the bar windblown snow has outlined what by quick count is a little less than a hundred chiru tracks, all pointing downstream. They are frozen in the mud, but because they are on a low bar that must be inundated after every rain or after every hot day that melts snow higher in the hills, we conclude they are unlikely to be more than a day or two old.

"This is definitely one of the ways they're heading," Conrad says.

We continue, and the wind begins to blow the snow in a slant that makes the landscape appear as though an artist using only diagonal brushstrokes had painted it.

"Another summer day in the Chang Tang," I quip.

It is cold, but dressed in our shelled jackets and pants, hoods up and mittens on, we are comfortable and, now that we have seen the tracks, relieved, at least regarding the chiru. A new concern, however, is slowly developing, as at every turn the canyon seems to be narrowing, and the size of the rocks over which we struggle to pull the carts seems to be increasing. I try to steer my cart around the larger rocks, but sometimes they are spaced too closely and then there is no choice but to muscle the cart over, taking care to do it as gently as possible, to minimize stress. The stream flows against a bank twenty feet high, and we can see on top what appears to be a terrace that might allow us to advance downstream with comparative ease a hundred or even two hundred yards; Conrad unbuckles and climbs the bank to investigate.

"There's chiru tracks up there," he says when he returns. "And it would be easy carting—if there was an easy way up this bank."

There is no easy way, however, and we are forced again to cross the stream, and this time we push our carts first. Getting a running start, I jump but land short, and my right boot splashes in the river. I can feel the icy water seep in, and I know I'll have one damp boot the rest of the day.

Galen now takes the lead, and Jimmy follows. They disappear around a bend, and when I turn the corner I am startled to see Jimmy sitting at the edge of the stream with his cart turned upside down, like a wrecked automobile on the side of a roadway. Conrad is immediately behind me, and we hurry to catch up.

"Tried to jump across without unbuckling," he says when we reach him, still sitting and leaning back on his arms. "One of the wheels hit a rock and whipsawed me over," he tells us, shaking his head and trying to smile.

This is what happened to me months earlier, when testing the carts in the hills near Galen's house and my cart had flipped. I had been astonished how quickly the rickshaw drove my head into the ground.

"You got a dent in your cart," Conrad says as he examines the upside-down rickshaw.

"I got a dent in my back," Jimmy replies.

Conrad looks up from the cart and realizes the reason Jimmy is still sitting may be that, despite his attempted smile, he is injured.

"You okay?" Conrad asks.

"I think so, but I hit my noggin hard," he replies. He is still leaning back on his arms, and he is still trying to smile. "This is a dangerous sport we're participating in."

We examine a cut on Jimmy's head and another short but deep one on his back. Neither is long enough for stitches, and soon we have him on his feet and his cart on its wheels. Conrad notes the boulders are getting bigger, and that we'll have to be even more careful.

"This is getting to be brutal terrain," Jimmy agrees. What he doesn't know then but will in months ahead is that the cut on his back, like the cut on his finger he suffered two weeks earlier, will leave a permanent scar, lifetime reminders of his rickshaw trek across the Chang Tang.

क

WE ALL REALIZE THE RISK IN CONTINUING down this canyon that, by all appearances, is constricting. But risk is an ingredient in our adventure we all agreed tacitly to accept. We all knew at the outset that if following these animals to their calving grounds were easy, others would already have done it. I also find it useful, to keep the carrot that dangles in front of me appealing, to recall a passage in Peter Matthiessen's *The Birds of Heaven*, a book on his travels pursuing the natural history and conservation of cranes, that I read just before departing on this trek. "Before any species can be systematically protected," he wrote, "its breeding grounds and migration routes must be discovered."

So it is motivating to remind ourselves, as Matthiessen said, that we are aiding in the systematic protection of the chiru by helping to discover its migration route to its calving grounds. It is also inspiring to consider how tenacious Schaller has been in this same effort, not only to discover the calving grounds, but more, to learn all he could about the chiru's natural history so he can use that knowledge to win the animal's protection. Or how Ashok Kumar, Belinda Wright, and others in India were so doggedly tenacious in their effort.

After Ashok and Belinda joined forces at the Wildlife Protection Society of India, one of their first efforts was to write an overview, titled *Fashioned for Extinction: An Exposé of the Shahtoosh Trade*, that described nearly all that was known at the time about the poaching of the chiru, the smuggling of the wool, the weaving of the shawls, and the retail trade in Delhi, Europe, the United States, and Hong Kong. After working on the report for a year and a half, they had researched most of the information, written most of the copy, and gathered most of the photographs. By then, however, they had run out of funds to publish it.

"About that time, George Schaller walked into the office," Ashok told me, "and we spoke to him about the report, saying it should be published. He hand-wrote a fax to his secretary [at the Wildlife Conservation Society] to wire us a thousand dollars."

When the booklet was published it was then distributed to the media as well as to law enforcement agencies, politicians, wool dealers and traders, fashion houses, and fashion designers around the world. Michael Sautman would later tell me that *Fashioned for Extinction* was really the turning point in bringing the shahtoosh issue "into the public domain."

ALL PHOTOGRAPHS BY GALEN ROWELL/MOUNTAIN LIGHT UNLESS OTHERWISE NOTED

ABOVE: We pull two-hundred-fifty-pound rickshaws two hundred seventy-five miles across a barren steppe that is completely uninhabited. "If we don't have it," Conrad said at the outset, "we can't get it, and if we can't get it, we don't need it." FOLLOWING PAGES: We make an auspicious departure from Lhasa during the festival of *Saga Dawa*; monks at the Drepang Monastery celebrate this triple anniversary of Buddha's birth, death, and enlightenment.

ABOVE: Stopped by mud a thousand miles from Lhasa, our truck and SUV can go no farther. We set up base camp and the next day the vehicles leave us utterly on our own: The closest humans are a day's drive behind us and we're setting out on foot the opposite direction, into the unknown. RIGHT: Conrad, left, and Jimmy put together a rickshaw, our only means of carrying the supplies needed to survive in this barren steppeland.

Our goal on this trek is to follow the chiru migration and hope they lead us to their hitherto unknown calving grounds. If we can document the nursery on film and video, wildlife biologists can use it in an attempt to persuade the Chinese to establish a nature reserve to protect the calving grounds before poachers can find them.

Elsewhere in the chiru's range, skinned and frozen carcasses are left to the vultures and wolves. The animals are being slaughtered for their fur used to make women's shawls that can sell for over $15,000. FOLLOWING PAGES: In any other place the gem-blue expanse of Heishi Beihu would be a World Heritage site. In the northwest Chang Tang, other than George Schaller, we are the only Westerners to have ever seen it.

ABOVE: The elevation of most of our trekking route is sixteen thousand to seventeen thousand feet and when the sun comes out, and the top inches of the permafrost melt, we feel the full weight of the two-hundred-fifty-pound carts. RIGHT: But mud is nothing compared to the slot canyon we call the Gorge of Despair. The welds on the carts crack and even break as we are trying to cross it. If we have to abandon them, there's no way we can carry everything we'd need to survive the trek in our backpacks, and no one we can call to rescue us.

ABOVE: We can't carry the weight of food needed to replenish the calories we are burning; each day we are withering. As the days wear on, the difference the rest stops make is less and less.

FOLLOWING PAGES: After nearly three weeks, we reach the calving grounds and an adjacent plateau that is like a high-altitude Serengeti, where in one sweep of the eye we count one thousand three hundred female chiru, nearly all pregnant.

(LEFT TO RIGHT: Conrad Anker, Rick Ridgeway, Jimmy Chin, and Galen Rowell.) Two hundred seventy-five miles later, and more than a few pounds lighter, our smiles reveal our success, and with it our hope the chiru will find the solace they deserve. For each of us, it was one of the most physically demanding expeditions of our lives, but also the most fulfilling: an effort to give back to the wild world that has nurtured us.

While they were writing it, Ashok and Belinda continued to press the Indian government to ban the sale of shahtoosh shawls, and to begin seizing the shipments of wool that for the most part were being smuggled from China into Nepal and then into India. To remove any doubt about the connection between the shawls in India and the chiru in Tibet, the Wildlife Protection Society arranged for Indian wildlife officials to send a sample of a shahtoosh shawl to the U.S. Fish and Wildlife Service's forensic lab in Oregon, where technicians compared the fibers in the shawls with samples of hair from wild chiru. The fur from any mammal is composed of thicker guard hair that gives the animal its color and texture, and much finer under-wool that provides insulation. The shawls were almost exclusively made of underwool, but there were nevertheless a few guard hairs that had escaped the tedious handwork required to separate the underwool from the guard hairs. Under a microscope, lab technicians observed that the guard hairs from the shawls and the guard hairs from the chiru had on the surface of each hair the same pattern of scales (the guard hair of every ungulate has its own pattern of scales unique to that species). Even the underwool of the shahtoosh shawls and the chiru had the same average diameter of less than ten microns. The lab could find no other wool from any other ungulate—even animals known for their fine wool such as vicuna, alpaca, and pash-mina—that was as fine. The evidence was conclusive: Shahtoosh shawls were made from chiru wool.

The Indian government, however, still needed proof the wool was-n't gathered from rocks and bushes, as the wool merchants in Kash-mir claimed.

"So the government, like all governments, appointed a commit-tee to look deeper into the subject," Ashok told me with an amused chuckle. "The committee went to Srinagar, met the traders, saw the weaving, then went to Ladakh in a helicopter supplied by the army to a place where there is a small seasonal population of about two hundred chiru.[iii] They spoke to the nomads, who told them the amount of chiru wool they could gather off of rocks and bushes wouldn't even make a pair of socks."

Even with this proof the government was slow in enforcing its own law. Then the Wildlife Protection Society served notice to the Ministry of Environment and Forests that they intended to make a legal complaint if the government didn't take action. A few weeks later authorities seized one hundred seventy-two shahtoosh shawls in Delhi valued at $285,000. The Indian government then sent two delegates to a workshop in Xining, China, organized in large part by the International Fund for Animal Welfare to raise the awareness worldwide of the true origin of shahtoosh, and the delegates returned to Delhi having pledged to step up efforts to stop the shahtoosh trade. The Indian government also released a statement to the public explaining that shahtoosh wool is from chiru, that the animal has to be killed to collect the wool, and because chiru are protected under Indian law, anyone selling the shawls could be imprisoned for up to seven years.

In addition to continuing to work with wildlife officials raiding high-end shops in Delhi selling the shawls, Ashok and his associates also developed programs to train border guards and customs agents in how to identify shahtoosh when they intercepted wool shipments coming in from Nepal. Even then, Ashok knew the most effective way to contain the trade was to go to the heart of the problem and ban the shahtoosh industry in Kashmir. The problem was that Kashmir, chartered as a semiautonomous region after partition in 1947, was the only state in India that had its own constitution. It also had its own wildlife laws, and unlike India's wildlife act, it did not list chiru as a Schedule I endangered animal, but only as a Schedule II species, meaning that trade in the animal's parts was permitted under license from the Kashmiri government.

Ashok knew the state government, however, was not issuing licenses to shahtoosh traders or weavers, and that gave him an idea. By then he had formed his own organization, the Wildlife Trust of India (WTI), and it filed suit claiming that the state government was not enforcing its own law. After a two-year court battle, WTI won the case. The Kashmiri government not only was ordered to regulate the shahtoosh trade, but further, the government had to honor India's support of the international CITES agreement: Even though the Kashmiris had their own constitution, the court ruled that in the case of international treaties, the national government trumped the state government.

Still, the Kashmiris did nothing, so WTI then filed a contempt of court petition asking the state government to follow the court decision. The Kashmiris complained that if the shahtoosh industry were to shut down, a hundred thousand artisans and support workers would lose their jobs. No one had surveyed the true size of the shahtoosh industry, so there was no way to verify this claim. But there was no doubt about the position of Kashmir's chief minister, whose political party had controlled Kashmir for nearly fifty years:

"Shahtoosh will be banned over my dead body," he told the Indian press.

क

WE DECIDE THAT EVERY HOUR ON THE HOUR we will rest for ten or fifteen minutes. At eleven a.m. Galen, who is still leading, stops for our scheduled break. I park next to him, unbuckle, and take my lunch from my pannier, deciding to eat part of it early in the hope I might increase my strength.

"It's not getting any easier," I say as I sit down.

Conrad appears from around the bend, and when he reaches us he keeps going.

"Conrad, time for a break," I call out.

But waving his arm as though to dismiss us, and saying something neither Galen nor I can understand, he keeps going. With both hands on his handlebar, he is pushing with force to get over every rock that otherwise might slow him, and he is going at a pace that I guess even he can't maintain.

"What's up with Conrad?" Galen asks.

"I don't know, but he looks frustrated," I reply. "Maybe it's the difficulty of getting the carts over these rocks."

Still chewing on a stick of jerky, I stand and fasten my waist harness, and then try to catch Conrad. It takes twenty minutes before I reach him, and then I do so only because he has paused to scout once again the best place to cross the river.

"Conrad, you doing okay?" I ask, trying to sound casual.

"Oh, I'm having a blast," he answers sarcastically as he pushes his cart across the river, then adds, "in my own little private hell."

He jumps the river and I follow, deciding to leave the conversation at that. He pulls ahead, and with Galen fifty yards behind me, and Jimmy another fifty yards or more behind him, we are each of us if not in our own private hells, then at least in our own individual struggles. An hour later Conrad, seeming to have worked out his frustrations, stops and pulls out his lunch sack and sits down, leaning against the back of his rickshaw. When the rest of us catch up we do the same.

After some discussion of how to measure an exchange, Jimmy and Galen trade each other dehydrated pineapple for jerky, Jimmy preferring the fruit to the meat, and Galen the other way around. Having already eaten part of my lunch, I'm the first to finish, and leaning against my cart while the others chew on their energy bars, I notice next to me a ceratoides bush. We have all been impressed how chiru manage to travel the distance of their migration subsisting in the main on this plant with its small leaves the shape and color of oregano; it's even more impressive considering how few of the plants grow on the otherwise barren ground. Continuing to stare at the bush, I ask myself that if it's good for them, why wouldn't it be good for me? With that I pluck a few leaves and sample them.

"Hey you guys, this stuff's good."

The others turn as I gather a handful of leaves, shove them in my mouth, and start chewing.

"Drokpa points," Jimmy says. "Rick's scoring drokpa points."

"One or two?" Conrad asks.

"Definitely two," Jimmy replies.

The ceratoides has a savory herb taste, and while the others finish their lunch I continue to graze. Finally Conrad says that we should probably keep going. Once more he takes the lead, and once more we struggle over increasingly large rocks. We stop in an hour for another scheduled rest.

"The carts are taking a beating," Conrad says.

"I don't know that we have a choice," I reply.

"We might, if there was a route up there," he answers, pointing toward the rim of the canyon.

"Think we could get our carts up that?" Jimmy asks, indicating the steep hillside.

"It'd be some work, but we could do it if it was worth doing. That depends on what it's like on the other side. Why don't I go up and check it out."

We wait while Conrad climbs to the rim of the canyon, then returns twenty minutes later.

"There's lots of chiru tracks leaving the canyon," he says, "and up on the rim there's some good stipa grass. I don't know if they're leaving for the grass or to shortcut it to the calving grounds."

"What's it like past the canyon?" I ask.

"There's still a series of steep hills, at least as far as I could see. It'd probably be harder to pull out of this canyon and then have to traverse the hills, than to just keep going the way we're going."

"That's not the news I was hoping to hear," I say. "But I guess we stay in the canyon."

"I just hope we're not heading into a dead-end trap," Galen says.

क

WE CONTINUE SLOWLY DOWN THE CANYON, fighting for every yard, and everyone is tired. Galen is again in the lead, and I know in his mind he wants to keep pushing through the day, until we get out of this gorge, but I also know that could take at a minimum several more hours. When he stops to rest and I catch up I suggest—even though I think I know his reply—that we go for another half hour to an hour, stopping between three-thirty and four-thirty at the first good campsite.

"It would be nice to get out of this canyon," Galen replies.

"I agree, but that might not be until six or seven or even later," I answer, turning to Conrad.

"I can go to six or seven or whatever," he says, but there is irony in his voice.

"Well, then, is there anyone too tired to keep going?" Galen asks.

"We don't need to make a macho thing out of it," Conrad replies sharply.

"I'm not making a macho thing out of it," Galen counters.

"Yes you are, by asking who's tired."

"I'm just trying to see if we can get out of this place," Galen answers in an appealing tone.

"I know," Conrad answers apologetically. "It's just that we're all getting pretty tired."

"I'll do whatever everyone decides," Galen says, and it is clear he means it. Jimmy, with endearing deference, hasn't voiced an opinion, but we all know that like Galen he too will be happy to go with the majority.

"Let's keep going a little while," I suggest, "then see if we can find a good campsite."

Everyone agrees, and we continue. This is the first direct conflict of our journey, and I'm not concerned; in fact, I'm amazed we haven't had more cross words considering the physical stress we have endured. I also have confidence that even when we heat up over our differing opinions, we have between us such a length of experience on difficult expeditions that we have learned how to cool down just as quickly. Now we continue to fight our way over the rocks, and we curse at them just as much as we did before our exchange. Then in a half hour, when I spot a terrace above the river and I suggest it would make an attractive camp spot, Galen agrees, and he does so with good cheer.

"This was a hard one," Conrad says to everyone, after we have the tents up. "Not just the difficulty of pulling, but the stress of taking care of the carts. We can't afford to have anything happen to them. Not here."

"Because if anything does," I add, "we'll be doing more than just practicing with those slingshots."

CHAPTER FIVE

क

JUNE 16

FOR BREAKFAST WE HAVE BEEN alternating between oatmeal and granola, and this morning is a granola day, my favorite. I savor the chewy oats and crunchy nuts slow bite by slow bite, rolling the freeze-dried blueberries on my tongue, and when I see Jimmy doing the same, I give him a knowing nod.

"Granola is to us what ceratoides is to the chiru," I tell Jimmy.

"I'm learning a new appreciation for the word 'migrate,' that's for sure," he replies, slowly chewing his cereal.

This morning we woke late, having agreed last night to start late knowing that the river bottom will be encased in ice from the night's freeze, and until it melts there is an increased risk of spraining an ankle or breaking a bone. Even with the late start, as we depart camp—descending carefully the steep bank surrounding the bench where we pitched the tents—we find there is still residual ice on the rocks along the river's edge, and we have to be careful where we place our feet. We also continuously have to look ahead fifty feet or so to judge the arrangement of the larger boulders and, like mapping multiple moves across a chessboard, decide the best route for the carts. Our jumps across the river become more frequent, but we manage to keep our boots dry. The canyon continues to narrow, and the turns are tighter. Entering each turn, we each hold an unvoiced hope the new view will reveal the canyon beginning to open; instead around each bend we see it continues to close. We round another bend to discover a contact zone with chalcedonous rock replacing the granite we have followed since yesterday, and with the new geology the steep walls of the canyon suddenly descend to both sides of the river, narrowing the gorge even more. We stop to consider the task in front of us.

"So much for dry feet," I say.

Conrad unclips from his cart, walks to the edge of the river, and, to open a corridor wide enough for the carts, rolls to the side a boulder the size of a beach ball. With Conrad pulling and me pushing, we then muscle his rickshaw into the river. Our feet crunch the ice that still lines the bank, and the water, just above freezing, floods our boots. We haul the cart over rocks, one of us on each side. The narrows is about a hundred feet in length, and when we reach the far end we park Conrad's cart and then return for the next one.

"My feet are singing," Conrad says as his feet, like mine, slosh through the ice water.

"Talk to me, toes," I reply.

Jimmy and Galen, who have been videotaping and photographing this latest challenge, have packed their cameras, and now we pass them as they struggle downstream with the second cart. Soon we have all four carts through the narrows.

"Yesterday was annoying," Conrad says, sitting on a rock emptying ice water from his boots, "but this is fun."

The rest of us smile, not because we think Conrad is displaying ironic humor, but because we know he means what he says about putting the best face on this latest turn in our fortune. It reminds me of one of the operating principles of the old British Antarctic Survey, in the days when most travel was by dog sled. Whenever a new recruit complained of severe conditions—blizzards and frostbite and suchlike—the old hands would say, "If you can't take a joke, you shouldn't have signed up."

When the banks of the river become too narrow or too choked with large rocks to navigate with our carts, we no longer bother, now that our boots are soaked, to jump across, but rather we simply slosh down the middle. It takes an hour to cover perhaps a quarter mile when we round another bend only to see another narrows even more constricting than the last one: The walls are ten feet wide and a hundred feet straight up, at which point they recline only slightly until they reach the top of the gorge several hundred feet higher.

We again shuttle the carts, one pulling while one pushes. Jimmy and I are returning from the first shuttle when we stop to rest. Leaning against the rock wall inside the narrow slot, there is suddenly a loud *kawhumpf!* and we spin to see that a basketball-size rock has exploded into the river not twenty feet from us.

"Oh wow!" Jimmy says.

"Let's keep going," I yell.

When the fourth cart is through and we are out of the narrows, Galen and I hug each other.

"Man, I'm glad to be out of there," he says, giving me a tight embrace.

By now my feet are so numb I have to take off my boots and shake one leg and then the other to force blood into my toes. Galen asks me to sit down, then starts massaging my feet, beginning at the ankles and working with fingers and thumbs toward the toes, then moving back to the ankles.

"Any feeling yet?" he asks.

"The pain is coming on."

"That's what we want," he replies.

When all ten toes burn to the point I feel queasy I thank Galen twice, to make sure he knows how deeply I appreciate his help. I pull on the wet socks and boots, and we continue. Past the narrows the canyon widens enough each of us can again pull his own cart. There is another contact zone and the chalcedonous rock gives way to a brick red conglomerate, and in another hundred yards the gorge once more narrows, this time to a constriction that we can see will leave only inches of clearance on each side of the rickshaws. Even worse, across the entrance of the narrows the river pours over a ledge forming a waterfall five feet in height.

"Welcome to R-4," Conrad says.

"The Gorge of Despair," I sigh.

The day has continued to warm, and no one has to say anything about the increased danger from falling rock. Before we enter this third narrows Conrad takes from his pack the yellow Rite in the Rain notebook where he has taped to the inside front cover a photograph of Jenny and the three boys. In the manner that Tibetan Buddhists venerate sacred objects and pray for good fortune, he holds the notebook for several seconds to his forehead.

"Today is Father's Day," Conrad says, returning the notebook to his pack.

"I'm sure the boys are thinking of you," I reply.

"And your kids are thinking of you," he answers.

This time we will have to triple-team the carts—one pulling and two pushing—while Galen or Jimmy, alternating, takes photos or video. Before we start we have to roll several large rocks aside to create clearance wide enough to get the rickshaws into the river. With that done, Jimmy then films while the rest of us lift the first cart into the river. We manage to advance it about ten feet downstream when our first obstacle, a rock four feet high, blocks us. We try to pull the cart around one side, but it doesn't fit. We try to pull it around the other side, but again the cart is too wide. We shrug our shoulders and grab the cart by the wheel frames.

"Okay," Conrad says, "One...two...three!"

We lift the nearly two-hundred-and-fifty-pound cart on top of the rock and balance it while we catch our breath. Jimmy points the video camera at me and says, "Can you please explain to the audience how this rickshaw has come to be sitting on top of this big rock?"

I shake my head, smile and say, "No, I can't."

"One...two...three!" Conrad says, and with a grunt we lift the cart and set it down on the other side of the rock. We advance ten more feet and encounter our next obstacle, the waterfall. We are now between the walls of the narrows, and despite the increasingly high sun the gorge is still in shadow, and ice coats the rocks on both sides of the waterfall. Conrad and Galen slide to the base of the waterfall and grab the cart as I lower it to them. The bottom of the river is now smooth enough to allow Conrad to pull the cart while Galen and I push, but the gorge is so narrow that at one turn Galen and I have to jockey the cart sideways to get it through: There is perhaps two inches of clearance on either side.

"I wouldn't want to be here in a flash flood," Galen says, his voice, mixed with the roar of the water, echoing off the rock walls.

We approach the end of the narrows, and Jimmy runs ahead to get a shot of us emerging. As we exit from deep shadow into bright sun, we pass Jimmy squatting down to get a low-angle shot.

"Granola for breakfast," Conrad says as he passes the camera. "Rice for dinner."

We park Conrad's cart and go back for the next one, this time Jimmy trading places with Galen so he can take photographs. We have the second cart through and are returning for the third when from around a narrow bend in the gorge we hear Galen scream, "Oh my God, no!"

"Galen's been hit by a rock!" I gasp.

We rush to the bend, and as we step over the iced rocks I tell myself in one instant to be mindful not to slip and sprain my ankle, then in the next instant I see a vision of Galen's head split open and bleeding and bone showing and I ask myself: How will we get him out? And I answer my own question: We'll have to cart him, but it will take two weeks, minimum, and that might be too long to keep him alive. We reach the bend in the gorge and turning the corner we see Galen standing in the river, his pants and shirt soaked with water.

"Are you okay?"

"No! I slipped on some ice and my camera's wet."

"That's all?"

"It's my camera!"

We climb the waterfall to the remaining cart, and Galen takes off his pack, retrieves a chamois he always carries, and dries his camera. In a few minutes he reports that the camera seems to be functioning. We lift the fourth cart over the rock and down the waterfall, and when it is through the narrows we continue down the Gorge of Despair.

While the canyon again opens enough to allow each person to pull his own cart, the frames nevertheless grind as we squeeze between rocks, and the wheels torque as we pull them over the large stones that choke the river bottom. Yesterday we would never have dreamed of putting the carts through such abuse, but yesterday we had no idea the Gorge of Despair would be so long, or so tortuous. At each bend we hope to turn the corner and see the opening to the basin, but instead each bend reveals another section of narrow, rocky riverbed.

"I feel like I'm in the Land of the Lost," Jimmy says.

"I think we're almost there," Conrad replies, pointing to a hill that has just come into view down the canyon.

"That hill is definitely more rounded," I agree with a tone of optimism that I wish reflected how I really feel.

"Yeah, that's what I said last night," Galen says, injecting more realism into the assessment.

In a few minutes we see a well-worn chiru trail ascending diagonally up the steep bank of the gorge. It's heading toward what on our map is a high plateau where a year ago Schaller's party, in their attempt by camel and donkey caravan to locate the calving grounds by coming in from the north, observed a large congregation of female chiru.

"They're probably shortcutting it to the calving grounds," Conrad says.

"Easy for them," Jimmy replies.

"Probably better to stay in the gorge," Galen offers.

"It has to end soon," I say, my tone of voice more of a prayer than a statement.

We discuss it further, and acknowledging it will be difficult either way—and knowing our decision is based more on guess than logic—we agree to stay in the gorge rather than try to pull our carts up the steep hill. Before we continue I ask Jimmy to retrieve the video camera and get a shot holding for a few beats on Conrad, Galen, and me continuing down the gorge, then panning up and zooming in on the chiru trail.

"Hold on the trail for ten seconds or so," I tell him, "to give the narrator time. I have a suspicion there will be a few things to say about the decision we just made."

क

SOON WE CAN SEE THE ENTRANCE to a fourth narrows, and it appears to be nearly as difficult as the previous one.

"We'll have to triple-team again on the carts," Conrad says.

We decide to take a break before we start. I lie on my back on a flat rock and spot an upland hawk spiraling in a thermal. It is in light phase and appears white against the blue sky, as bright as an angel. Earlier this morning we saw a lammergeyer, and later a tawny eagle, and as it has been over a week since we've seen any birds of prey other than a couple of falcons, we take heart these raptors are surely signs there is food in the area; and as we have seen no pika, marmot, or rabbit, the only other likely prey for the hawks and eagles are baby chiru, and for the vultures the remains of babies as well as females taken by wolves. Now I watch the hawk until it is only a whitish dot, and when I look away for a moment and then back I am unable to find it. I know, however, it is likely still watching us.

We stand and stretch, and I am adjusting the bungee cord that holds one of my water bladders when I notice what appears to be a crack in the weld that attaches the wheel frame to the bolt plate that secures it to the cart. I quickly examine the other side.

"Oh no. I've got two cracked welds," I say to the others.

"Uh-oh," Conrad says as he comes over to have a look. Everyone then pauses to inspect his own cart.

"Mine are okay," Galen says. "But the frames are definitely bent."

"Three of my four welds are cracked," Conrad reports.

"I've got one weld broken all the way through," Jimmy says.

This is serious. Conrad looks at me, his brows furrowed, his eyes fixed on mine in a way that gives silent voice to his thoughts.

"I don't need to tell you guys," I say, "we are in deep doo-doo if these carts break."

We decide the most sensible response is to unload each rickshaw, stuff the contents in our backpacks, and portage everything downstream. We will then come back for the carts, and even though they will be empty we decide nevertheless we will lift them over any big rocks.

We each have empty backpacks that we have brought just for this contingency, and we now load them until they each weigh seventy-five pounds or more. Still, a pile of camera equipment, food, and other gear will have to be carried in a second shuttle. As we depart with the first carry, I consider how the exercise only underscores the predicament we will be in if the carts break beyond repair: There is no way we could pack everything in a single carry, and no way we could afford the time, and with the time the food, to double-carry.

We walk a quarter mile downstream, unload the food and gear in a pile, and return for the second load. As I pass Jimmy recording our efforts with the video camera, I tip back my cap, look in the lens, and say, "It's the way you eat an elephant: one bite at a time. We'll get there."

After I deliver a second load to the cache I ferry my empty cart, stopping to lift it over the larger rocks. In the center of the narrows I pause to look up at the two rock walls only six to ten feet apart and at least a hundred feet high. The smooth polish on the walls is testament to the power of the water that must on occasion flood this high-altitude desert. Once out of the narrows I park the cart and look back to see Conrad exiting from the slot that is cut into the rock wall like a narrow passageway in a medieval city. Once we have our carts to the cache we can see that downstream the riverbed is littered with rocks that Conrad says are "TV and sofa size." We agree the best strategy is to continue to portage. Once more we strap the packs to our shoulders and slowly work our way downstream.

"What do you think if we camp when it gets to be five or six?" Conrad asks me. "Whether we're out of the canyon or not."

"That's fine by me," I agree. "We can't push ourselves until somebody slips and sprains an ankle, or worse."

In another quarter mile we find a flat bench twenty feet above river level. It's close to six o'clock.

"This looks like a good campsite," Conrad says. "What do you think?"

"Fine by me. Let's see what the others say."

We cache our loads and are returning with empty packs when we approach Galen and Jimmy, bent under the weight of their packs. When we reach each other I tell them about the idea to camp.

"I don't think that's such a good idea," Galen says.

"It's almost six," I reply, "and if I knew it was an hour to get out of here, I'd say yeah, absolutely, let's do it. Even an hour and a half. But it'll take three or four hours, and that's too far to push. We're too worn out."

"Yes, three or four hours might be," Galen says. He's taken his pack off while we talk, and now his arms are folded and his hands clutch his biceps. "It'd also be a real mistake to get caught in here in a flash flood, or get in a snowstorm, or to have the rocks ice. We'd do more damage to the carts moving them over iced rocks than we would burning ourselves a little more today. We've got decent weather, and my vote is to go at least another hour, hour and a half, and see where we get."

"But we don't want to end up in another slot canyon with no place to camp," I counter.

"We have five hours of daylight, and we don't know what the weather is going to bring."

"Look up at the sky," Conrad says, hands in the pockets of his jacket. "The weather is better today than it was yesterday."

"I wouldn't be so adamant if it weren't for three things," Galen says, unfolding his arms. "Ice, cold water, and flash flood." With each point he slaps first one finger to his palm, then two, then three, then he clasps his hands in front of himself in a gesture firm yet polite.

"There is no flash flood," Conrad says, enunciating each word. "The weather is solid. It snowed all day yesterday and stormed during the night, and the creek didn't rise an inch."

"It didn't snow until four," Galen replies.

"Galen, we woke up and it was snowing. Recall?"

"Okay, you guys," I say. "I'm not worried about a flash flood. My biggest concern is pacing, and making sure nobody gets so tired they twist an ankle. It's well said about ice and cold water, although cold water is something we can put up with. Ice, we have to be careful, but we have to be careful with exhaustion, too. Listen, maybe we should take fifteen or twenty minutes and make a reccy."

Jimmy, who has been quiet until now, says he agrees that's a good idea. Galen volunteers to finish shuttling his load, cache his pack, and continue down the canyon until he gets to its end, then come back with a report. Meanwhile Jimmy will also finish his shuttle to the lower cache while Conrad and I return to the higher cache to bring two more backpack loads from there.

"It's appropriate the hardest day of the trip is on Father's Day," Conrad says after we reach the higher cache and start downstream with our packs once more fully loaded. "It's kept my mind on my family, and that's kept it all in perspective."

As we pass Jimmy returning for his second load, I ask how he is doing, and he admits he's getting tired. When Conrad and I near the terrace where we have deposited the lower cache, we see Galen returning from his scout.

"It's only ten minutes or less to the end of the canyon," he says. "We can definitely make it today."

"That's ten minutes without a load," Conrad says.

"There's one more narrows, and it will take time with the carts," Galen counters, "but we can definitely do it."

"Galen, I think we should camp right here, on the bench," I say. "We're too tired."

"Conrad, is that how you feel?" Galen asks.

"Yep, that's my vote," he replies.

"And Jimmy?"

"He's tired, too," I add.

"I don't think it's a good idea," Galen says, "but if that's the majority, I'll go along with it. But I'm going to portage all my camera gear and film out of here."

"Galen, why don't you just do it in the morning, with everything else? Relax and have a cup of cocoa or something. We've got to pace ourselves."

"I don't think it will be safe in the morning."

"Okay, but first help me get the rest of the carts to the campsite while Jimmy and Conrad get the tents up and start dinner."

"Okay," he says, and his tone is sincerely amenable. Conrad and I dump our loads at the lower cache, and while Conrad starts to set up the tents, Galen and I walk upriver to get the carts.

"I understand your reasoning," I tell him, "but I have to balance everyone's opinions, including my own, and as I said before, I think we're risking an accident if we push too far. We have to pace ourselves, like Amundsen did in Antarctica."

"But this isn't Antarctica, with one expanse of polar ice. This is different geography, and it has different demands."

"Well, that's a good point," I concede.

But we both know the decision has been made, and the discussion ends. We pass Jimmy shuttling his last load, and he agrees to help Conrad set up camp. Meanwhile Galen and I shuttle the rickshaws, and after we have the last carts delivered, Galen departs downriver, his backpack filled with his cameras and film, making sure the gear that safekeeps his livelihood—more, that embodies his dreams and aspirations—is secure from whatever trials the morning brings. I watch him disappear around a bend in the gorge, amazed how, at age sixty-two, he can push himself so hard, even when the rest of us—including Conrad, at age thirty-nine, and Jimmy, at age twenty-nine—are calling it a day. What is his secret?

But I no more than ask myself the question than I tell myself the answer. There is no secret. There is only commitment, passion, and hard work.

क

CONRAD AND JIMMY HAVE DINNER READY by the time Galen returns, and everyone is cordial, experienced enough from years of doing these trips not to let the issue taint our evening. We go to bed agreeing to sleep in until 8:00 a.m. and then, once the ice on the rocks has melted, we will begin the final portage.

After dinner I'm outside my tent when I spot four chiru grazing on the hillside opposite our camp. The bank is steep, and the animals have worn into the slope goatlike trails that belie the common perception chiru are comfortable only on open steppe. When they wrote *Fashioned for Extinction*, Ashok Kumar and Belinda Wright noted, "Unlike Asiatic Ibex, the chiru prefer the plains and valleys, lacking the agility to climb the steep and often rocky mountain slopes."

Schaller was more accurate in observing that chiru "prefer flat to rolling terrain, although they readily ascend high rounded hills and penetrate mountains and cross passes by following valleys." Still, I'm not sure even Schaller has observed chiru on a slope this steep (from mountaineering you get a knack for estimating the angles of slopes, and this one to me looks to be about 50 degrees); and watching them I wonder if perhaps they are revealing that connection dating back to the Miocene when their lineage split from their goatlike ancestors.

Ashok and Belinda were not wildlife biologists, and the information in *Fashioned for Extinction* about the chiru's natural history was taken mostly from Schaller's observations. If they were inaccurate in this small detail about chiru, the booklet was nevertheless vital in bringing the plight of the chiru to the attention of officials and politicians in Delhi. In Kashmir, however, the politicians in power remained entrenched, including the chief minister who was also leader of the incumbent National Conference Party, which had ruled the state of Kashmir and Jammu since partition fifty years before, the same chief minister who, reacting to the efforts of Ashok, Belinda, and others, had said, "Shahtoosh will be banned over my dead body."

When I interviewed Ashok in Delhi, I asked him what his reaction was when he heard the chief minister so emphatically draw the line in the sand.

"I thought, 'Oh very well then. We will simply ban it over your dead body,'" Ashok replied, his eyes squeezing in amusement at the thought.

But Ashok knew this would be a major effort: It had taken two years even to obtain the favorable court ruling he had received. Meanwhile, the popularity of shahtoosh shawls in Hong Kong, Europe, and the United States was increasing rapidly. British *Vogue* called shahtoosh a "survival tactic" to "get through the parties and holidays." *Harper's Bazaar* ran an ad for the New York outlet of the Italian company Malo advertising shahtoosh shawls for sale for $2,850. A web site specializing in high-end luxury goods called shahtoosh a "status-symbol that has turned into an addiction," and a high-end New York designer listed shahtoosh on her published list of "most useful travel clothes." Zoe Tay, Singapore's top star, was described in a fashion bulletin as being a "well-known clothes-horse...often swaddled in a khaki shahtoosh," and in another on-line bulletin the Italian fashion femme Antonia Dell'Atte, when asked to give "the 5 basic pieces of the modern wardrobe," included shahtoosh. A wealthy Hong Kong department store owner was quoted as saying he liked to have a shahtoosh spread on his lap when he ate his TV dinners.

As the popularity of the shawls increased, some women who had exclusive Rolodexes but presumably proletarian bank accounts, began hosting, usually in their houses or apartments, shahtoosh sales. They were like Tupperware parties for the wealthy. This was also popular in Hong Kong, where upper-class women known as tai-tais were having their own apartment sales. An article in the South China Morning Post titled "Christmas Wrapping" reported, "Some tai-tais are known to have a collection of at least 30 to 40 [shahtooshes] in different colours...a devotee has even arranged... with some of her friends...to fly to New Delhi for a shahtoosh shopping trip."[1]

Even with the government crackdown in India, many high-end shops in Delhi's best hotels and shopping areas were still selling shahtoosh to anyone who made a discreet inquiry, and Ashok and the Wildlife Trust had a number of spies doing just that. "When you are in my line of work," he told me, "you either sit in your office and write papers, or you are proactive. Here in India, I am an adviser to the wildlife officials, so I can call them up and say, 'I have learned that such-and-such a shop is selling shahtoosh, so let's go in there together and catch some people!'"

In addition to raiding shops, Ashok and his associates continued to assist customs agents seizing shawls at the borders and airports. In one bust at Indira Gandhi International, Delhi agents seized twelve shawls being shipped to a certain Renaissance Corporation in London. Ashok's group notified the Wildlife Crime Unit of Scotland Yard's Metropolitan Police, and agents traced the shipment to a high-end shop in London's exclusive Mayfair district. Suspecting the shop had additional shawls for sale, Scotland Yard obtained a search warrant to raid the shop, but then realized none of their officers knew how to distinguish a shahtoosh from a pashmina. No problem. Ashok was scheduled to travel to England to attend a conference, so the officers postponed the raid until he could join them.

क

"ANYTHING CAN TURN UP HERE IN LONDON," Ian Knox, sergeant in the Wildlife Crime Unit of the Metropolitan Police told me as he zipped open a bag under a table next to his desk that revealed a large head with an open maw and big white teeth. "Here's a complete polar bear head and skin that we seized."

At the other end of his office in Scotland Yard was a cabinet with shelves containing a mounted kestrel, a gorilla skull, a stuffed tiger head, a grizzly bear skull, and several shahtoosh shawls. He pulled out one shawl that had extraordinarily fine embroidery and let me rub it between my fingers.

"This one still has the price tag," he said. "See?"

"Eleven thousand three hundred and five pounds?" I said questioningly. "Is this from the Mayfair seizure?"

"Yes, and it was the most expensive shawl of the bunch."

"And you were involved in the raid?"

"There were five of us. It was our first raid. Before we received the tip we didn't know anything about shahtoosh, what it looked like, what it felt like. Then Ashok contacted us saying twelve shawls had been intercepted in India, being exported to a company in London. We executed a warrant and then scheduled the day for the raid to coincide with the time off that Belinda and Ashok had from a conference they were attending, so they could come along. That sort of thing wouldn't be allowed now, everyone would have to have protective vests, pepper spray, extendable batons, etc. In those days all we had were wooden truncheons and common sense.

"The shop was called Kashmir, on South Audley Street, right across from the American Embassy, and it carried all sorts of exotic Indian carpets and furniture, and shawls. On arrival the police constables and I secured the exits. I don't mean we handcuffed people and herded them into one room, we just established where they were and politely asked them not to touch anything. The staff appeared quite nervous until they realized we had come to search for shahtoosh. There was plenty of evidence in the form of brochures that shahtoosh was on sale in the shop, but Belinda, Ashok, and I were not prepared for the amount we found. One section of the shop was given over to the display and storage of the shawls, hundreds of them. Belinda and Ashok diligently began rubbing them between their fingers and declaring 'shahtoosh, pashmina, shahtoosh, pashmina.' The search took several hours. In the end we seized one hundred thirty-eight shawls that they identified as shahtoosh. And that's when our problems started.

"We claimed they were shahtoosh, but we had to establish that shahtoosh was chiru. We had no forensic test available to us at that time, but at one of our conferences that we attend, the American Fish and Wildlife laboratory in Oregon had offered to test any substance for us, free of charge. We contacted one of the technicians, Bonnie Yates, and learned she had already developed a test to identify chiru guard hair. So I thought, 'Oh, we have one hundred thirty-eight shawls and that will require someone to personally take them to America, and that should be me!' But then the court told us we only needed to send a sample of ten shawls, so I didn't get to visit America, but we did get our proof when all ten shawls were shown to be chiru wool."

"Then you got your conviction?"

"Yes, but the company was fined only one thousand five hundred pounds for a seizure that was worth three hundred fifty-three thousand pounds. That was the largest seizure in the world at the time. But we shouldn't comment on the decisions of the court."

"Have you made any more seizures?"

"Nothing like that one. But based on that conviction we started a campaign to increase public awareness about shahtoosh here in the U.K., and using samples cut from the shawls we confiscated, we developed a shahtoosh identification kit that we distributed to law enforcement agencies around the world."

"I have one more question for you," I said. "I've been curious about this for some time now. You see, these chiru, they live out in the most remote corner of one of the most removed ends of the Earth. It's very,

very unlikely—as in next to impossible—you are ever going to see one in flesh and blood. So here's my question: What motivates you to work so hard to try and save them?"

Sergeant Knox grinned, leaned back in his chair, and rubbed his chin.

"It doesn't matter, I suppose, that I won't see one," he answered. "They're there, we're here, and what we do is making a difference, a small difference, but a difference. But that article that you wrote about your trip, the one in NATIONAL GEOGRAPHIC, we all passed that around the office, and it was very important to us, to see your photographs of the animals in the wild. It was very encouraging."

"They weren't my photographs," I replied. "They were my buddy's, Galen Rowell. But I know he would be pleased if he could hear you say that. Very, very pleased."

CHAPTER SIX

क

JUNE 17

"It feels like Sunday morning," I say.

"Who knows, maybe it is," Galen says.

"Yeah, I have no idea what the day of the week is," I chuckle. "That feels good, too."

It's eight a.m., and even though we had all agreed we would wake by this time, there's no sound of the stove from Conrad and Jimmy's tent so we assume they are still asleep. Galen and I lie in our sleeping bags, enjoying the late start and chatting about the book publishing business. Galen is explaining how he and Barbara have packaged her upcoming book, hiring a designer and doing the layouts themselves, when Conrad unzips the door on our tent.

"Morning, Conrad," I say. "I thought you guys were still asleep."

"The coffee's been ready for a half hour," he replies.

"We didn't hear the stove," Galen says.

"That's because the river is roaring louder this morning," Conrad answers. "It came up during the night."

I can see there is concern in Conrad's eyes.

"I guess it is louder," I say. "I'm not paying attention."

"I woke up at one and heard it," Conrad says, "so I got up and I saw it was rising. It's nearly twice as high as yesterday."

"You think we can get down?" Galen asks.

"Yeah, but it might take some work. We saved some coffee for you, and some granola."

"Granola two days in a row?" I ask.

"Yeah, we thought we'd celebrate."

Conrad leaves and Galen and I dress.

"Sounds like we should have listened to you," I say to Galen as we leave the tent.

"We'll figure it out," he replies.

The river is a rushing mud torrent, and as Conrad said it's twice as high as yesterday. Galen and I study it for a moment, and then go to Conrad and Jimmy's tent for breakfast. Jimmy is outside the tent loading his backpack.

"Where's Conrad?" I ask.

"I'm not sure," Jimmy answers.

"Has he left with a load?"

"I guess so."

Galen and I crawl in the tent and have our breakfast, and we are outside loading our backpacks when we see Conrad coming down the steep slope behind the terrace on which we are camped.

"I made the portage," he says when he reaches camp, "but the water's high and there's another tight narrows, so it'd be a full goat wrangle with the carts. So I came back looping around, coming down this slope."

"How was that?" I ask.

"The steep part is right here, up to the crest. Then it's gradual out to the basin. Probably the same calorie expenditure as going down the gorge considering we'd be cold, but a lot less frustration and potential damage to the carts."

"You think we can get the carts up that?" Jimmy asks, indicating the hill.

"Empty carts you could," Conrad answers.

"I think it's a good idea," Galen says. "Last night when I went down it wasn't that deep, but now I've been dreading going through that cold water."

So Galen's position yesterday afternoon to push out of the gorge was valid, and while we are huddled I feel it's important to recognize that.

"You had some good points, Galen," I tell him. "If the river had come up even more, and we didn't have an escape route, we could be in trouble right now."

"But we do have an escape route," he replies.

"And we have to continue to learn from our decisions," I answer.

क

CONRAD LEAVES WITH ANOTHER LOAD, and the rest of us return to loading our packs and breaking camp. Soon Galen leaves, then Jimmy. I follow, and I'm only a short distance above camp when I pass Conrad. I'm aware that I am beginning my first shuttle as he is returning from completing his second, and I apologize for my slow start.

"Don't worry," he says. "The good news is we'll soon be out of the Gorge."

"And this time we're in all agreement. But I don't think Galen feels any ill will from yesterday."

"Everybody's fine," Conrad says. "I've realized we're all Type A's on this expedition. And Galen? He's a Triple A. But you know, if we weren't this way we wouldn't be who we are, and we wouldn't have done what we've done, and we wouldn't be here doing what we're doing."

He nods his head and waves his hand in his loose-wristed parody of the Hindu salute to the acceptance of things as they are, then turns toward camp. I watch his tall, strong frame descend in loping, athletic strides, and then I return to my task. When I'm at the top of the hill I get my first view into the desert expanse of the wide Shor Kul basin, and beyond, a glacial-covered subrange of the Kunluns called the Kaxtax Mountains.

"We're here, all right," I tell myself, grinning at the thought. "Doing what we are doing."

I reach our cache, dump the contents of my pack, and go back for my second carry. After completing that, I am returning toward our now dismantled camp and our next chore—getting the carts up the hill and into the basin—when I come over the crest and look down to see Galen struggling on his own to pull his cart up the steep slope.

"Galen, wait right there. We'd better belay the carts."

Conrad has left our rope in a coil on top a small rock that will make a good belay platform. Jimmy is down at the campsite with the rest of the carts, and when I call to him he starts up as I descend to the rope. When Jimmy reaches Galen I toss the rope and Jimmy ties it to the cart, and I put Galen on belay.

"Conrad will be back in a minute," I call to Galen. "He can help push the cart while I belay and Jimmy films."

"Okay," Galen replies, nodding his head with a firmness that suggests he realizes he is in a fix.

Jimmy returns to our campsite to get his video camera, and when Conrad arrives he pushes the cart while Galen pulls and Jimmy films. When they reach my position we balance the cart on top of the rock, then Conrad and I climb uphill, stringing the rope as we go. When we reach the end of the rope we kick another belay platform into the hillside. Conrad then goes back down to help Galen with the next stage. When they have the cart up to my new position we still have one pitch to go, and this time Conrad takes a turn at belaying while I push the cart. From there we traverse the slope, holding the cart level so it rolls on the uphill wheel only.

"R-4 or R-5?" I ask Conrad.

"R-5," he says.

In three hours we have all the rickshaws out of the Gorge of Despair and into the Shor Kul basin. At the cache we spend another hour repacking and also repairing the carts: Conrad has to remove his disk brakes because the wheel frames on his cart are bent so badly the brakes are irreparably out of alignment and rub with each rotation against the calipers. If we have any more steep terrain between here and our rendezvous with the vehicle that will pick us up, it will be more difficult without brakes for him to control his cart, but he has no choice. When his brakes are removed, Conrad then tapes and wires his wheel frames in hope such reinforcement might prevent the cracks in the welds from breaking the rest of the way.

"Let's see if that works," he says.

"And if it doesn't?" I ask.

"R-6," he answers. "Abandon carts and walk."

क

IN THE NEAR DISTANCE sand blows in banners off the tops of dunes around which we soon must cart; in the middle distance, heat waves, rising then catching the wind, cause the floor of the basin to shimmer as though it were on fire; and in the far distance the snow slopes of the Kaxtax Mountains, a range all but unknown to the outside world, are bright white against bright blue. We have completed the transition from the alpine steppelands of the Tibetan Plateau to the high desert expanses of Central Asia, and as we pull our carts into the basin, my earworm returns. I hear the first brushes of the snare drum, like the stirring of the sand on the dunes in front of me. I hear the flute play the theme, evoking a distant caravansary, then the clarinet followed by the bassoon, and in the distance I imagine a long line of approaching camels. The tenor sax and the soprano sax and then the French horn, and the caravan nears, the oboe invoking the sounds of the animals protesting the desert heat. Then the woodwinds and the violins and the horns build with each repetition, layer upon layer, until finally Ravel's *Bolero* crescendos and the camel caravan arrives.

My reverie over, I look up and there is Conrad, Galen, and Jimmy pulling their carts past the dunes, the only humans for miles in any direction.

"Here we are, doing what we're doing," I say to myself, smiling once more at the thought.

We head west by southwest, the first time on our trek our route has contained a southerly vector, and we walk parallel to the base of the range of hills from which we have just emerged. When we last saw the chiru tracks leaving the Gorge of Despair, they were heading toward what appears on our Russian map to be a high plain nestled in these hills; it is the vicinity of the place where, a little over a year ago, members of George Schaller's party, searching for the elusive calving grounds, had seen a dense congregation of female chiru that appeared to be loitering instead of migrating. Schaller was then, in 2001, attempting to find the calving grounds by coming in from the north, through the back door. While he and his party were then unable to wait to see if the animals gave birth, it was his opinion that the area is likely to be the calving grounds, and our own observations of the direction of the animals' tracks only strengthen his supposition.

Our next challenge is to figure out how to get there. The topographical lines of the map outline a valley that begins in the hills near the plain and ends in this basin, and while the floor of the valley appears to have only a moderate grade, and the sides seem to be comparatively open, we have learned that a lot can happen between the 50-meter contours: None of the four narrows that we encountered in the Gorge of Despair, for example, were indicated on the map. Anyway, the entrance to the canyon is too far to reach today, so our plan is to get as close to it as we can, and then tomorrow learn whether it can accommodate carts. If it can't, we will have to cache the carts and food in the basin, and try to reach the plain on foot. That is not our first choice, however, as we are wary of leaving our food: Even if we were to put our food sacks between two carts and strap them together with our climbing rope, the result would be no match against a bear's prying claws.

The afternoon heat brings with it a desert wind, and soon we see bearing down on us a dark screen of sand rising three hundred feet into the air. We have only time to zipper our wind jackets and strap our ski goggles across our eyes before the sandstorm hits. For the next ten minutes visibility is thirty feet or less. The sand stings any exposed skin, but I manage to strap a surgical mask across my mouth and nose—an item we had packed in anticipation of dusty roads on the drive out—and when my face is fully protected I raise my arms and yell in delight at our privilege to witness such natural power.

"Real *Lawrence of Arabia* stuff," I yell to Galen through my mask, and I can see in the glimmering black beads of his eyes that he too is enjoying it. My comment brings to mind the film, and I recall the scene in King Feisel's tent when the Arab says to Lawrence, "I think you are another of these desert-loving Englishman."

When the sandstorm abates we continue, and in late afternoon we arrive at a collection of mudstone outcrops that rise out of the desert floor like a Central Asian Stonehenge. The formations offer the only protection from wind visible for miles, so we decide to make camp. After dinner we stand on top of the mud hillock adjacent to what we have decided to call Druid Camp, and using marble-size rocks we practice shooting with our wrist rockets at neighboring outcrops. Our accuracy with the slingshots is improving, and we still feel we made the right decision bringing them, but if anything were to go wrong and we were forced to forage for food, they might not be as useful as we had hoped: We haven't seen a marmot, pika, or rabbit for days.

After dark we gather in Conrad and Jimmy's tent while hailstones pummel the fly. A lightning flash is so intense it illuminates the interior of the tent as brightly as a lantern.

"One thousand one, one thousand two, one thousand three," Jimmy says, stopping when the volley of thunder reaches our camp. "That's pretty close."

"The smell of rain in the desert," Conrad says, smiling. We listen to the hail hit the fly. There is another flash of lightning, then another clap of thunder that rolls across the valley like the boom of artillery.

"Then the other side of lightning," Conrad continues, "is that the only metal in this huge basin eight miles wide and fifty miles long..."—and he pauses while he points toward the rickshaws parked between our two tents—"is about ten feet that way."

JUNE 18

AFTER BREAKFAST, while the rest of us break camp, Conrad walks a full mile across the desert pavement to intercept the same river that we had tracked through the Gorge of Despair, and that since debouching into the basin has been flowing down a broad alluvium at a diagonal to our own route. It has also been little by little percolating into the parched floor of the Shor Kul, and what yesterday was a turbid torrent is now a remnant trickle that nevertheless has sufficient flow to allow Conrad to fill our water bladders. By the time he returns we have the carts packed and ready to go. We consult our Russian map and take a compass bearing on the entrance to the canyon we hope will afford us access to the plain we hope to reach today.

"I get two hundred ten degrees, so we head for the right margin of that hill over there," Conrad says, pointing to a landmark in the foothills he proposes we use to keep our bearing. "It's a little over two miles to the canyon."

As we get under way the sun shines through thin clouds and casts pale light over ground dusted with snow from last night's storm. Today the weather is stable, and there is no wind. My health also seems improved: I can now breathe deeply without triggering a paroxysm of coughing. I'm in the lead, and as the ground is hard we make good time. To our relief we see that the entrance to the canyon is wide, at least compared with the notch in a rock wall that marked the entrance from the basin into the Gorge of Despair. To save time I decide to cut a corner across a mud bar that I know looks questionable, and sure enough the wheels of our rickshaws sink into the soft surface.

"Sorry, guys," I apologize. "Let's backtrack and try the other side of the canyon."

Although we can see another mud bar awaits us at the opposite entrance to the canyon, when we get there we are relieved to find it dry enough to support our wheels. Then to the side we notice what appears to be a single line of animal tracks. We alter direction to investigate and discover in the hardened mud the single track of an animal larger than even a yak.

"What do you think?" Jimmy asks.

"Camel tracks," I answer. "And look, over here. Footprints. Human footprints."

"Schaller's party?" Galen asks.

"Must be," Conrad answers.

क

THE FACT SCHALLER TOOK his camels up this canyon increases our hope it will be favorable terrain for carting. Ahead of us the canyon seems to narrow, but the floor remains smooth and other than a few soft spots it continues to be an easy pull; compared with the Gorge of Despair it feels like a Sunday stroll. As we pull our carts alongside the camel tracks, our bicycle wheels leave parallel lines next to the large cloven prints. Seeing the tracks side by side makes me wonder what—if somehow all the tracks were preserved in this mud—some future visitor might conclude, trying to deduce what sort of bizarre caravan had passed through here.

Following these camel tracks through this canyon as remote as any place in Central Asia brings with it an even deeper admiration for the tenacity of Schaller's effort to trace the chiru's migration. The idea for his expedition started after Schaller's failure in 1992 to follow the migration north of Heishi Beihu, when he began to consider the possibility of trying to locate the calving grounds by coming in from the opposite direction. He knew the birthing area had to be somewhere north of Heishi Beihu but south of the Kunlun Mountains because the higher summits of that range, all between twenty thousand feet and twenty-three thousand feet in elevation, created a natural barrier the chiru were unlikely to cross, especially since there was nothing to cross to: North of the Kunluns is the great Taklimakan Desert.

Only two or three expeditions of outsiders before him had explored the region immediately south of this section of the Kunluns.[1] The first was the intrepid Capt. H. H. Deasy, the same British surveyor who had reached the basin north of Toze Kangri that he had named Antelope Plain after the vast herds of chiru he had sighted there. In 1897—the year after his exploration of the Antelope Plain—Deasy left the old Silk Road caravansary of Yarkand and headed east across the southern margin of the Taklimakan. Hiring a mix of horses and donkeys from local villagers, he then followed a deep riftlike valley that cut through the Kunluns, reaching a huge basin on the south side of the range called, after a salt lake in its center, Shor Kul. On the map inserted in the front of his book In Tibet and Chinese Turkestan—Being the record of three years' Exploration, Deasy labeled the Shor Kul basin "barren and waterless." Even then, Schaller suspected that the margins of the basin, or the foothills on its south side, were the most likely places the chiru were going to have their babies.

On his 2001 attempt Schaller organized an expedition that would retrace much of Deasy's 1897 route. Schaller had four companions, the expedition-seasoned Canadian filmmakers Pat and Baiba Morrow and Jeff Boyd, and the Asian scholar Jon Miceler. A mixed staff of Uighur and Kyrgyz locals worked as guides, camp personnel, and caravan tenders. Near the same place where Deasy obtained his pack animals, Schaller's team hired twenty-six donkeys and two camels to freight the expedition's camping equipment, filmmaking gear, and food for two months. They also had several loads of fodder for the pack animals—they knew there would be insufficient graze for much of the route. Schaller had brought a photocopy of Deasy's map, and they followed it, ascending the same fifty-mile-long "rift" valley the earlier explorer had transited. The floor of the rift ascended gradually to a sixteen-thousand-five-hundred-foot pass, where it then descended in the opposite direction toward to the Shor Kul basin. Schaller could only hope that somewhere ahead lay the calving grounds.

Jon Miceler had been with Schaller on a previous expedition searching for wildlife in Arunachal Pradesh (the remote northeastern corner of India), and there Miceler had learned quickly to appreciate what he called Schaller's wordless way of tempering excitement without appearing jaded. Watching him now, Miceler thought he could see something different. There was hope, but this time it was mixed with trepidation. After so many years of trying to follow the chiru to their calving grounds, Schaller was poised to make the discovery, but he didn't know if he would find the thousands and even tens of thousands of females with their young calves that he knew once existed, or instead witness only pocket remnants of chiru decimated by a mix of illegal poaching and an expanding population of Tibetan nomads encroaching on their winter habitat.

Then they were dealt their first setback. They learned from their Uighur guide that somehow there had been a miscalculation of the fodder they would need for their pack animals, and they had brought less than intended. They had planned to stay in the field for six to eight weeks, and now that time had to be reduced to five to six weeks. They pressed on, and as they descended into the basin Schaller spotted a herd of fifty chiru. They were all female, and most of them were pregnant. Schaller still didn't feel there were enough animals to conclude they had found the calving grounds, but he did suspect these females at a minimum indicated the migration made it this far north. When they reached the salt lake of Shor Kul they divided into three teams and fanned out, spending two days exploring the basin, where they saw more females but no single congregation larger than about sixty animals. They broke camp and continued by caravan to the west end of the basin, where, continuing to follow Deasy's route, they ascended into foothills where Schaller hoped they might see larger concentrations of chiru.

The following day they climbed to a small pass and descended a dry riverbed. As was his habit, Schaller was walking several minutes ahead of the caravan so he could view any animals they might encounter before the procession spooked them. Ascending a rocky ridge, he peered over the other side to discover in an area of about three square miles, grazing on grassy hills, roughly a thousand female chiru. Most of them were pregnant.

Still, unwilling to conclude he had found the calving grounds, Schaller and his team continued into the foothills, arriving at day's end at the confluence of three rivers with no names. That evening at camp the dinner conversation was tense. Even though they had found one large herd, they didn't know if perhaps even larger herds were in the area. They didn't know if indeed this was the place the animals had their young, and of more concern, Schaller said there would be no way to know for certain unless they stayed a week or longer, until the date arrived when the chiru began to birth. Their Uighur guide, fearful their caravan animals were continuing to weaken, preferred to keep going. Schaller warned that if they left this area they might not find any more chiru; this could be the only place they were congregating. Putting off the decision, they decided to stay one more day, and in the morning to divide into two groups, Schaller and the Morrows going one way, Miceler and Boyd another.

They left before dawn. Miceler and Boyd elected to explore hills southeast of their camp. The weather was clear and still, and at dawn Miceler nearly tripped over a female chiru sleeping on the ground. He looked around and saw there were perhaps fifty other animals in the vicinity, and for five or ten seconds the animals stared at him as though in disbelief, then bolted. Continuing their ascent, the two reached a rocky summit at seventeen thousand feet, and now it was their turn to stare in disbelief: Across the grass-covered hills there were hundreds and hundreds of grazing female chiru, nearly all pregnant.

In camp Schaller reported his group found only scattered groups of female chiru, but when Miceler and Boyd told him of their discovery Schaller surmised that the hills to the east and southeast were in all likelihood the calving grounds. To prove that, however, he pointed out again they would have to witness the calving, and further, Schaller explained such proof was important because it would give him the evidence he needed to persuade Chinese and Xinjiang officials to extend the borders of a proposed reserve to include this area. The others in the party concluded, however, that to wait for the birthing would be too risky. The next day, validating their concerns, two of the donkeys collapsed as they were being loaded, and refused to stand. They had no choice but to abandon the animals to certain death.

"I would have liked to stay another three or four days," Schaller told me in a conversation I had with him after they had returned. "There was talk about what to do, I take a few donkeys and stay and the others go on, but we decided it wasn't desirable to split up. You start together, you finish together. So the conclusion, very amiably achieved, was to go on, and we were not going to see the births."

Schaller stated this as simple fact, with no tone of regret. By then I was getting to know him well enough that this complete lack of remorse or even self-reproach was not a surprise. His will to learn all he could of the natural history of the chiru was implacable, and I realized this trait was behind the success of his studies over his lifetime of so many of the world's keystone species. I could also see his ability to accommodate setbacks to his goals was both flexible and resourceful. Even though he was nearing seventy, he considered many of his unrealized goals—including confirming the location of the calving grounds of the western population of chiru—to be open projects. There was always another day.

AFTER A QUARTER MILE the castings in the mud of the camel and its human companion disappear, washed out by an interim flood. The mud and gravel river bottom is soft in some places but hard enough in most areas that pulling the carts remains easy, especially measured against what we have been through this past week. The canyon continues to narrow, however, and we can't help but fear that ahead of us are more slot canyons that may force us to park the carts and continue on foot. We approach a bend in the watercourse around which we can't see. Galen is in the lead, and as he nears the blind turn I know Conrad and Jimmy are saying to themselves the same thing I am: "Please, canyon, please continue to be open." Galen reaches the corner, and as he looks around it the rest of us watch in anticipation. He stops, look back at us, raises his arm, and cheers.

"Yeah!" Conrad yells back, and Jimmy and I also let out a shout. The canyon is a go. We maintain our steady pace up the gradual incline, heartened by our progress, by the blue sky, by the hills around us now under a mantle of alternating white and brown patches of snow and earth. Looking up I see two Himalayan griffons—vultures with wingspans of eight feet and more—and when they see us they circle back close enough we can see their naked necks. They are scruffy, with open slots on their wings where they have lost feathers to the summer molt, but that doesn't impede their ability to catch a thermal, and we stop to watch as they spiral upward in tight gyres, quickly gaining several hundred feet.

We still haven't seen any more of the camel and human tracks, but at noon we reach a side valley that we surmise is the point where Schaller and his party continued in a southwesterly direction. Both the terrain in front of us as well as our map suggests the better route for us is to follow the main watercourse. Before we continue, however, we spot a group of fifteen female chiru in the side valley, grazing on a hillside spotted with patches of grass.

"Be very quiet," Galen whispers, motioning us to move slowly.

We unbuckle our waistbelts and slowly lower our carts until they rest on the balloon tires tied to the backs.

"As long as we're stopping, let's have lunch," I suggest quietly.

We slowly open the zippers on our panniers, remove our lunch bags and, leaning against the balloon tires, sit on the ground and pass among us our one pair of high-power binoculars. In the half hour we take to finish our nuts, dried fruit, candy bar, and jerky, the animals never notice us, but when we stand to continue one of them looks up and alerts the others, and they run from our view.

In a hundred feet we stop again to examine the prints of a wolf heading in the direction of the chiru we just saw, and then in another hundred feet we stop once more when we see first one group of twenty chiru, and then another group of thirty.

"This is the most animals we've seen since Dispersion Camp," Conrad says.

"Wow, look over there," Jimmy exclaims, pointing in the opposite direction toward an enormous herd of so many animals that the hillside they are on seems to shift under their movement.

"I have a rough count of about a hundred and thirty," I say as I watch the animals through our binoculars. "Give or take ten or fifteen, because they're running."

"That's the biggest herd we've seen yet," Conrad says.

"It's like watching wind blow across hillsides of wheat," Galen adds.

Conrad records the sightings in his pocket notebook, and we resume our steady pull up the gently inclined gravel floor of the canyon. Two hours later we reach the edge of our goal, the high plain, and beyond it we can see a glaciated massif that, according to our map, is over twenty-three thousand feet in elevation, making it one of the highest in the western Kunlun. Somewhere across the plain, toward the massif, is the place where last year Schaller's party reported seeing over a thousand chiru. Although there is nothing like that number visible to us now, we do see in the middle distance several scattered herds of twenty to thirty females, their tawny coats blending with the dun plain so that the more distant animals are difficult to distinguish.

"There could be a lot more animals around here," Galen says as he studies the panorama with our binoculars. "In low areas of the plain hidden from our view, around the corners of these foothills."

"We'll need to spend some time reccying the place," I reply. "Especially those hills on the far side of the plain."

"That looks like a good campsite right there," Conrad says, pointing to a nearby knoll rising above the plain. "If you want to wait here I'll go check it out."

When he returns, Conrad tells us it would be a perfect campsite hidden from view of the chiru, with a nearby stream for fresh water. But I'm undecided whether to take advantage of the campsite or to try to get closer to the place where last year Schaller's group reported seeing so many animals.

"If we do camp here we would have to walk an extra five or six miles in the morning," I say.

"We would also miss the best time for photography," Galen adds.

"But if we keep pushing we might also end up in a place with no water and no cover," Conrad counters.

The three of us turn to Jimmy.

'Oh, man, don't look at me like that, you guys," Jimmy pleads.

"Sorry, Jimmy, you're the tiebreaker," I say with a grin.

Jimmy is also grinning, but his teeth are closed in a gesture that pleads to be let off the hook.

"Okay," he says reluctantly when he realizes it's his call. "I guess if I have to, I'll vote to keep going."

"Veddy well, sahib," Conrad replies with his Hindu accent and nod, returning Jimmy's grin. "We keep going then, I think."

We cross the plain on its northwestern side, keeping against bordering foothills in hope of finding in them another good campsite with water and cover. In a mile we see about two hundred yards in front of us a group of thirty chiru that are as yet unaware of our approach.

"Do you mind staying here for a few minutes?" Galen asks in a hush. "This is a perfect place to try something I've been thinking about for a while."

He removes his tripod from his rickshaw, and extends two of its three legs. He then hangs his camera with its long lens around his neck, clips into his rickshaw, and with one hand on the rickshaw trace, he takes his other hand and holds the tripod upside down on top his head. With his "horns" in place, he then starts slowly to pull his rickshaw toward the chiru, who are still grazing.

"He's trying to make himself look like a male chiru," Jimmy says.

"The tripod legs are at the right angle," I say, "but if you didn't know what he was up to, you'd think he'd lost it."

"I have to get this on tape," Jimmy says as he slowly retrieves his video camera, then shoots Galen trying to shoot the chiru. Conrad and I watch as Galen continues slowly to approach the herd. He's within perhaps a hundred yards when one of the animals looks up, and then the entire herd stops grazing as they fix their eyes on Galen, who nevertheless continues slowly to advance.

"They're going to bolt," I say skeptically.

"It looks like it," Conrad agrees.

Then one by one the chiru lower their heads and go back to grazing. Galen continues to advance, and when he is within fifty yards he stops, lifts his camera with his free hand and starts taking pictures.

"Whoa," Jimmy exclaims as he continues to look through his viewfinder. "Look at that. It's working!"

We watch Galen finish his roll of film, and when he returns he is grinning widely.

"Can you tell me what just happened?" Jimmy says, pointing the video camera at Galen.

"I've tried this on caribou," Galen says to the camera, lifting the tripod and setting it upside down on top his head. "And I've been wanting to try it on chiru, to make my tripod look like the profile of a male's horns as much as possible. Did you see me get close to that herd of twenty-eight females? They went back to grazing and I got really close. It worked!"

क

AN HOUR LATER we park our carts and each go different directions looking for any site that might have water, not to mention seclusion from the view of the chiru. I'm feeling bad I countered Conrad's suggestion to camp at the earlier location.

"It was the navel of the plain," Conrad says. "Everything converged there."

I know he's teasing me, but that isn't helping my guilt. I walk around the base of a bare hill with no flat bench, no water, and no place to hide the tents. Conrad finds a slight depression where all but the tops of our tents would be hidden if any chiru did happen to cross the plain in this vicinity.

"We've got enough water in the bladders for tonight," Conrad says. "It looks like there might be water against that bluff over there."

He is pointing toward the west end of the plain, where a high cutbank crossing the open flat suggests at least a seasonal streambed. We pull the carts up a short hill to the depression Conrad has located, and set up the tents. Despite the mediocre campsite, we are all in a good mood. From inside Conrad and Jimmy's tent I hear the stove roar to life. Galen crawls in our tent, no doubt to complete his camera notes for the day. It's time for me to transcribe my notes from my tape recorder, but before I do that I decide to scan the foothills across the plain to the west, beyond the cutbank where in the morning we hope to find water. I focus the binoculars on what appear to be dozens if not hundreds of rocks on the otherwise bare hillsides. They are shimmering in the heat still rising off the plain, and as I study them I begin to realize they are not only shimmering but slowly moving. I pan over to an adjacent group of hills, and there I see hundreds and hundreds, no, at least a thousand, additional moving rocks.

"The hills are covered, you guys!" I yell to the others. "Get out here, quick. There are chiru. Hundreds of them. No, a thousand, even more. It's the calving grounds. We've found the calving grounds!"

ॐ

AFTER EVERYONE HAS A LOOK through the binoculars, we gather in Conrad and Jimmy's tent for dinner.

"Now all we need is some calving," Jimmy says.

"I think our timing may be perfect," I reply. "We started the trek early enough there were still animals to follow, and I think we've arrived late enough I bet the calving's already started."

"Hope you're right," Conrad says.

"I'm still not a hundred percent those are the calving grounds," Galen adds. "It could be just a good grazing area, and the calving is happening in the hills farther to the west."

"We'll find out tomorrow," Conrad replies.

We finish dinner, and while Conrad prepares our evening hot chocolate Galen says he is going to put the spotting scope converter on his long lens and have another look at the foothills.

"It turns it into a fifty-power scope," he says. "So we should be able to see the animals pretty clearly."

Galen leaves, and in a few minutes, as Conrad is serving the chocolate into our mugs, we hear Galen yell.

"I've got a calf! I'm sure I saw a baby chiru."

We scamper out of the tent. Galen is bent over his spotting scope, and he looks up when I rush to his side.

"I'm sure it was a calf," he says. "Here, have a look, see what you think."

Galen has the scope locked off, and careful not to bump it I look through the eyepiece and see the female chiru he has been watching, as well as a small dot behind it.

"I see what you're talking about," I say. "It's right behind the female, but it's too small to tell. Could be a rock."

I watch the dot and then it appears to shift, but I'm not sure if it is moving on its own or because of the heat waves.

"Is it moving?" Galen asks.

"Just a second. It still looks like a dot, but yeah, it's moving. There it goes. It's definitely moving. In fact, it's running. The dot…it's running…running to catch up to its mother."

CHAPTER SEVEN

क

JUNE 19

THIS MORNING ALL I HAVE TO DO to get ready is dress. I don't have
to stuff my sleeping bag, and I don't have to place my personal belongings into my duffel and load everything into my rickshaw. It's a small
pleasure, but out here small pleasures feel big. To celebrate our brief
repose even more, I decide to curl into the warmth of my bag for ten
more minutes, knowing the only travel we'll do today is to walk from
here to the hills where last evening we saw the concentrations of
chiru and the mother with her baby. I nestle in my bag, close my eyes,
and then through the nylon wall of the tent I hear Galen's voice.

"It's beautiful light out here. You shouldn't miss it."

I open my eyes, take a breath, and as I exhale I say to myself, "Fuck."
Galen has already been up for half an hour, and so far on this expedition he hasn't missed a single sunrise or sunset. Despite this morning's ten minutes of circumscribed leisure, I consider myself
reasonably disciplined about getting up at the beginning of each day,
and reasonably tenacious about pushing myself until the end of it,
but I'm no match in either attribute alongside Galen, and I can't think
of anyone else I know who is, either. And I know quite a few people
who know how to push themselves.

"I'll be right there," I call back to Galen after I sit up. I maneuver out
of my warm bag and into my cold pants, pull on my jacket and boots,
and crawl out the door of the tent. Galen, twenty feet away, is changing

the filters on his camera, which is mounted on his tripod and pointed toward the Kunlun, whose central massif is as pink as a flamingo.

"Isn't that beautiful?" Galen says with a grin that he has worn each time I've seen him witness a beautiful sunrise or sunset. (And it's a grin I suspect he has worn with every beautiful sunrise or sunset he has ever witnessed.)

"That it is," I reply.

"Coffee's up," Conrad calls. I go to our tent to get both Galen's and my insulated mugs, and then hand them through the door of the tent to Conrad, who fills them with Major Dickason's Blend, our supply of which, thank God, is holding out. I walk back to Galen, who smiles even more broadly when I hand him his mug.

After the pink glacial snow on the massif fades to white, Galen disassembles his camera, and we head for Conrad and Jimmy's tent to eat breakfast and also to discuss our strategy for stalking the chiru and, if we are so lucky, for capturing on video and film any newborns that may be ambling across the hillsides on the heels of their mothers.

"I've noticed the chiru are much more sensitive to movement than they are to form," Galen says as we eat breakfast. "That's a trait that's true for a lot of animals. It's what Konrad Lorenz discovered in his famous experiment when he determined goslings would respond to the most minimal outline of their goose parents, and it's also why my trick with the tripod worked. So I think we can use that to our advantage."

"How so?" Jimmy asks.

"We approach them very, very slowly and use any natural features we can to hide our movements. We also want to remember to bring the camo netting."

We all agree to the strategy, and we also remind ourselves that if it doesn't work we'll have to come up with something else, quickly: We can only stay here two days, three days if we stretch it.

"It's a little over a hundred miles from here to the roadhead," Conrad says, holding up the map. "I figure that will take us nine days, including two days if we stop to climb a peak. We've got eleven days of food left, counting today."

Conrad refers to a notion we had when planning the expedition to stop as we cart along the south side of the Kunluns and, if we still had the food—not to mention the energy—attempt to climb a mountain. Apart from just doing what we like to do, scaling a peak is also part of our strategy of surveying the region: If the weather is clear when we made a climb, we might be able to see across these foothills and judge whether there are any other potential sites for calving grounds.

"So if we do need an extra day here, we could take it out of the food set aside for the climb," Galen says.

"Yeah, we could do that," Conrad replies. "Plus having those two days of food is a nice padding for any contingency."

"Still, cutting it down to two days when you're in the middle of nowhere isn't exactly extra fat," Jimmy says.

"Yeah," Conrad agrees, "but on this trip any fat feels kind of luxurious."

क

I WALK WITH A LIGHTNESS that I realize is a combination of the weight I've lost and also the fact that for the moment, anyway, I am free of what Jimmy has referred to as that extra two hundred and fifty pounds strapped to our asses. Then I notice that both Jimmy and Galen are walking in a curious way with their arms bent and hands cupped, and I realize I am doing the same thing.

"You guys, you're still walking like you're pulling your rickshaws," I call to them.

They both look down at their arms and hands, laugh, and then self-consciously try to walk with a natural stride. We reach the cutbank we spotted yesterday from camp, and to our relief find a stream running at its base. We have our empty water bladders in our packs, and we'll fill them on our return to camp. For now we continue toward the foothills where yesterday we saw the concentrated herds, knowing today could be our big day. The sun breaks behind our shoulders and edge-lights on our left a company of thirty chiru running toward the same foothills. We stop to glass them, in case they have any calves. We don't see any, but Jimmy points out any mothers with calves probably stay in the hills until the little ones can walk better. Once the herd achieves a distance from us with which they are comfortable they slow to a walk, but pause frequently to glance back, making sure the separation is still sufficient.

"We're doing what our ancestors did," Galen says. "Stalking game animals. But the result is an image instead of a roasting carcass."

"I'm beginning to favor the roasting carcass," I reply, the mention of food reminding me of the main reason I am walking so lightly. To the right we see another herd also walking toward the same destination, confirming our impression we are heading to the calving grounds.

"This is like summit day," Conrad says. "All the effort, all the time, all the expense, reduced to this one moment."

While our own effort is coming to what we hope will be a successful climax, I have over the last couple days, as we have neared what we now are confident is the calving grounds, considered how nevertheless it is a small piece of a much larger endeavor. If we succeed in our goal of photographing and taping baby chiru, and if subsequently we complete the magazine article and the TV show and the book, our efforts will help publicize the plight of the chiru, and it will give Schaller an additional tool in his initiative to persuade the Chinese to create a new reserve. Since National Geographic's reach is global, both with their magazine and their television shows, the publicity presumably will also help Ashok Kumar's group in India trying to outlaw the production of shahtoosh in Kashmir, and Ian Knox and his associates in the Wildlife Crime Unit at Scotland Yard in their continued efforts to crack down on the illegal sale of shahtoosh in England, and perhaps as well the law enforcement arm of the U.S. Fish and Wildlife Service in its effort to control the sale of shawls in the United States.

क

OFFICIALS IN THE UNITED STATES were only tangentially aware of efforts in India and Europe to control the trade in shahtoosh, until in the mid-1990s they began to receive requests from their international counterparts to investigate shipments of the shawls that were either leaving or entering the United States. One of these requests arrived in March 1995, when French authorities asked the U.S. Fish and Wildlife Service to investigate an exporting company based in Bombay named Navarang, as well as an importing company, retailer and marketer of high-end luxury items based in Hong Kong named Cocoon. Several months earlier French wildlife agents had made several raids in Paris that had netted 404 shahtoosh shawls. The French subsequently learned that some of the retailers they raided had obtained their shawls from the New York office of Cocoon—best known as a source of silk quilts and satin sheets priced at $3,000 a set—and that Cocoon in turn had imported them from Navarang.

The U.S. officials then raided the New York office of Cocoon and found evidence that indeed the company was receiving the shawls from Navarang (eventually they would discover that Navarang had brought three hundred and eight shawls into the United States, representing the lives of one thousand to one thousand five hundred chiru). Fish and Wildlife also found a paper trail leading to a public sale of shawls in November 1994 that had totaled more than $100,000, and perhaps most intriguing to the officials, included supermodels, spouses of real estate barons, social critics—some of the biggest names in New York's social circles. Investigators soon learned the sale of the shawls was organized in part by the well-known New York hostess Nan Kempner, and it was designed to raise funds to support a program to make the wishes of dying cancer patients at the Memorial Sloan-Kettering Hospital come true.

"We're called the 'dream team' because we learn about the patient's dream or wish from a doctor or a nurse, or from someone who is close to the patient, and then we make it happen," Nan told me when, following our trek, she invited me to tea in her New York apartment. "It's an anonymous society—we are very sotto voce—because we don't want to be thanked. The patient has no idea; it's a complete surprise; it just happens. It can be a visit from a famous rock star, or relatives suddenly arriving from some far corner of the world who otherwise couldn't afford the trip."

We were sitting in the library of Nan's apartment, the walls beautifully hand-stenciled in a floral pattern against a warm red background, the room full of objets d'art that Nan had collected over her long life-time. She told me she had lived in the apartment for forty-seven years, and that it had "sort of designed itself around me." She was suffering from what her doctor had confirmed was pleurisy, and I thanked her for seeing me, despite her illness. "The least I could do, since you've come so far," she replied, patting the back of my hand.

"So how did it come about that the dream team sold shahtoosh shawls to raise money?" I asked.

"I can't remember precisely, it was so long ago, but I think it was one of our members who knew this company, or perhaps it was the company who asked us if we would like a percentage. Either way, I remember my reaction was 'And how!' because the best way to raise money is to sell something people want. So we sent flyers out announcing the sale of the shawls, and asking people to please come and do their Christmas shopping with us. And believe you me, they came in and bought them. They were thrilled to see them, to feel how wonderful they felt, and to hear the story about how they were made from the hair of the chin of a goat that rubbed against stones and how all these poor people picked the hair off the stones."

"You heard that story from the company that provided the shawls?"

"Yes, and I had heard the same story when I bought my first [shah-toosh] shawl thirty years before. I had been at a party in Delhi with an Indian friend who was a member of parliament, a very attractive, won-derful man. I saw this other man at the party who had a lovely red shawl, and I told my friend I would love to have a shawl like that. My friend said, 'Maybe we can get it,' so he called over the other man and we bought it from him right then and there. And I was told the same story about the hair coming from the chin of a goat, and how it's plucked off rocks."

"Since I finished my trek I've been researching shahtoosh," I told Nan, "And I've communicated with one researcher who found a ref-erence to that story in a book published in 1839."

"You see, there! And we certainly didn't know the shawls were ille-gal when we sold them at the fund-raiser. I bought a few of them myself, as Christmas presents for my daughter and my daughters-in-law. I was very excited about it, and they were too. They had never seen them before, seen shawls so soft and warm and light, and they were thrilled. And the records [of my purchase] were right there, on my American Express card."

As were the records of most of the other people who had purchased shawls at the sale, receipts that were on file at Cocoon when the agents searched the office, receipts that eventually would be used to create a list of subpoenas requesting people who purchased the shawls to appear in court in Newark, New Jersey.

क

AS WE APPROACH THE FOOTHILLS we stop to glass the slopes and see three groups of chiru, each with perhaps twenty animals. They all are lying down, presumably waiting until it grows warmer before they begin to graze, but none of them appear to have babies.

"The calves might be too small to see," I say.

"And the birthing is probably just starting," Conrad points out. "So there might not be that many, anyway."

The sun is now an hour above the horizon, but it is shining through thin clouds so that it has around it an iridescent halo—what Galen earlier told us is called a solar parhelion—that almost certainly portends bad weather. We can only hope we have time enough to spot any baby chiru already born—and to get close enough to film them— before the storm arrives. We stop to examine one of the groups of chiru that we had spotted earlier, and now they are on their feet and starting to graze.

"Wait," I say as I study them with our binoculars. "There's a calf. With its mother, at the rear of the group. Here, look."

I hand the binoculars to Galen.

"Yep. There's one calf in that group."

We head toward a ravine that bifurcates the foothills and looks like it will provide cover as we approach the small herd. We enter the hills and find the ravine is indeed narrow enough that we remain hidden. A small stream of clear water flows out of the steep-sided gully, and we note along its banks two kinds of grass other than stipa, and several small forbs, including one cushion plant with small white blossoms—more variety of potential graze than we have seen in over a week. Several lateral runnels enter the ravine, and Galen stops in front of one that looks favorable.

"What about going up there?" he whispers.

"That looks good," Conrad replies.

We slowly ascend the runnel and near its top, as the sides fold open, we crouch in case the chiru herd is close on the other side.

"Galen, what if Conrad and I stay here," I whisper, "and you and Jimmy go ahead?"

"That's a good idea," he replies.

Jimmy and Conrad agree, so we unshoulder our packs, and while I retrieve two lengths of camouflage gauze we have brought all this way to use just for this moment, Galen and Jimmy prepare their cameras. Galen mounts his 1000-mm lens with extender while Jimmy puts on a 400-mm that, because of the video camera's small frame size, is equivalent to a 2800-mm lens on a 35-mm still camera. While they work I pause to consider the team effort required to carry this heavy camera gear all this way in the hope of capturing on film a few baby chiru. We all had a part in it: While Galen and Jimmy carried the camera gear, Conrad and I, to compensate, carried part of their portions of the food and fuel.

"Image stabilizer on?" I ask Jimmy in a whisper.

"Yeah, got it on."

"You have that camo netting?" Galen whispers.

I unfold the camouflage fabric and then help Galen put it under his hat so that it hangs down his shoulders and back. Jimmy grabs his cloak and drapes it over his head and body like an Arab's burnoose.

"How do I look?"

"Like a homeless sheikh that hasn't been getting enough to eat," I tell him.

"You ready?" Galen whispers to Jimmy.

"Yeah."

"Okay, let's go."

"Good luck, you guys," Conrad whispers.

We pat them each on the back, and, cameras in hand, they crab-crawl the remaining distance up the runnel, like extras in a B-grade war film. In a few minutes they are skylighted on the ridge, and then they disappear.

"Nine thirty," Conrad says, checking his watch. "I give them two hours, maybe a little more."

"Fingers crossed," I reply, holding up my crossed fingers.

We each find a comfortable place to sit and enjoy the first daytime break more than an hour long since starting the trek. We wait. Occasionally we stand and walk around the confined area in the bottom of the runnel, careful not to venture up the hillside in case Jimmy and Galen are stalking animals near us.

"Ten thirty," Conrad says.

The sun fills into the runnel and we are thankful for the warmth it brings. I've brought my journal, so I catch up on my entry for the day. Conrad stands again and investigates a stunted plant that we haven't seen outside this calving area. He sits back down and waits.

"Eleven," he says.

I finish my entry and put my journal back in my pack. We wait. Ten more minutes. Twenty.

"Here they come," Conrad says.

They are no longer crawling, but walking down the slope in jaunty strides and talking in full voices. Jimmy has his wide smile, and I hear him laugh. Galen is grinning, too, and he has a large feather in his cap—presumably lost in molt by some passing bird of prey—and whether intentional or not, I note the symbolism.

"I've got a good feeling," I say to Conrad.

"Me too," he answers.

Conrad picks up the small video camera that we carry as a backup, and turns it to tape their arrival.

"I got a scene with a calf suckling on his mother," Jimmy says, his grin irrepressible. "Then romping around, cruising."

"I got some good shots with my 1400-mm lens," Galen adds, referring to his long lens plus extender. "A mother and calf, and for a few seconds they walked on the skyline in silhouette."

"We'll look at the video tonight," Jimmy says. "But I know I got some good stuff."

क

WE STILL HAVE NINE HOURS OF DAYLIGHT, and even though it sounds like we have some good shots, we all agree we need more, especially images of the animals large in the frame. To achieve that, however, Galen and Jimmy would have to stalk even closer to the calves and their anxious mothers.

"Galen, I don't know if maybe you agree," Jimmy suggests, "but for me it's almost easier if I'm by myself."

"I would agree," Galen answers. "Plus if we both go in different directions we might end up flushing some of the chiru toward each other."

Galen wants to continue westward, deeper into the foothills, so Jimmy says he'll go in a more southerly direction. Conrad and I, with no specific task, decide that if we were to stay in one place and lie still, the chiru might come to us, especially if Jimmy or Galen were to flush any in our direction.

After Jimmy and Galen leave, Conrad and I hike to a nearby hilltop where we lie down and cover ourselves with a piece of the camouflage netting. After a half hour two lammergeyers fly overhead, close enough we can see their eyes and feather beards. I doze a few minutes, then wake and turn my head slowly to see crossing a hill at fifty yards distance a herd of twenty female chiru.

"Conrad, you see them?" I whisper as softly as I can.

"Yeah," he answers.

Both of us remain still, and the animals graze at a slow amble in our direction. There are no calves with the group, but it is nevertheless a privilege to be this close and undetected to these skittish creatures. Soon I can see the white markings on the inside of their alert ears, the dark eyes framing their pug snouts, the sheep-skin texture of their fawn coats covering the bulge of their bellies. Suddenly they stop and in near unison raise their heads. For a moment I think they have sensed us, but then I realize they are looking not toward us but to our side, perhaps in the direction of some perceived danger.

"A wolf?" I whisper.

"That'd be my guess."

Nothing happens and the chiru, one by one, return to grazing. In five minutes they have crossed the hill, and then they disappear down the far side. By now the sky has clouded and the air is noticeably colder.

"The storm's getting close," Conrad says.

"Maybe we should head back to camp."

We walk off the hilltop toward camp and pick up an incipient runlet that soon becomes a deepening ravine. We are passing a chest-high rock when I notice, in a small alcove at its base, a curious bed of matted grass and protruding from it what appears to be a small black knob. Looking closer I see it is an animal's hoof, and as I lift it the grass falls away to reveal the hindquarter remains of a half-eaten chiru.

"A wolf's den," Conrad says.

"This carcass is fresh," I reply as I hold up the hindquarters with one hand and pick away the grass sticking to it with the other. "Looks like good meat, doesn't it?"

"I don't think we're that desperate," Conrad says, "Not yet, anyway."

With some reluctance I put the meat back where I found it, and cover it again with grass. We continue descending the gully, and what starts as a small spring turns into a small stream. A light wind cants the first flakes of snow that soon veil the surrounding hills so that a group of chiru on our flank who are also descending appear as ghost creatures. As we near the base of the hills, both in front of us and to our sides we make out through the falling snow the dark shapes of more chiru taking the same direction we are, leaving the impression that like us they are abandoning the hills before the coming storm.

By the time we reach the plain, visibility is reduced to a few yards. I chide myself for forgetting my compass, and Conrad has failed to bring his as well. We use the angle of the snow on our faces to maintain direction, and soon we reach the cutbank, although not in the same place we crossed it this morning. We descend to the stream, and despite the closing weather we take the time necessary to fill our water bladders. We climb the opposite counterscarp and, using it as a benchmark, set our bearing.

"Camp is in that direction," Conrad says, pointing into the opaque whiteness.

"The wind direction has been steady," I say, "so let's use the angle of the snow to maintain our heading."

Conrad leads and I stay immediately behind him, mindful to keep the snow hitting the right side of my face at a constant angle. We walk for an hour. Neither of us talks, but there is nothing to talk about. This is not life threatening, but it would be debilitating to spend the night out in a storm, and we need to husband our remaining strength for the walk out.

"There're the tents," Conrad says.

The two yellow tents are just visible through the gossamer screen of falling snow.

"Maternity Ward," I say, repeating the name that this morning, as a term or endearment, we chose for this camp. As relieved as I am, now I'm wondering how Jimmy and Galen are doing. Then, as we near camp, I hear Jimmy's voice call out from inside his tent.

"Welcome back," he says, sticking his head out the door.

"Is Galen here?"

"Not yet," Jimmy replies. "I haven't seen him since we left you guys."

"I'm sure he's okay," Conrad says assuredly. Then to Jimmy, "Did you see any more baby chiru?"

"A couple more, but I didn't get that close. I think I got my best stuff this morning."

It is snowing heavily as I crawl in my tent, and I am conscious of the empty sleeping bag next to me, and the personal belongings arranged alongside it. A half hour passes, and then with great relief I hear approaching footsteps. I poke my head out the door and see Galen nearing our tent.

"I'm glad to see you," I say.

"I almost lost my direction back there," Galen reports. "I had to wait until it cleared for a second to see which way to go."

"Come in and warm up," I tell him.

"Welcome home," Conrad calls through his tent wall. "Dinner will be ready in a few."

When he has his jacket, pants, and boots off Galen sits on top of his sleeping bag and rubs his face and eyes.

"How did you do?" I ask.

"I saw a few more babies, but I'd still like to try and get closer."

"I think Jimmy feels the same. Let's figure a plan for tomorrow while we're having dinner."

In a few minutes Conrad announces dinner, and Galen and I crawl to the other tent to find Conrad frying falafels, everyone's favorite. Jimmy hands us our daily portion of salami and Parmesan, and as he does each evening, he moans as he eats his ration. Conrad serves the fried falafels, and now we all sigh as we eat our portions. We take turns scraping the pot and then fill it with water for our evening cocoa. As it heats Jimmy browns over the stove's flame the Parmesan rind, then quarters it and doles each man his small wedge. A few minutes later, while we drink our cocoa, Jimmy rewinds some of his tapes and we view them on the flip screen of our small video camera. While he has some good shots we all agree we would prefer more.

"The film editors are going to want as much variety as we can give them," I say.

"Same for the magazine," Galen adds.

"We've only got food to stay here for one more day," Conrad reminds us. "Two days and we'd have to forgo the climb."

"So let's stay one more day, take stock of what we have, and then decide whether or not we need to stretch it one more."

Everyone agrees, and when we finish our cocoa Conrad says we have enough powder mix to treat ourselves to a second cup. As he heats the water I zip open the tent's door and crawl outside.

"It's stopped snowing and the clouds are lifting," I tell the others.

When the cocoa is ready Galen hands me my mug, and I walk toward a small hill in front of camp that offers a view across the plain to the calving hills in the middle distance. The wind has stopped, and the sky is a smooth wash of blue-gray. As I reach the top I see the cloud layer has lifted sufficiently that my view encompasses the entire plain—seven miles long and five miles wide—and, to my astonishment, brackets a spectacle that even as I see it I realize is etched indelibly in my memory. I stare transfixed for a full minute, then hurry back to the tents.

"You guys, come out, right away," I call, careful not to yell too loudly. "The plain, it's covered with chiru. It's unbelievable, hundreds of them, maybe a thousand or more. Bring your cameras."

I return to the hill and gaze across the plain dusted with snow tinted the same blue-gray as the sky. Across this luminiferous expanse, like the negative reversal of stars in a nightsky, are the manifest black dots of the chiru who fled the foothills as the storm descended. They seem to be spread evenly from foreground to as far in the distance as I can make them out. The others join me, and after initial exclamations we are for a moment quiet.

"This is what the pioneers talked about when there were buffalo as far as you could see," Jimmy says quietly.

"It's Africa with snow," I reply. "A high-altitude Serengeti."

While Jimmy and Galen prepare their cameras, I start counting, beginning where the foothills of the calving grounds edge the plain, and working toward the other end where it drops away toward the Gorge of Despair. It takes me several minutes.

"I get about one thousand three hundred," I report. "And that's just what I can see; there are no doubt more in the distance, too far to make out."

JUNE 20

"I STILL THINK I'LL INCREASE MY CHANCES," Jimmy says, "if I'm on my own, like I was yesterday."

"No problem," I say. "Galen, you want to go alone again?"

"I could, but it might be nice to have somebody to help me carry gear, especially the tripod."

"I'm happy to do that," Conrad offers.

"If you don't need me," I say to everyone, "I wouldn't mind going by myself. I'd like to try and get close to a baby, even if I don't have a camera."

We all agree, and when everyone has their gear ready we leave camp. We stop for a moment on the crest of the hill where last evening we watched the chiru spread across the snowy plain. In the sky above us we see to the south and west remnant wisps of high cirrus, but to the north and east there are only innocuous puffs of fair weather cumuli. Across the plain below us, from far left to far right, illuminated in the soft light of morning, are group after group of female chiru, all in slow movement, walking, stopping to browse, walking again. The animals, no doubt sensing the return of stable weather, are returning to the calving grounds. We gaze at this spectacle in silence, and I offer mute thanksgiving to the circumstances in my life that have allowed me to be standing on top of this hill at this moment, with three close friends, paying homage to this epochal migration that, like a tide pulled by the gravity of the seasons, has flooded and ebbed across this plain year before year.

We cross the plain, walking at a jaunty pace four abreast, and by midmorning we reach the base of the calving hills, where we stop and choose routes.

"I wouldn't mind going west again," Galen says.

"I'll head north for a while," Jimmy replies, "then cut west."

"Then I'll go south and then west," I offer.

We wish each other good luck and go our different directions. In a few minutes I stop and look back. Galen and Conrad have disappeared behind a foreground hill, and Jimmy is a small dot rapidly diminishing. I continue, following the small stream that Conrad and I descended yesterday. I turn a corner and in ten more steps my companions suddenly exist only in memory. The only sound is the crunch of my feet in the gravel and the soft purl of the stream. I enter the calving hills feeling utterly alone.

As I walk I consider how for nearly three weeks we have been crossing this huge open that is as yet unoccupied by humans, yet we have had each other for company. What if I were making this journey by myself, attempting a solo crossing of the Chang Tang? How would I react, week after week, alone in this barren vastness? No, more than alone, because here there are in some directions no other humans for hundreds of miles. How would I have faired when I came out the other end?

I tell myself that while I am generally gregarious I have an inner nature that enjoys solitude enough that I could probably have managed such a challenge, but I also understand why, in biblical times, banishment to the desert was the ultimate punishment. Still, at this moment I am relishing walking these hills on my own. As I stop for a moment to decide the route I will follow, I consider how in our own culture silence such as this is more often feared than welcomed. The adjectives we use to modify the word "silence" reveal our attitude toward it: eerie, stifling, dreadful, painful, disturbing, forbidding. But on this side of the world, to both Hindus and Buddhists, silence is bliss.

I decide to ascend the same draw where yesterday Conrad and I found the wolf's den. As I enter the narrowing gully I can see in the mud next to the stream fresh prints of a wolf, likely the same animal that owns the chiru carcass. I continue walking, studying the ground for more prints, and then I look up and there it is, only a hundred feet away. The wolf is facing me so that I can't tell if it's male or female, but it is large and healthy. I have my binoculars in hand—as I usually do when I am hiking—and I slowly raise them to my eyes, and as I bring the wolf into focus I see its vigilant eyes focused back on me. A slight breeze lifts the end hairs of its coat. For a full minute we both remain motionless, eyes locked on each other. Then the wolf turns, lopes up the steep hill, stops, and studies me again.

I lower the binoculars and see to the side a herd of thirty chiru, and although they watch me carefully they pay the wolf no mind. Then, as I begin to move, the chiru also move, decreasing their distance to the wolf to increase their distance from me. The wolf, however, remains still until finally it turns and lopes unhurriedly to the top of the hill, stops and eyes me once more, then disappears.

क

I REACH THE WOLF'S DEN and see the chiru carcass is still buried under the grass. The wolf is probably satiated, and I have the thought that if I were to filch its food it could easily take another chiru. Schaller states that although snow leopards, lynx, and "probably even brown bears" prey on chiru, the wolves are their principal predator; and as we have seen no sign of any of these other predators, this wolf has no competition, and at least during the calving season it is making a very easy living.

I rest at the wolf's den for a moment and consider how the chiru were seemingly unafraid of this fierce canine, but very wary of me. I suspect they knew the wolf was satiated, and perhaps even knew it still had a substantial meal hidden under this rock. I also suspect they knew that among their predators, Homo sapiens are definitely the animals to fear most. That raises the question of whether by publicizing our confirmation of the calving ground's location we may unwittingly lead poachers to it. I make a note in my tape recorder to suggest to the National Geographic Society they purposely remain vague when they produce the maps that will accompany the magazine story, film, and book about our discovery, at least until a reserve is created to protect this area.[i] But even if the maps are ambiguous, will the poachers, simply by being alerted to the existence of the calving ground, find it on their own? I admit that is a risk, but also I realize it is one that has to be taken, for if we do succeed and the reserve is created, the western population of chiru have a much better chance of survival; without a reserve, it is likely to be a matter of time until the poachers discover this place, with or without the publicity of our expedition.

But what are the chances of the reserve becoming a reality? I admit at times it seems fantastical to think our effort, combined with Schaller's journey through here a year ago, could help persuade the Chinese to afford at least nominal protection to another fifteen thousand square miles of the planet. Then I have only to remember that it was the results of Schaller's initial surveys of the Chang Tang in the late eighties and early nineties that spurred Chinese and Tibetan authorities to create the Chang Tang Reserve.

Like so many reserves in the world—including, as we have seen recently in the United States, places like the Arctic National Wildlife Refuge—the Chang Tang Nature Reserve is under threat from development, especially mineral exploitation.[ii] Even then, the fact the reserve exists at all is testament to the growing number of Chinese scientists, government officials, and members of the general public who are becoming increasingly committed to safeguarding what remains of their country's wildlands. This is a comparatively recent development. For the first thirty to forty years after the revolution, the government's policy in the main was not only disregard, but also what must be called aversion to wildlands and wildlife. "Especially since 1949, China has been afflicted with appalling abuse and mismanagement of its land and life," Peter Matthiessen has written, "with consequent public alienation from its wild creatures."[iii]

That's not to say disregard for wildlife was ubiquitous in China after the revolution: There has always been a compassion for nature reflected in Taoist and Confucianist writing that was translated into a moral code prescribing harmony with nature's order and pro-scribing wanton killing of its wild creatures. Beginning in 1928 and finishing in 1974, the Chinese writer and painter Zikai Feng produced a six-volume work called *Love for Animals*. "He poured his heart and soul into the collection, especially during the Cultural Revolution," Ping Mang, professor of journalism at the Academy of Chinese Culture, noted. "To Zikai Feng, all things are created equal: be it a dog, a sheep, an eel, a blade of grass or a bunch of flowers." In his writing, however, Feng also acknowledges the opposite attitude toward animals so prevalent in China, describing, as an example, a restaurant in the Shanxi Province that sold donkey meat that was cut from the flanks of live animals.[iv]

China is infamous for the national passion for eating exotic animals. In many major cities there are outdoor markets where vendors peddle snakes, wild birds, and turtles. This appetite extends to rare animals such as masked palm civets and pangolins, an Asian species of scaly anteater. In one recent seizure, Thai wildlife agents confiscated one hundred thousand snakes and ten thousand turtles destined for restaurants in China. A *Wall Street Journal* article on the wild animal market in China reported that the dishes on a single restaurant menu can run in the dozens. "The Heavenly Fragrance Mansion in Shenzhen offers a meal of nine creatures in one sitting, from deep-fried baby pigeons, to soy-braised civet steamed with ginger and garnished with coriander."

In addition to eating wild animals, the Chinese fascination with medicines made from wild animal parts also seems emblematic of the culture's traditional arrogance toward its fellow creatures, and it is unquestionably the central reason for the demise of many of the world's most charismatic endangered species, from rhinos to tigers. I saw an example of this disregard for wildlands and wildlife when I first traveled to China in 1980. Along the eastern margin of the Tibetan Plateau I found an endless train of green Dong Fengs laden with fresh-cut logs of fir and pine descending roads muddied in monsoon rain. Some of the trucks had the bloody carcasses of freshly killed wolves tied across the vehicles' hoods. Another friend who traveled to China in 1985 had a more poignant experience while traversing the eastern Chang Tang in a place that likely had seen few if any previous visitors. He and his companions had stopped in their vehicles when they saw in the distance an animal trotting toward them. It maintained its unwavering approach, and when it was close they could see it was a fox. It appeared as though it had never seen a human being. When it arrived at their vehicles it stood looking at them, transfixed in its gaze—until the Chinese army officer accompanying the expedition raised his rifle and shot it.

Schaller also has many anecdotes of Chinese officials shooting wild animals, and of the unease so many Chinese seem to feel when they are in wilderness (a reaction that you suspect may be linked to the national mandate to tame it). Having said that, it is also necessary to say that this collection of anecdotes seems no different from the lore passed by Americans generation to generation of their ancestors' taming of the West, from the massacre of the buffalo to the damming of the major rivers. And if that is true, then it also invites the question whether this Chinese attitude is shifting, just as the American attitude toward the wilderness has evolved these past hundred years. Could there even be evidence that instead of evolving, the attitude is actually changing rapidly? If the Chinese can transform their economy so fundamentally as they have in the past twenty years, might they also have the ability to remake just as fundamentally—and just as rapidly—their attitude toward wildlands and wild animals?

"There is a growing appreciation of wild country which was not there twenty years ago," Jim Thorsell, the IUCN's senior adviser for World Heritage sites, told me. Jim has worked in China extensively for the past two decades on missions to protect wildlands. "The phenomenal rise of a middle class in China," he said, "has led to a corresponding boom in domestic tourism to many of the remaining natural areas in the country. Tourism pressures in such areas as Emei Shan, Huangshan, and Juizhigou—all World Heritage sites—has reached 'Yosemite' levels. This is a 'good problem:' use it or lose it."

This growing interest in wilderness and parks was corroborated when, following our trek, I returned to China to interview people involved in the effort to control the poaching of chiru. One of them was William Bleisch, a wildlife biologist specializing in Asia who for several years worked for the Wildlife Conservation Society, under George Schaller's supervision. Now he is the China program director for Fauna and Flora International, an over-one hundred-year-old organization that may be the oldest conservation group in the world. Bleisch is based in Beijing and married to a Chinese woman, and he confirmed that unquestionably the Chinese attitude toward wildlands and wildlife is changing rapidly.

"There is now a big backpacking movement in China," Bleisch told me when I met him in Beijing. "Bird-watching has suddenly become a popular pastime for city people. There are also many well-organized conservation NGOs such as Friends for Nature. They don't yet have that much influence, but there is real commitment. We advertised for an assistant's job in our organization, for example, and had seventy-five applications, with many people telling us they would be willing to volunteer. Then there is the story of Ya Ya."

Ya Zhang, nicknamed Ya Ya, was a twenty-seven-year old Chinese woman working for Fauna and Flora International who, during my visit, volunteered to help me as a translator when I interviewed other people involved in the anti-poaching effort. She wore glasses and a plain white blouse, and her medium-length hair was parted in the middle. She looked like a graduate student, and she had that polite deportment common to Chinese that is easy to confuse with diffidence. So

I was surprised when she told me she had just returned from the Congo, where she had been doing field research on chimpanzees.

"When I was a little girl I read a picture book featuring Jane Goodall and her chimpanzees," Ya Ya told me. "Her story made me want to be a field primatologist. When I had finished my master's of science degree, going to Africa to study apes was still my dream. So I contacted a project for a field assistant position, but I did not get in. Then a year later I got another opportunity to go to Salonga National Park, in DR [Democratic Republic] of Congo. I conducted a pilot study of the bonobo's use of other animals as food. My work involved tracking bonobos, taking fecal sample analysis, making mammal, termite and ant surveys, as well as behavioral observations. It was really fun."

"Ya Ya's example may be unusual," Bleisch told me, "but it represents how among a rapidly growing number of Chinese the attitude toward nature is changing fast. And then there's Zhang Huibin, in the Arjin Shan [the nature reserve in the eastern Chang Tang]. On a weekend he'll leave his wife at home and drive out into the desert just to do it, just to be there, outdoors, outside."

Zhang Huibin is currently the vice director of Arjin Shan, and he has worked in the reserve since 1988, following his graduation as a wildlife biologist from the university. The reserve itself was created in 1983, very early in China's nascent conservation movement, and it owes its genesis to a government geological team that was given the task, in the late 1970s, of surveying the region for potential mineral and oil reserves. The team operated in the area for two years, and they learned early in their study that nomads in the area had been hunting the region's abundant wild yak, selling the meat in local markets. Soon the geologists followed the nomads' example, poaching what would eventually number hundreds of wild yak. They consumed some of the meat, but sold most of it in nearby towns and cities. When the team was exposed they were fined 200,000 yuan ($25,000), and the bonus otherwise due them for their two years of work was canceled. Subsequent studies revealed that, despite the poaching, Arjin Shan still held some of the biggest herds of wild yak in the Chang Tang, and several scientists, as well as local officials, pushed to create the reserve.

In the beginning of his tenure, Zhang was assigned the task of surveying the reserve's wild ungulates including wild yaks, chiru, antelope, kiang, and argali sheep. In the summer of 1992, he and his associates were crossing the western extreme of the reserve, near the base of Ulugh Muztagh—the twenty-three-thousand-foot peak in the north-central part of the Chang Tang—when they came across a herd of female chiru and, to their surprise, a female that had just given birth to a calf. Zhang managed to get a photo of the youngster, still wet with natal fluid, as it balanced awkwardly on its two front knees, then managed to stand on all four of its hooves. Zhang didn't realize it at the time, but he had discovered one of the calving grounds of the eastern population of chiru.

Later Zhang Huibin happened to mention his encounter with the baby chiru to a photographer named Wong How Man, who lived in Hong Kong and traveled extensively across China. Wong, an avid wildlife enthusiast, was familiar with George Schaller's work, and when he saw the photograph he realized Zhang had discovered one of the calving grounds that had long eluded Schaller. In 1998 Wong organized an expedition to the Arjin Shan, and invited the wildlife biologist William Bleisch, whom he had met when he was a student in the United States, to accompany him.

The expedition had to drive hundreds of kilometers cross country before they finally approached the slopes of Ulugh Muztagh, where Zhang Huibin told them he had taken the picture of the baby chiru six years before. Zhang directed them through the foothills surrounding the peak, and as they approached a secluded valley where Zhang told them he had found the calving area, they saw that the sky ahead of them was full of vultures.

"Zhang had told us that poachers had been shooting chiru," Bleisch told me. "But he said they had been doing this further to the south, and that the poaching was mostly in the winter, when the male chiru are in rut. So at first we didn't know why the vultures were circling. But then we came over this ridge and found the carcasses of six dead female chiru. Their hides had been cut off, and their babies were lying next to them, also dead."

That first year Bleisch found a total of seventy carcasses of freshly killed females, mostly with their dead babies next to them. The following year he returned, and once more Zhang Huibin led the expedition. This time when they reached the calving grounds they found the carcasses of over nine hundred dead females. They set camp in a valley sheltered from wind, and Bleisch thought he could hear vehicles. In the morning, as they prepared to count antelope, they saw through their spotting scope the vehicles Bleisch thought he had heard. They knew they were poachers, and Zhang was furious. The team had with them only one semiautomatic rifle and one collecting gun. Zhang ordered Bleisch to stay in camp, and with the men he had available Zhang left to confront the poachers. Bleisch could hear the gunfire. Most of the poachers escaped, but one of Zhang's men, aiming the collecting rifle, managed, at a hundred-yard distance, to put a bullet through the back window of one fleeing vehicles, and two poachers were apprehended. They tied them up, but that night one of them escaped. Fearful the poachers might attack, Zhang radioed for support, and two days later more police arrived, but they had to drive so quickly to high altitude that the lead officer suffered pulmonary edema and had to be evacuated. Other than the one prisoner, the other poachers escaped.

"You don't need to be a wildlife biologist to know that killing mothers with newborns is a guaranteed way to decrease a population in a hurry," Bleisch told me.

I REACH THE TOP OF THE GULLY, close to the hilltop where yesterday Conrad and I watched the herd of chiru pass within fifty yards of us, then continue west across hills pocked with mounds of earth marking the excavations of burrowing pika. I stop to eat lunch, and while I rest I notice a flock of eighteen females on a small flat between two adjacent hills. They don't see me, and looking through binoculars I am thrilled to spot at the end of the group a colt-legged calf. As the herd ambles across the flat, the youngster stops to inspect something on the ground, and when finally it looks up and discovers the gap between it and its family, it scurries in a wobble-legged run to catch up. It passes the first female at the end of the group and continues to the second, who turns and noses the suckling. The calf tries to nurse, but the mother moves on, stopping to eat snow from a remnant patch while the calf again runs to catch up. The mother continues, and then stops to graze, and with her head bent to the ground the youngster then begins pushing with its nose on its mother's ears and throat. Finally the mother rubs the calf with her nose, and apparently satisfied with the attention it has received, the baby chiru folds its over-long legs and lies down, its alert black ears sticking up as the soft hairs of its downy coat turn in the light breeze. Then it plops its neck and chin on the ground ready for a nap.

I finish lunch and continue west, then follow a long descending ridge northward. I see several more groups of chiru, and three of them have newborns. In midafternoon I turn eastward toward camp now two hours distant. I am descending the slope of a small runnel when I notice on the opposite hillside an adult female lying by herself, her legs folded under her. While she eyes me warily I slowly sit, and when I focus my binoculars I see about ten feet from her a baby that is also resting. I stand to continue, and my movement spooks the mother and she runs up the hill two hundred feet, but the calf remains motionless. It's odd that the mother is by herself, and that the calf didn't run after her, and both things make me wonder if the youngster is so recently born that it has yet to stand and walk. I decide to see how close I can get to it, but also to do it quickly so it isn't separated from its mother for more than a few minutes.

I cross the drainage and start up the opposite hill, looking up to see the erect ears and alert eyes of the mother chiru peeking above the crest, watching my every step. When I am no more than ten feet from the calf, I stop. The calf's head is curled on its front legs, and if it is aware of me it is making no reaction. I take two more steps and still it lies motionless. I wonder if it is alive. I watch its flank, and although I'm not positive, I am reasonably sure I can see it breathing. It is as endearingly cute as a young puppy, and for the second time on our journey I regret the decision I made at the outset to leave my camera.

Moving as slowly as possible, I make one more step forward. Although I have no intention of doing so, I am now nearly close enough to reach down and touch the baby. I don't want to torture the mother any longer—she presumably receives enough anxiety in her life from poachers—but out of curiosity to verify the calf is okay, I decide to make one more half-step forward. In slow motion I lift my boot, and I have it only an inch or two off the ground when suddenly the calf jumps up, and on legs that are wobbly but surprising swift, it runs toward its mother. In only a few seconds the two are rejoined, and together they disappear behind the crest of the hill.

क

THE OTHERS ARE ALREADY IN CAMP by the time I return.

"Join us in here," Conrad says, motioning me to his tent, where Jimmy and Galen have already gathered.

"Did you see any babies?" Conrad asks.

"Did I ever," I tell them, relating my experience getting within five feet of the calf that now I am convinced was only an hour or two old. "Up to now I've been okay with my decision not to bring a camera, but today I could have had the all-time closeup. Anyway, how did it go with you guys?"

"Kind of so-so," Galen says.

"We just couldn't seem to get close enough for good shots," Conrad adds.

"That's too bad," I reply. "How about you, Jimmy?"

"I'm afraid it's the same with me. I tried to belly-crawl up to a mother with a baby, but I just kept spooking them."

"Oh!" I groan, more to myself than the to others. "That makes it even worse I didn't have a camera."

"We've been waiting for you to have dinner," Conrad says, "so I'll go ahead and start cooking."

"At least I got some water," I say, trying to sound like I did something useful.

I crawl out of the tent and retrieve the bladders from my pack that I filled at the stream on my way back to camp. I hand the bladders through the tent door to Galen, then go back to my tent to get my pen and journal, eyeglasses, and the small earphones for my tape recorder. I return to Conrad and Jimmy's tent, sit in the vestibule, take off my shoes and crawl in. Jimmy has finished cutting the salami and Parmesan, and he hands me my portion. I plug the earphones into the recorder, rewind to the starting point of my day's entries, and begin transcribing them to my journal, adding annotations while my memory is fresh. But after a minute I stop, lacking enthusiasm at the moment, anyway, to complete the task: I still am chiding myself for not bringing a camera, and also concerned we have enough good shots for our film and our magazine story. I set down the earphones, take off my glasses and slowly chew my slice of salami. Meanwhile Jimmy is using our small video camera to review the tapes he shot today with the larger camera. He turns the flip screen toward me.

"What do you think?" he asks.

I look at the screen but without my glasses the image is blurred.

"I don't know. What is it?"

"Put your glasses on."

I reach down and place my glasses over my nose and look at the flip screen, where I see, from one side of the frame to the other, a baby chiru, its over-large eyes and big lashes looking directly at me.

"Conrad got this shot," Jimmy says, "with the small camera."

"Galen and I got within a few feet of the calf," Conrad says.

"And I got a full roll of stills," Galen adds.

"Check this one out," Jimmy says, putting in another cassette. "This is a shot I got with the big camera."

I look in the flip screen and watch as a baby chiru, nearly full frame, runs on its long, skinny legs, then stops and turns and looks directly into the camera as though it were a freeze frame designed for rolling credits.

"What are you talking about? This stuff is fantastic!" I blurt.

Jimmy's grin turns into a laugh, and the others join him.

"I'm sorry," Jimmy says. "We shouldn't have teased you like that, but we couldn't help it."

"Here, see if this makes you feel better," Conrad says, reaching to a corner of the tent and producing a can of Pabst Blue Ribbon beer.

"Where in the hell did that come from?" I ask.

"They're even chilled," Galen says. "Chang Tang chilled."

"I've had them hidden in my rickshaw," Conrad says. "There were four, but the Gorge claimed one. We had to appease the river gods; otherwise our carts never would have made it through. Anyway, we've got three cans, and we've got our footage, so let's have a little celebration."

Conrad hands me the can, but I tell him that if he carried them, he gets the first one. Then we decide with only three we'll share them one at a time.

"There's solidarity in passing a beer," Conrad says as he cleans the can with one of the socks he's been wearing since we started the trip. He pulls the tab and the beer foams. He lifts the can to his lips.

"Salud," I say.

"To the chiru," Conrad replies, taking a long, slow drink, then handing it to Galen.

"Hhmmm, that's good," Galen says, handing it to me.

I take a slow drink, the effervescent fizz in my throat like a refreshing breeze, the yeasty taste on my tongue like a pleasant memory.

"Unbelievable," I say as I pass the beer to Jimmy. He takes a slow drink and then shakes the can to indicate it's empty.

"So where does that leave us?" Jimmy asks after he's swallowed his swig of beer.

"Out of here before dawn," Conrad says as he pops the top on the second can.

"Homeward bound," Galen adds.

"It's like we've reached the summit," I offer. "And now we have to get down. Extending the metaphor, in our case that means we still have to walk another hundred miles."

Conrad takes his swig and passes the beer to Galen.

"Here's to the final leg," Galen says.

Galen finishes his draught and passes the can to me. I tip it in a toast to the others and take a swig. "I think I'm appreciating the calories in here," I tell them, "as much as I am the beer."

PART THREE

THREAT AND HOPE

CHAPTER EIGHT

क

JUNE 21

I ZIP OPEN THE TENT DOOR and all I can see is a blackness so absolute it has absorbed even the outline of Conrad and Jimmy's tent only ten feet away. I reach for my headlamp and shine it outside.

"How does it look?" Galen asks.

"Three to four inches of snow," I reply.

The flakes are still falling, crossing the cone beam of my headlamp like white tracers.

"Good morning," Conrad calls from his tent.

"Morning," I reply. "Little wintry out here, at least for the summer solstice."

"Is that today?" I hear Jimmy ask.

"June twenty-first," I answer.

"And I suspect we got ourselves an adventure getting out of here," Conrad calls back cheerfully.

It's four a.m., and we had decided last night to wake early with the hope that today we could log twenty miles, perhaps more. With this snowfall that may be ambitious, but it doesn't seem to dampen the good mood that prevails as we convene for morning coffee. When breakfast is finished, we fold open the map and measure the compass bearing to the entrance of the canyon that will lead us back to Shor Kul Basin.

"Three forty-five," Conrad says.

"Then let's drink some coffee and get after it," I reply, quoting a phrase that was one of Alex Lowe's favorites. Conrad gives me a nod of recognition, and when we have finished our coffee we crawl outside, break down the tents, and pack the rickshaws. When we're ready, Conrad consults the compass function on his wristwatch.

"That way," he says pointing into the blackness.

"Lead on," I reply.

Jimmy, Galen, and I follow Conrad's rickshaw into the black predawn, our visual world reduced only to the small sphere of illumination from our headlamps. In our audible world, extending farther, we hear animals shuffle and run, and changing course to investigate, our lights reveal a dozen dark circles in the snow, wallows of bare earth that mark the sleeping positions of a herd of chiru that apparently we have just flushed.

"I feel kind of bad we made them get up early," Jimmy says. "Now they don't have any place to lie down that isn't cold."

"And they don't even get granola for breakfast," Conrad adds.

"Given the choice between sleep and granola, I'd take granola," I reply in what occurs to me may be a non sequitur, but at five thirty a.m. I don't have the mental acuity to think it through.

"In that case, let's keep going," Galen says.

That reply has my brain in even more of a pretzel, but rather than question it I follow Conrad into the darkness, turning off my headlamp to save batteries, and then staying close to the wheels of his rickshaw. It continues to snow, and with the nearing dawn a movement of air causes the flakes to drift obliquely. After another fifteen minutes I have a vague sense that the direction of the flakes has reversed, and I am about to say something when Conrad stops.

"Well, look at that," he says.

"What?"

"We just crossed our own tracks."

I turn on my headlamp and sure enough I see our tire marks in the snow coming from the right and disappearing to the left.

"We've gone in a circle?" I ask.

"Looks like it," Conrad replies.

"How could we do that?" Galen asks.

"It had to be only the last couple of minutes," Conrad says, "because I checked my compass not too long ago."

I'm the only one with a compass on the handlebar of my rickshaw, and since I can't read it without glasses I suggest to Conrad we switch carts, as that will make it easier for him to monitor our heading. I strap into his harness, and we keep going. It feels odd to be pulling someone else's rickshaw. Conrad has more weight in his cargo bin than I do, but it's more than that, perhaps a difference in the load distribution or the harness adjustment. Whatever the reason, it's like wearing someone else's shoes: They feel odd, even if they are supposed to be the same size.

The black fog through which we pull our carts thins to dark gray, and soon we are able to turn off our headlamps. With dawn the snow stops, and the clouds begin to lift so that the surrounding terrain is revealed in the way that a photographic image slowly emerges in a developing tray.

"There's the entrance to the valley," Conrad says, pointing ahead.

"Good navigating," Galen replies.

The rising clouds spread like thin gauze over the sky, softening light from the sun breaking above the rim of the valley. We follow a stream of pellucid water that purls over rounded stones, and despite the snow vigor fills our stride. Conrad, with his long legs and strong arms, stays in the lead; Jimmy, with his straight back, pulls his traces with hands just behind him in "trad rickshaw style"; Galen, running ahead with his cart, stops to photograph us.

"This could be a cover shot," Galen says as we cart past him. "Keep going so I can get you with the basin in the background."

We pull our carts at a jaunty step down the white-carpeted floor of the valley. The crystal snows of the Kaxtax Mountains, fifteen miles distant, frame the top of Shor Kul Basin, and the air is as clear as a vacuum. Above the basin a horizontal cloud, balanced on an inversion, is suspended at the same altitude we are, invoking a sense that we ourselves are floating. Enlivened perhaps by our success recording the birthing of the chiru, and also by this midsummer dawn that has revealed this midwinter landscape, I have the thought that we are lungpa, the mythical flying monks of Tibet that glide just off the ground as they speed across the steppe with no purpose beyond the meditative joy of movement.

क

IN LESS THAN TWO HOURS we reach the gear we had cached at "Druid Camp," and we take a break to sort our equipment and repack.

"Doesn't a cup of coffee sound good?" Conrad asks.

We all heartily endorse his proposal, and while I retrieve from my rickshaw the stove and fuel bottle, Conrad takes from his cart the coffee and small cloth filter that each morning he carefully cleans after breakfast. He aligns our mugs in a row, and when the water boils he pours it over the ground coffee, taking care to rotate the filter mug to mug so no one receives a brew stronger or weaker than another.

"That smells so good," I say, breathing deeply to capture the aroma that diffuses into the air around our parked carts. Conrad hands each of us our mugs, and I hold mine with both hands, breathing the aroma again, then sipping the brew and pausing to make a vow to esteem this moment of common pleasure in such uncommon circumstance.

Energized by coffee, we pull our carts into the fifty-mile-long expanse of the great Shor Kul basin. Backlit by sun, steam rises off the land as the snow sublimates. By midmorning the floor of the basin is a checkerwork of snow white and sand brown; by noon only scattered patches of snow survive the building heat.

"I think the river that comes out the Gorge of Despair is in that depression straight ahead," I say.

The others agree, and in a half hour we reach the watercourse only to discover the parched floor of the basin has absorbed the river.

"It's going to be a long walk back to the hills," I say.

"There's one snow patch left over there," Conrad says, pointing ahead. "We could melt some on our pads."

Everyone agrees that is the better alternative. At the snow patch we park our carts and spread Conrad's two sleeping mats made of closed-cell foam. We place our cooking pot and water bottle under the two ends of the pads, sprinkle snow on top, and in a few minutes there is a steady trickle into each container. When the water bottle is nearly full I lift it to take a drink.

"Did you look in there?" Conrad asks.

I peer in the bottle and examine the flotsam that has washed off the sleeping pad.

"Some Synchilla fuzz, couple of UFO's and one, maybe two pubes," I report. I look in again, shrug my shoulders and then take a long swig.

"Wow, Ridgeway scores some drokpa points, big time," Jimmy says.

"What do you think?" Galen asks. "Two?"

"Three at least," Conrad counters.

"How come I'm the one getting all the drokpa points?" I ask when I finish my drink and hand the bottle to Conrad.

"Just look in a mirror," Jimmy replies with a laugh.

I did see my reflection the other day in the lens of Jimmy's camera as he was interviewing me, and I know that while we all with justification can be called crusty, I alone with accuracy can be called grizzled. My hair juts out in ratted bunches in the first evolutionary step toward dreadlocks, and my beard is a mat of gray hair. I am aware that with each day I seem incrementally to stoop forward in my traces, a simian position that is making me appear to have clocked even more than the fifty-two years I have actually passed on this Earth. The cough I suffered for so long may have something to do with my haggard state, but I sense the larger reason is simply the wear on my body. As Indiana Jones said, "It's not the year, it's the mileage."

Conrad takes a swig from the bottle and passes it to Jimmy, who drinks and passes it to Galen, who, when he is done, replaces it under the catchment. While the containers fill, we have lunch. Then we leave, keeping to a small rise on the flank of the basin in case the center is soft sand. When the rise ends we have no choice but to angle into the basin, and we are relieved when we find the floor is firm. In the middistance to the right is the range of hills that separates our present position from "Dispersion Camp." Recalling that extra day we took from our trek to reconnoiter the area around Dispersion Camp, we all agree that because we saw so many tracks of animals heading north in what appeared to be a more direct route to this basin than the one we followed through the Gorge of Despair, it seems likely that at least some of those animals are birthing in the hills now to our right. It's even possible there is another concentrated birthing ground, but because on our map there are no topographical lines suggesting a plain similar to the one that fronted the calving grounds we recorded, we all agree that the one we visited is most likely the principal birthing area.

Still, we all wish somehow we could rise into the sky to have an aerial overview, and that brings up the possibility we had talked about earlier of climbing one of the summits in this Kaxtax sub-range of the Kun Lun. We stop to examine the summits, rising five thousand vertical feet above the basin, and we look closely at one peak on the far end of the range that on our map is about twenty thousand feet high.

"If we waited to try that one we could assess our food situation once we got to it," Conrad suggests, "and then decide if it still makes sense to climb it."

Everyone agrees to Conrad's proposal, in part, I am guessing, because we all share a desire to delay thinking about climbing a peak until we have to. At the moment it seems like we will need all our energy just to get our carts and ourselves to the rendezvous with our vehicles. We continue, pulling the carts down the center of the basin, grateful that the desert pavement is hard, thankful we are surrounded by this stunning landscape.

The ground in all directions is a tessellation of alkaline deposits. On our left the snow peaks rise like a white wall. On our right the foothills are patterned in zebra stripes where snow has melted off the tops of runnels. My earworm returns and ahead, complementing the music, a rising convection lifts the ceratoides plants so they appear as shimmering dots suspended in the air, as though the scene were a pointillist painting come to life. Farther in the distance, a building cumulus drops rain into the basin that creates a screen behind which the snow mountain we may consider climbing appears as though its features were made with a wet brush dabbed in soft-hued watercolors.

My perspective on the Kaxtax changes at the rate of footsteps, one peak slowly disappearing behind a ridge while another emerges, step by step by step. This is how travel was in the last century across the steppes of Central Asia, on foot and by camel from one caravansary to another, when the rate of your thinking was set by the metronome of your stride, and you would watch a camp or a town appear on the horizon and then grow larger with the passage of hours, as slowly as the mound of sand in the bottom of an hourglass grows below the trickle of grains.

क

THROUGH BINOCULARS WE CAN SEE at the base of the foothills a few small groups of chiru. A company of seven females crosses at a run in front of us, a diminutive newborn racing to keep up, its long legs elongated even more in the shimmering air. Judging by the size of the calves we saw in the birthing ground, this little one is probably only a day or two old, and it is amazing to witness the speed with which it can run. Once more on our journey I have the thought that if the mavens of fashion and entertainment who wear shahtoosh could see the spirit with which this tiny chiru is speeding across the steppe to keep up with its mother—and feel as I do this affinity for this little creature—I can't imagine how any of them could continue to wear the shawls. But as Galen said—when I voiced to him this same sentiment over two weeks ago—it is with our images and our descriptions of the Chang Tang that we hope to impress on such people the epochal grandeur of this wild place and its wild creatures, and with that the importance of preserving all of it.

When conservationists and wildlife champions have in the past made efforts to save a species endangered because it was the victim of a fashion craze, public opinion and the potential opprobrium that attends it has been one of the most, if not *the* most, effective weapon. This was the case over a hundred years ago when the efforts to contain the demand for egret feathers to decorate women's hats—a fashion craze that nearly resulted in that bird's extirpation in Florida—began to succeed. This was the case twenty to thirty years ago when the craze for spotted cat fur began to subside once public opinion turned against women wearing fur coats. So in the late nineties the World Wildlife Fund, the Wildlife Conservation Society, the International Fund for Animal Welfare, the Wildlife Trust for India, and other NGOs around the world that had by then joined the anti-shahtoosh campaign sent letters, press releases, videos, pamphlets, and booklets to fashion magazines, newspapers, clothing manufacturers, television studios, and radio stations, hoping the subsequent publicity would begin to turn the public against shahtoosh.

The effort to publicize the plight of the chiru received perhaps its biggest boost when agents of the U.S. Fish and Wildlife Service followed up on the credit card receipts they had confiscated when they raided the offices of Cocoon, the company that had supplied shahtoosh shawls to the sale to raise funds for the Memorial Sloan-Kettering Hospital.

"Nobody paid much attention [to the plight of the chiru] until the New Jersey grand jury began to investigate some socially prominent women," George Schaller would later tell the *New York Times*. He also would tell me that more than anything it was the publicity from an article in *Vanity Fair* about the subpoenas and the illegal sale of the shawls that would have a tremendous impact on raising awareness about the illegal shahtoosh trade. Titled "OK, Lady, Drop the Shawl," the article by Bob Colacello came out five months after the subpoenas were delivered. At the beginning of the piece Colacello wrote:

> It is probably safe to say that the last thing the dowagers, heiresses and trophy wives of New York's high society were expecting as they lunched on lobster salad at the Bathing Corporation in Southampton this past summer, or worked out with their

personal trainers by their pools in East Hampton, or packed their Vuittons for the Paris couture shows, was a flurry of subpoenas from the United States District Court in Newark, New Jersey, of all places. But that is exactly what more than one hundred socialites and celebrities…had hand-delivered to them at their country houses or Manhattan apartments by U.S. marshals.

Colacello then described how one subpoenaed woman went on a rampage, "calling everybody and raving that we've got to fight this…she's not about to bring tens of thousands of dollars of her property to some courthouse in Newark." Others were similarly indignant:

"I haven't heard of anything so ridiculous in a long time. Some of our friends will have to call a moving van."

"Tell me they're going to bring in the closet police."

"Don't mention my name, but—no pun intended—could they make someone a scapegoat."

"Darling, everyone I know has one or two. Or three or four or five. This is the first time I hear it's illegal."

Indeed, a U.S. Fish and Wildlife officer told the press that all the people who bought shawls at the fundraiser "had absolutely no idea or knowledge that it was prohibited." But the officials needed the depositions for their case against Cocoon and Navarang. When the trial concluded, two women from Cocoon who had supplied the shawls to the sale were found guilty, and each fined $32,000 and placed on probation. Navarang, the company in Delhi that supplied the shawls to Cocoon, was also fined. Some people in wildlife organizations were disappointed the sentences were comparatively light, but because so many celebrities and well-known high-society women were involved, the attention in the press brought by the subpoenas probably did more to publicize the plight of the chiru than all other media campaigns combined.

Even though they were all exonerated, the women who had purchased shawls at the fund-raiser were then asked to forfeit them to

Fish and Wildlife. "I was told to go and get my shawls back that I had given away," Nan Kempner told me when we had tea in her New York apartment. "I said, 'No, I won't be an Indian giver.' This was then quoted in Women's Wear magazine, and I was called a bigot because I had used the phrase 'Indian giver.' I tell you, they are out there waiting for something they can nail you for. I spend a lot of time trying to do good things, and then it backfires and there's simply not a goddamn thing you can do about it but weather it through. We didn't know we were doing anything illegal. Believe you me, I was shocked when I learned the horrible things that were happening to the animals. I love animals. I'm a West Coaster, born and raised in San Francisco, and I spent a good deal of my time on a ranch in Reno, Nevada. So I respect animals. What I can't understand, though, is why they can't clip the fur [of the chiru] so they wouldn't have to kill them."

"When I returned to China about a year after our trek to do more research," I told her, "I learned that people have tried to keep chiru in captivity, but all the efforts have failed. I was also told there is a university in China trying to splice chiru genes to pashmina goats, to improve the cashmere of the domestic animals."

"How brilliant! Clone 'em! I like that," she said as she lifted the ends of the claret-colored shawl draped around her shoulders. "This shawl is a pashmina, and it's nice, but the others [the shahtoosh shawls], they really are a better mousetrap."

"But, Nan, to tell you the truth they are kind of plain-looking. So tell me, why are people willing to pay so much for these things?"

"It's because they are so light and so warm. You don't need to wear so many other warm things. They are thinner, and because they are thinner they can be wider and longer and still so light and so soft. And I just love being wrapped in soft things. Who doesn't?"

ॐ

"IT LOOKS LIKE WATER in the distance," I say.

"That's probably Shor Kul Lake," Conrad replies, referring to a large saline lake that our map shows positioned in the midpoint of the basin. In his transit of the basin in 1897, H. H. Deasy had labeled this lake salty, but some of Schaller's party had told us that on its north shore we could find a spring that we are now counting on to refill our depleting water bladders.

"It could be a mirage," Galen cautions.

Mirage or not, I convince myself we will find the spring. Another hour passes, and as we walk we tend to spread apart until there is a hundred yards or more between each of us. Overhead the sky is cloudless, and I consider how in the last weeks not only have we seen no other human beings, but we have seen no contrails from jets; other than our footsteps on the hardpan, the squeaking axles of our carts, and our voices there have been no human sounds or noises. I remember reading once that after a long search someone found only one place in the lower forty-eight states—somewhere in Montana—that was outside of all flight paths, so you could sit there a full day and neither see nor hear evidence of our species.

My calf muscles begin to cramp, but on this vast steppe I nevertheless feel a deep contentment that aids me in an effort to ignore the pain. I keep walking—feeling a certain pleasure in this pain that comes from walking—and recall a passage from Bruce Chatwin's *Songlines*: "Natural Selection has designed us—from the structure of our brain-cells to the structure of our big toe—for a career of seasonal journeys on foot through a blistering land of thorn-scrub and desert."

Natural selection has also designed us to become anxious in the absence of water. What I thought might be the lake—and with it, the freshwater spring—turns out, as Galen cautioned, to be nothing more than a mirage. Finally, in late afternoon—with lower light and fewer heat waves—we see what is unmistakably the lake, but it is too far to reach today. Between the lake and us we note what appears to be an embankment that we hope marks a stream course, and we decide to make that our goal. It is six p.m. when we reach it, and while it is a watercourse, there is no water. Apart from a few short breaks, we have been pulling our carts for over twelve hours, and we are too tired to continue; even Galen agrees it's time to stop. We pitch our tents at what we call "Sahara Camp," and Conrad, always the one to volunteer to make the extra effort, gathers our water bladders and starts walking toward the Kaxtax Mountains. In fifteen minutes he is a small dot on the broad floor of the basin, and in twenty minutes he is too small to see.

JUNE 22

"I DREAMED LAST NIGHT that we were back at the Telluride Mountain Film Festival," I tell the others over breakfast, "celebrating the successful completion of our expedition, and the owner of the restaurant next to the Opera House hosted us to a free steak dinner."

"I dreamed of trees," Conrad says. "I was just someplace where there were trees."

"I was too out of it to remember my dreams," Jimmy says, "but they had to be food dreams, for sure."

"Same here," Galen says. "Whatever I dreamed about, the theme was deprivation."

We all report that we slept well, however, and that we feel refreshed after yesterday's pull of twenty miles, a record so far for our journey. Since the ground is hard and the weather solid, there was no reason this morning to get up early, and it's seven thirty by the time we leave Sahara Camp. A high-pressure cell has moved over the Kaxtax Mountains, and from horizon to horizon the sky is a seamless sea of azure. We set our course on the snow peak at the eastern terminus of the range that we have talked about climbing. As our map indicates it is still nearly twenty miles away, our plan is to try to reach its base either today or tomorrow, and then take stock of our remaining food—not to mention our remaining energy—and decide whether to attempt to ascend it.

Meanwhile, we parallel the midsection of this unexplored range where the nearer summits, according to our map, are only five miles from our present position. Later Jimmy would tell me that for him it was like walking on a nude beach where you know you aren't supposed to look but nevertheless you keep stealing glances. For my part, I keep looking at one peak that on our map is about twenty-one thousand feet in elevation, higher than the summit we have selected to consider. If we were to climb this nearer mountain we could even begin the approach today, thereby taking advantage of this good weather. Moreover, this peak is directly opposite the foothills that we think could harbor additional calving grounds, and from the summit we would have a better overview that might reveal any topography attractive to female chiru.

The downside of the idea, however, is that we would have to decide to climb the peak within the next hour or two—before we walk past it—and I'm just not sure I have the energy to do that. Then I tell myself that if I don't the energy now, what makes me think I'll have it tomorrow or the day after? Maybe we're naïve to think we could muster the wherewithal to climb anything. Or perhaps foolish to even consider expending the extra day or two of food reserves the task would require. I decide not to say anything to my companions about the idea, at least not for now.

An hour later we reach a point abreast the west end of Shor Kul Lake, the shoreline of which is yet about a mile from us. Holding our present course, we should intercept the lake at its midsection, a point that also happens to be the reputed location of the freshwater spring. Then, in the distance, I see something that looks out of place, like the top of a tower, and I stop and retrieve my binoculars from my pannier.

"What is it?" Galen asks when he arrives at my position.

"I don't know. It looks like an oil derrick."

The others join us, and although no one can discern what it is, we alter course toward the lake to investigate it. A half hour later we are close enough to see it is indeed a tower in the shape of a miniature oil derrick, and we conclude it is most likely a marker from some past Chinese survey.

"I bet it also marks the location of the spring," I tell the others. "It would be a perfect place to cache the carts."

"What do you mean?" Galen asks.

"I'm not sure I have the energy, but if we still wanted to climb a peak, maybe it makes more sense to climb that one right there," I reply, pointing to the mountain I have been eyeing.

"That's an interesting idea," Galen replies.

"Let's look at the map," Conrad says.

He opens the map and spreads it on the ground, placing a stone on each corner, and we huddle around it.

"Six thousand four hundred and five meters," Conrad says. "That's nearly a hundred meters higher than the one we've been looking at."

"So your idea is to leave the carts at that tower?" Jimmy asks me.

"Yeah, and mainly what I'm thinking is that we could take advantage of this good weather. The last time we had a high pressure like this was back at Kansas Camp, and it lasted two days. So if that's the pattern, tomorrow should be good weather. Then we could get a great view over these foothills to see if there is any other place that might have a calving area."

"Why don't we go to the tower and have lunch and then decide," Conrad suggests.

We all agree, and in another half hour we arrive at what is indeed a survey marker. It is rusted and presumably years if not decades old. Through binoculars I can see at the lakeshore what looks like a discarded fuel drum, and while Conrad assembles the stove to brew coffee, I go to investigate. When I get to it I see it is instead an empty propane tank, and also scattered in the vicinity are shreds of discarded shirts and pants, a solitary shoe with a curled toe, and thousands of shards of broken glass turning purple under the desert sun. The garbage appears Chinese-made, and I conclude a survey crew or a geology team must have used this site as a camp.

I am about to return to the tower when I notice near the lake what looks like a small pond in a green meadow, and walking to it I discover in half a dozen places springwater gurgling from the ground. I follow one flow as it merges with another and then another, and in a few more yards I am on the bank of a small creek of crystal water flowing through this desert. Looking up, I can see it travels perhaps a half mile and then empties into the salt lake. I bend down, cup my hand, and dip into the stream. The water is cold, and when I lift it to my lips it is as delicious as any water I have tasted. I stand and look at a green, grass-covered flat next to the stream—a perfect place for tents. I walk back to the tower and tell the others that in spite of the nearby garbage dump, I have just seen what would make the prettiest campsite of our trip.

"It's twelve right now," Conrad says. "That's too early to camp."

I look back at the campsite, then up to the peak I have proposed we consider climbing, and I realize that despite my fatigue I am about to talk myself into this loony side excursion.

"If we did leave our carts here," I tell the others, "we could be at the base of the peak by nightfall, get an early start, reach the summit tomorrow, and get back here before dark. That way we wouldn't have to pass up this campsite."

"The southwest ridge looks like a good route," Conrad says, handing me the binoculars.

"There's a cornice," I say, studying a lip of windblown snow that guards the summit ridge. "But it looks small. We could probably find a way through it."

I hand the binoculars to Galen, and he studies the route while Conrad makes coffee. Galen then hands the binoculars to Jimmy, who agrees the ridge makes sense, although he would tell me later he was silently wondering where we were going to get the energy to pull the rickshaws the eighty miles we still had to cover in order to return safely to civilization, much less climb a mountain twenty-one thousand feet in elevation. But, of course, he kept his doubts to himself.

When the water boils, Conrad pours it over the coffee in the filter, and the aroma once more lifts into the air.

"Like a close friend of ours used to say," Conrad says with a grin as he hands me my mug, "let's drink some coffee and get after it."

क

WE HANG OUR FOOD BAGS from the center of the tower so they are over ten feet off the ground, in case there are bears in the area, lash our carts to the tower, in case there are any windstorms, then shoulder our backpacks and leave. We are taking with us Conrad and Jimmy's tent, which we intend to crowd into for the night, food for one dinner, one breakfast, and two lunches, our sleeping bags and pads, and our climbing boots and crampons. We are several hundred yards from the cache when Conrad stops.

"We forgot our passports," he says. "Think they're safe?"

"That reminds me I forgot the ten grand," I add, referring to a large packet of hundred dollar bills that we will use to pay for the remainder of the trip once we get out.

"Think we should go back?" Galen asks.

We stop and gaze at the desert basin and the hills and the peaks, with the nearest human habitation in any direction days or weeks away by foot or caravan. We look at each other, shrug our shoulders, and keep going. By late afternoon we are deep in the Kaxtax, following the main fork of a stream swollen by afternoon melt and tinted by brick-red silt. We maneuver around large boulders, climb out of the deep wash to a bench near the base of the southwest ridge of the peak, and pitch our tent. We inflate and arrange our sleeping pads on the tent floor, then find a large flat stone to set in the middle on which we position our stove. Conrad starts cooking our dinner of black beans and TSP, aka baby clams. After dinner we prepare our lunch for the climb, fortifying our otherwise meager rations with an extra Butterfinger candy bar for each of us.

"More calories per ounce than any other over-the-counter bar," Conrad, who had purchased the candy bars, says as he holds one in his hand and points to it.

"I'm not sure Butterfinger would use that endorsement in their ads," I reply.

We spread our sleeping bags, arranging them head-foot-head-foot, and even though it is still light, we crawl in and zip them.

"So what time are we getting up?" Galen asks.

"The alarm goes off at two forty-seven," Conrad replies as he checks the alarm function on his wristwatch. "And we're out the door at four."

"Wow, that'll be early," Galen replies.

"The four musketeers, like sardines," Jimmy says, rolling over and covering his head with the hood of his sleeping bag.

JUNE 23

"TIME TO WAKE UP," CONRAD SAYS.

"Already?" Jimmy asks in a pleading tone.

"It's four a.m.," Conrad answers. "I must have slept through the alarm. Sorry, you guys."

We sit up each in our corner, and Conrad starts the stove to make coffee. None of us are concerned about the late start, as we have all done climbs like this enough times we are confident we still have time to ascend the three thousand vertical feet to the summit, return here and break camp, then hike back to the survey tower before dark. We drink our coffee, eat our blueberry granola, and crawl outside, where we stuff our backpacks with lunch, water, crampons, and camera and video gear.

"We should leave while we still have some moonlight," I suggest.

A gibbous moon, low and yellow above the western ridges, imparts to our tent a ghostly luminance, but as we get under way we find that moonlight alone is insufficient to navigate through rocks of a moraine that we must cross, so we turn on our headlamps. By the time we reach the base of a buttress that leads to the ridge we will ascend, the moon has dropped below the surrounding crest, but higher it must still be visible, as the snow on our peak is tinged pale yellow. The air is calm and cold, the nightsky is cloudless, and the only sound is the clanking of my ice ax against rock. The W shape of Cassiopeia is positioned above the summit of our peak like a crown, the Milky Way arcs across the sky like a nocturnal rainbow, and Sagittarius, suspended above the basin, dims as the glow on the eastern horizon brightens.

At first light we stop, and Jimmy videotapes us as we strap on our crampons. I purchased a new set for this expedition, and as this is the first time I've used them I discover, to my chagrin, they are adjusted incorrectly. I'm trying to get them to fit as Jimmy puts the camera in my face.

"You know the real reason I climbed K2 without oxygen?" I say to the camera as I fiddle with the crampon. "It was because I got up to about twenty-seven thousand feet and I couldn't figure out how the oxygen mask adjusted. I put it on one way, then another, but the straps were wrong."

I position the crampon on the bottom on my boot, but it still doesn't fit.

"Back then nobody had climbed K2 without oxygen, and I thought I might get brain damage if I tried. My partner was sure he could do it, and finally he got tired of waiting and took off. I looked at my mask again and said to myself, 'Well, you probably already have brain damage or you wouldn't be in this position.' So I left the mask and bottle and climbed it without oxygen."

I place the crampon on my boot again, and this time it fits. By now there is wind filling from the west, and we are all getting cold. We leave as soon as I'm ready. Conrad sets a fast pace, in part, I'm guessing, to warm up; in part, perhaps, because we had a late start; and most likely, because he is incredibly strong. I manage to keep up, but I notice I am also breathing so quickly I am getting dizzy.

Despite my difficulties, I am exhilarated. Everything around me confirms why we disciplined ourselves, short on food and short on energy as we are, to make this climb. To my right and over my shoulder the Shor Kul basin is painted by dawn light in mineral hues of ochre and terra cotta, and beyond the Chang Tang plateau stretches to the far horizon like a great inland sea, the snow ranges and peaks like white archipelagos. The wind increases, and looking up I see madcap vortices of spindrift scud off the summit cornice. The sun crests the ridgeline, and the direct light refracts through the spiraling snow to create galaxies of iridescent sparkles.

"Conrad, let's stop and film this," I yell, thankful for a legitimate reason to rest.

Galen and Jimmy are also thankful for the chance to record the scene. In ten minutes we continue, and soon we are ascending in switchbacks the final slope toward the summit cornice. Even though the angle is steep, we have sufficient experience we feel confident climbing without a rope. I plant my ice ax in the hard snow, move one foot, then the other, and when I'm balanced I once more move the ax uphill. Conrad is still in the lead, and he heads toward a notch in the cornice that looks like it will allow safe passage through the overhanging snow. When he reaches it I can see that while the notch is vertical it's only chest high. He plants his arms over the crest, pulls up, and disappears. Jimmy follows. When I reach the notch I stand in it and look over the lip. There is Jimmy and Conrad, ten feet away. I stretch my arms, plant my ice ax, then pull up with both hands on the head of the tool as I swing my feet over the lip.

"Welcome to the summit," Conrad says.

"We made it," Jimmy exalts.

I grab Jimmy in a hug, and then step over and embrace Conrad.

"Our second first ascent together," he says, referring to our previous first ascent, when we had climbed the granite spire in Antarctica, the adventure that we had also shared with Alex Lowe.

Galen has taken another route around the cornice, and now, ascending the summit ridge, Jimmy takes a photograph of him as he makes the final steps to the top.[1] Once again we all embrace, then stand together gazing southward across the Chang Tang.

"Being up here brings it all together," Conrad says in a voice that is reverential.

"You can see our entire route," Galen adds, also with a tone of awe.

"Way in the distance, those are Schaller's Aru Mountains," I say.

"And there's Toze Kangri, and the peaks above Heishi Beihu," Jimmy adds.

"Mount Cook, the Twin Peaks, the Gorge of Despair," Conrad continues. "And just off there you can see the calving grounds, where the chiru are milling around today, with their babies at their sides."

Looking westward we also can see the tip of another singular summit that appears, using the Aru Mountains as a gauge, to be much farther away; because there are no other high mountains in that direction, we conclude the peak must be Ulugh Muztagh.[ii] The wind dies, and we kick into the snow a platform large enough for all of us to sit and eat our lunch, including our celebratory Butterfingers bar. I remember how I used to relish this brand of candy when I was a kid, but I don't think I ever savored it then as I do now. We finish lunch, and as it is only midmorning, there is plenty of time left in the day to descend all the way to our cache.

"I'm going over there to check out the view," Conrad says, pointing along the summit ridge to a rock outcrop fifty yards away.

"Stay away from the cornice," I say, forgetting for the moment I am talking to one of the world's foremost mountaineers.

"Don't worry," Conrad says with a grin.

He lifts his pack over his shoulder and sets out along the ridge. Galen is leaning against his pack napping, and Jimmy is chewing slowly on the second half of his Butterfinger, rationing his lunch as he does each day so that he can enjoy it as long as possible. I gaze across the north side of the Kun Luns toward the Taklimakan and what I know is the location of the southern fork of the ancient Silk Road. I turn and see that Conrad has reached the rock outcrop. I watch as he takes from his pack a white Buddhist prayer scarf that he must have carried all the way from Lhasa. He carefully arranges it on the most salient rock, and then weights it with stones. I know what he is doing because I have seen him do this before when I have been with him in other wilderness places that he deems significant. He sits down, gazing across the Chang Tang, next to the scarf that he will leave in memory of his best friend, his wife's former husband, and his adopted children's first father.

क

BY MIDDAY WE REACH OUR HIGH CAMP, brew four cups of coffee, then disassemble the stove and break down the tent, dividing it —rain fly, tent, and poles—so we each carry equal portions of our community gear. As we descend toward our cache Jimmy asks what we should name the mountain we just climbed.

"How about Chiru Peak?" Conrad offers.

"Chiru Kangri," Galen replies, adding the Tibetan word for "mountain."

We all agree, although we all know the name will remain as reference, as well as homage, for our use alone. We won't be reporting the ascent in any of the annals that record such things, nor will we be petitioning to make the name official with any of the agencies that register such things (if indeed there is even a way to do that in China, which seems unlikely). We climbed the mountain because that's our passion, because it offered us a view of our entire route, and because it allowed us to survey the hills that extend west of the calving grounds, to see if there were any other plains or plateaus likely to harbor additional calving areas.

While we could see no other flat area similar to the one we found, looking across the rest of the subrange it seemed likely there are additional calving areas, although probably not as large as the one we documented, for the simple reason there are not enough animals in the western chiru population to fill another major calving area. Any definitive answer will have to wait a future survey. Even then, I find it interesting to try to visualize what these hills were like a hundred years ago, when C. G. Rawling described the animals returning from these calving areas as an endless stream that passed by all day long, when at one sweep of the eye "there could not have been less than 15,000 to 20,000 visible." I also remind myself that these hills were dotted with tens of thousands, even hundreds of thousands of female chiru not only one hundred years ago, but as recently as thirty or forty years ago, before the beginning of the shahtoosh craze.

ॐ

MAYBE THERE'S A SILVER LINING in the fact the shahtoosh craze is just that: a fashion trend that, like fur coats and feathered hats, presumably will go out of style as fast as it came in. This is what Ritu Kumar, one of the leading fashion designers in India, told me when I met her in her office in Delhi.

"The shahtoosh craze will die because fashion always dies," she said. "But the trouble is, if we don't speed up the death we may lose the species."

Ritu, fifty-nine years old, is celebrated in India's fashion circles for her elegant traditional Indian wear as well as for designing gowns worn by Indian women in international beauty pageants, including the Miss Universe, Miss World, and Miss Asia Pacific contests. I thanked her for finding the time in her busy schedule to see me, and she apologized that I had to drive to the outskirts of Delhi, where her office is located. She invited me to sit in a deeply cushioned couch in her wood-paneled office, and then left to prepare tea. I knew from her web site that many of her designs have reflected an Indo-Western fusion, that she is well known and widely respected for embracing the textiles of traditional Indian craftsmen, and that she is credited in her country with giving the term "fashion" a uniquely Indian look.

I also knew from interviewing Ashok that, as a former business-man, he understood the importance of marketing, whether it's a product or a conservation initiative, and how recruiting celebrities and personalities as spokespersons can be a powerful tool in trying to capture the attention of those you are trying to reach. He told me he had persuaded Ritu to hold a series of press conferences at India's major fashion events, publicizing the plight of the chiru and asking her colleagues and clients to shun shahtoosh.[iii] The press had responded, and soon word spread in India's upper classes that the shawls were no longer fashionable. The increased awareness even resulted in political sniping when Maneka Gandhi, daughter-in-law of Indira Gandhi, accused her estranged sister-in-law Sonia Gandhi—leader of the opposition Congress Party—of wearing shahtoosh shawls in public.

"Now at a party if you wear one," Ritu told me, after serving tea, "someone will come up to you and say (with a critical undertone), 'Oh, is that shahtoosh?' People don't want to be seen in it. So to some extent the effort has been successful. But my involvement has been very small compared to what the issue is all about."

"I'm not sure I agree with that," I replied. "It seems to me the con-tributions of prominent people in the fashion industry like yourself have cumulatively been very important. As you said, if the goal is to speed along the death of a fashion fad, then your contribution has been very significant."

"That's nice of you to say, but I am a small cog in the wheel."

I was going to tell her that the wheels of such efforts turn only when they have cogs, but then I chose not to counter her charming lack of pretension. But from my research at that point, it was evident that Ritu's effort, combined with similar contributions of other celebrities in Europe and the United States, was beginning to shift the awareness of the nexus of a fashion trend that might last twenty years with the extinction of an animal that had been roaming the planet for eight million years. The World Wildlife Fund had recruited the supermodel Shalom Harlow to head its campaign, for example, and the Asian Conservation Awareness Program had asked actress Minnie Driver to appear in their anti-shahtoosh video that then aired on Discovery, Animal Planet and other cable channels around the world.

I was also beginning to see more clearly the scope of the contribution that Ashok, Belinda, and all their associates in India was having on the worldwide effort to save these animals, and how their dogged tenacity was perhaps the single most important factor in their effort. In addition to the initial success of the "Say No to Shahtoosh" campaign, Ashok and his group continued to press their strategy of achieving an outright ban on the manufacture of shahtoosh shawls in Kashmir, no matter what the roadblocks. After the chief minister had claimed, "Shahtoosh will be banned over my dead body," the Kashmiri press took up the debate, claiming that hundreds of thousands of artisans would be out of work in a state already suffering the loss of tourism from the conflict with Pakistan and the Muslim insurgents. Ashok's response was to have his Wildlife Trust of India obtain funds to survey the shahtoosh industry to find out exactly how many people would be affected if a ban was imposed, and also to study what alternative work they might pursue. The survey would be "exact" because instead of taking a sample of the artisans, Ashok wanted to interview every person involved at every step in the manufacture of the shawls across the entire state of Kashmir. It would take a couple of years, but he knew the results would also be incontestable.

Ashok had already received the favorable ruling in his suit against the Kashmir government for not following its own law requiring it to regulate the shahtoosh industry, and when the Kashmiris did nothing he filed a contempt of court petition. He also quietly began to recruit contacts in the Kashmir government who he felt were perhaps open-minded to rethinking the shahtoosh issue. He started a covert effort feeding them information about seizures in Delhi, developments to contain the poaching in China, and efforts to curtail the sale of the shawls in the United States and in Europe.

"Some good officers saw the light of day," Ashok told me, "and they started telling their government, 'Look, do something.'"

Ashok and his group received another boost when, for the first time since partition fifty years earlier, the ruling party—including the chief minister who had said shahtoosh would be banned over his dead body—lost the election in Kashmir. Then in May 2002, about the same time we were setting out with our rickshaws, the legislative assembly of the state of Kashmir and Jammu passed a law upgrading chiru to a Schedule 1 protected species, effectively outlawing all trade in the animal or its parts. The manufacture of shahtoosh shawls in Kashmir was by law banned.

CHAPTER NINE

क

JUNE 24

THIS MORNING THE HAZE hanging over the basin is so thick the sun is a pale disk that I am able to look at comfortably without sunglasses. I crawl out of the tent in bare feet. It's seven a.m., and I can tell already the day will be warm, at least compared with other days of our trek. I hear the stove going in Conrad and Jimmy's tent. I raise my arms over my head and stretch, and as I relax, my eyes focus on the bleached white skull of a donkey sitting outside Galen's door of our tent. Yesterday, after we had returned from the climb and set up camp, Galen had walked to the lakeshore to take photos and found the skull, which we think likely belonged to one of the two donkeys that Schaller was forced to abandon when the animals had refused to continue.

I walk across a green lawn of cropped grass to the creek, stoop, and splash cold water on my face. The filtered light, reflecting off the riffles in the spring creek, creates a sparkling dance of diamond glints, while beneath the water long strands of moss, moving slowly in the current, wave in emerald banners. Water in the desert is an incongruity always to be celebrated, and a cold spring percolating out of the hardpan and gathering into a crystal stream supporting a surrounding oasis of green grass is a wonder worthy of worship. The only thing I can find wrong with this place is that soon we must leave it.

"Bring your coffee mugs," Conrad calls out.

We gather in the cooking tent, sitting in our habitual corners and enjoying for the first time on the trek temperatures warm enough we can leave both doors fully open. All of us are wearing only our long underwear, and it feels like the beginning of summer when you open the windows for the first time and listen to the birds. In our case we do indeed have a Tibetan sandgrouse that releases a series of loud squawks as it lands fifty feet from our tent, then cranes its neck to stare at us as we stare back.

Today is an oatmeal morning, and after breakfast we study the map. Our goal for the day is to reach the terminus of Shor Kul Basin and the opening of the fifty-mile-long, riftlike valley that cuts diagonally through the Kunluns; after that we estimate it will take another three or four days to reach the other end, which will also be the end of our trek. We measure the bearing to the beginning of what we nickname "the rift," and once outside I use the compass on my handlebar to get a fix on a distant butte to use as a navigational goal. When the carts are packed, I lead the way, passing a few yards from camp the forlorn skeleton of what we presume is the second donkey from Schaller's caravan. Even though they were left to their fate over twenty miles from here, if these remains indeed are the two animals Schaller's party was forced to abandon, they likely walked back to this place because they recalled the green grass around the spring. They would have had a month or two of good grazing before winter came, unless wolves shortened what at any rate was a brief reprieve from their inevitable fates.

Our map shows the hills at the end of the basin are seven miles away, and our eyes confirm that even though it is a gradual incline, every step nevertheless will be uphill. Yet I don't find the challenge discouraging in the least; in fact, rather than dread the task, I find myself at moments wistful knowing the trek itself soon will end. The only preoccupation we have now is water. We topped off our bladders and bottles at the spring, and we have marked on our map the few places where last year the Schaller party found water, but they warned us that the water in some of the holes—if there was water at all—could be "pretty grody."

Even though the challenge of finding water—and the threat of thirst if we don't—adds another measure to the degree of self-reliance that this trek has required, I know I speak for the others in saying there is satisfaction in solving these problems. Lack of water also adds to the windblown rawness of this landscape, and gives it an austerity I find appealing. I am beginning to have at least an intuitive understanding of why so many of the world's religions have been spawned in the desert. Perhaps it induces mysticism because, as Galen says, the lack of perspective that attends big opens makes it difficult to compare one thing with another. Or maybe it is as simple as the mirages that cause the horizon to liquefy. Or even simpler, perhaps, as another friend who has spent most of her life in the deserts of eastern and southern Africa believes, the desert spawns prophets because they have visions induced by dehydration.[i]

An hour later I am still in the lead, holding a hypnotic pace that, dehydration notwithstanding, seems itself capable of inducing a prophetic vision, when I look up and I am startled to see straight ahead, in all apparent reality, what can only be called an apparition. Through shimmering heat waves, elongated as though distorted in a carnival mirror, I see three figures walking directly toward me. Are they people? After seeing no other humans for such a long time, even the possibility comes as a shock. I retrieve my binoculars, and I am looking through them as the others arrive.

"What is it?" Galen asks.

"Three figures. They're really distorted, but each of them only has two legs. They must be people. Three people, coming straight toward us."

"You're kidding," he answers. "Out here?"

"Do they have any pack animals?" Conrad asks.

"No, they're just walking, right toward us."

"Whoa!" Jimmy says.

"Da-do-do-do, da-do-do-do," Conrad replies, mimicking the theme from The Twilight Zone.

I hand the binoculars to Galen.

"They do look like people," he says, handing the binoculars back to me. I adjust the focus again, and then the figures stop. Do they see us? I am studying them intently when all three in unison turn so they are in profile.

"Wait a minute, you guys. They just turned sideways."

"What do they look like now?"

"They look like they've each suddenly grown an extra pair of legs."

"Chiru?" Conrad asks.

"Yeah, chiru," I reply sheepishly as I hand the binoculars to Conrad.

"Hallucinations are starting to happen," Jimmy says with a grin.

क

FOR THE MOST PART the desert pavement is firm, and even though we continue to ascend a gradual incline, pulling the rickshaws is straightforward. Occasionally, however, we encounter sections of sandy soil and then each step requires a pull on the waist harness or a tug on the traces. I stop every hour to rest for ten minutes, and then in some unspoken consensus I continue to lead. As he often does, Conrad takes a course off the side and sometimes behind; I have assumed he enjoys the solitude. I stop at twelve thirty for lunch, and resting against my cart I watch Conrad approach, his lean figure even leaner through the distorting heat waves. When he arrives he unbuckles his harness, turns around, and removes his lunch from his pannier. His thick blond beard and hair are coated with dust; his wind-chapped skin is deeply tanned. He reaches for the tube connected to his drinking bladder, sits against his cart in the little shade it offers, and places the water hose in his mouth, looking for all the world like a weathered traveler taking a break at an opium den in some caravansary along the Silk Road.

We are now following tracks in the hardpan of two camels and several donkeys that have to be from Schaller's caravan a year ago. An hour later, the sun overhead, I am still in the lead when I see to the north something on the hardpan that is white and out of place. I am chary of calling attention to any more apparitions, but I also remember how on the Antarctic icecap when you see a dark object it is always foreign and likely to be a meteor.[ii] I have read that in deserts it can be the same. Once Saint-Exupéry was forced to land his biplane in what in those days was Spanish Africa, on a tabletop mountain guarded on all sides by cliffs. Confident he was the first human ever to set foot on the plateau, he stumbled on a black rock that was set on a surface that otherwise was composed, in all directions, of broken shells. "A sheet spread beneath an apple tree can receive only apples," he wrote in Wind, Sand and Stars. "A sheet spread beneath the stars can receive only star-dust."

Even though this object is white—and, of course, not a meteor—maybe the same concept holds here. I stop and point out the odd object to the others.

"It's something foreign, all right," Galen says, looking through the binoculars.

We park our carts and walk more than a hundred yards to the object, and as we approach we can see it is a large skeleton. When we arrive Galen lowers to his knees to photograph the skull.

"It's definitely a camel," he says.

The bones are as white as the meridional sun, and the mouth is frozen in that ironic grin skulls in the desert seem always to make.

"If a camel can't make it out here," I say in partial jest, "it doesn't bode well for us."

क

As we near the end of the Shor Kul basin and the beginning of the long rift, the tracks of Schaller's party merge with the wider and more aged tracks of many previous animals, and we guess they mark the path of past caravans. The sun is warm enough today that it seems to take from me more energy than it gives. I visualize myself as the equivalent of the cartoon caricature with the long beard and ragged clothing crawling across the desert. At three p.m.

we stop for a ten-minute break. I have saved from my lunch half an energy bar, and retrieving it from my pannier, I lean against my cart and slowly nibble on it, saying to myself, "Okay energy bar, live up to your name." Conrad lies supine on the empty hardpan, his hat over his face as though it had been placed there by some passerby covering a corpse. Jimmy walks slowly to me, squats, and turns on the video camera. In the corner of my eye I can see that he has framed the scene with me in the foreground and Conrad's corpse in the background.

"Every hour," I say, turning my head slowly toward the camera, chewing even more slowly on my energy bar, "we stop for five minutes...or ten...to rest...but as the afternoon wears on... and on...the difference that the rest stops...make...grows less...and less."

After ten minutes we stand like old men getting up from their rocking chairs, buckle into our harnesses, and, without saying anything to one another, leave. In another half hour I have to pee, but I am so enervated that for the first time on the trek I don't bother to unbuckle the waistbelt connecting me to my rickshaw, and instead just stop and pull down my shorts. Before I am finished first Conrad, then Jimmy arrives next to me and stops.

"Look at Ridgeway," Conrad says. "He's not even bothering to unclip."

"Awesome," Jimmy answers. "Just like a horse tied to a wagon."

"What do you think? Two points?"

"Oh man, three at least. Like this is real beast of burden stuff."

We slowly pull the carts into the foothills, and at a cairn marking this old caravan route, we enter a canal scoured by flash floods. Half buried in windblown sand, and desiccated under the desert sun, is the skeleton of another camel, and nearby the brittle remains of a camel saddle. We continue up the wadi, stopping on the hour to rest. A stiff wind blows up, carrying with it sand and dust.

"Sand in your eyes," Conrad says. "Sand in your throat. Sand in your nose."

Conrad leads for an hour, and the wadi narrows. He passes an even narrower lateral gully only fifteen feet wide.

"It's protected from the wind," he says. "What do you think?"

"Looks good to me," Galen replies, looking more exhausted than I have yet seen him.

We unload our carts and pull the tents from their stuff sacks. We have pitched camp so many days in a row that we each know our roles by rote, and despite the wind, in only a few minutes we have the tents up, the food and gear organized, and the stove roaring.

"What if we call this Quickdraw?" Conrad asks.

We all agree to the name for this camp. Conrad fills our pot with precious water taken this morning from the spring, and he has dinner ready in a half hour: falafels and black beans spiced with a dash of Chinese hot sauce.

"We have dessert this evening," he says as we finish.

"Dessert?" Jimmy asks incredulously.

Conrad produces a chocolate bar.

"Where did that come from?" Jimmy asks.

"Left over from my lunch. I didn't eat it, so now we can share it."

We each get two squares to eat with our hot chocolate, and we each thank Conrad at least twice. Galen and I return to our tent and I write in my journal for a half hour, recording that while on the map we made only nine miles for the day, most of it was uphill.

"Just moderate progress today," I write, "but we needed that after yesterday's climb of the mountain. We're all feeling the lack of food. Everyone is more visibly exhausted, especially Galen. I've never seen him looking this worn-out. But all of us still seem to be enjoying it. Despite my enervation, I'm loving crossing this desert on foot, Bolero playing in my head, pulling my cart toward that 'ever-receding horizon' that shimmers in the heated air."

I return my journal to its plastic bag and place it alongside the wall of the tent. Galen finishes his camera notes and zips up his sleeping bag.

"See you in the morning," he says.

"Sleep well."

I listen to the windblown sand gravel against the nylon fly of the tent, my last perception of the sentient world as I leave it and drift into the other world of dreams.

JUNE 25

THE NORTHERN HALF of the Chang Tang, as well as this Shor Kul basin, seems to pass through alterations in weather as rapidly as any places I've been. Yesterday we woke to a smoglike haze that cleared by midmorning, by which time we were pulling our carts under hot sun and over sunburned earth. This morning we woke to snow scudding over the barren ground, and now—midmorning again—the floor of the wadi, the sides of the enclosing hills, the sky, all are cold gray. Yesterday was the first day of the trek I was able to wear shorts; today I am back in my insulated trousers feeling my sunburned legs chafe against the pants' liner. And even though I am working hard, I am still cold.

In another hour the snow stops, and the clouds lift but the sky remains leaden. On the north bank of this dry wash are scattered clumps of ceratoides, and we see occasionally the prints of chiru. Perhaps they are a resident population, and perhaps they are even small groups of males wandering the area apart from the migration of the females. No one knows. But there are no animals to be seen, and although no one voices it, I am guessing my three companions miss as much as I do having the chiru around us.

On our map this valley that we have nicknamed "the rift" looks like a diagonal cleft dividing the Kunluns. In addition to our map we also have with us a photograph of the northwestern Chang Tang taken from the space shuttle, and there as well, even from outer space, the valley is so pronounced it looks as though it were a cut made through the mountain range with a giant cleaver. Even though we call the valley "the rift," however, it is more precisely a graben, a fault line where one side has dropped lower than the other. And even though it cuts so deeply through the mountains, it nevertheless drains in two directions, with the divide of the valley more or less in line with the crest of the mountain range.

At ten thirty a.m. we reach a narrow pass marked with a cairn that we can see from the topo lines on our map is the divide of the valley as well as the crest of the Kunluns. This is what in 1897 H. H. Deasy recorded as Atish Pass, "an easy one, 16,500 feet high." The trail through this rift is also the same track a Japanese team followed two years ago when it came through here to climb the highest peak in this end of the Kunluns, and the same one Schaller's team followed one year ago. The trail is worn enough to suggest that in addition to the Japanese and the Schaller parties, there have been other caravans that have traveled this route, and Schaller thinks they most likely were local miners venturing into the Shor Kul looking for gold. As for us, this Atish Pass offers other riches: Even though there will be a few ups and downs as we cross intermittent hills, the overall gradient from here to the finish of our journey will be downhill.

"So let's see what a little downhill feels like for a change," Conrad says.

"You going to be okay without brakes?" I ask, referring to the surgical triage Conrad had to perform on his cart the day we exited the Gorge of Despair.

"I'll have to be," he replies.

With that we descend into a twisting gully that although narrow nevertheless has a hard sand bottom with a floor that is only moderately declined, so that soon we find ourselves being pushed gently by the weight of our carts, with no braking necessary.

"R-o," I say.

"I don't know," Jimmy says. "Maybe R-o is we somehow get in the carts and ride."

By noon the trail of past caravans that we follow merges with a lateral stream flowing from the snow mountains on the opposite side of the rift, and we stop to eat lunch and also to fill our water bladders. Finding water is a relief, for even if this small stream disappears later into the dry floor of the rift, we should now have a sufficient supply for two days—three if we stretch it—and that should give us sufficient time at least to get close to our planned rendezvous with the vehicles that will transport us across the Taklimakan through the former caravansaries of Hotan and Yarkand, along the old Silk Road to the city of Kashgar, where we will catch a flight home.

In midafternoon Jimmy loans me his compact digital music player and earphones, and listening to the *Best of the Rolling Stones*, I pull my cart quickly down the hard, sloping desert pavement. By the time the player cycles back to the first song, I turn and discover I am a quarter mile ahead of the others. While I wait for them to catch up, I finish the portion of my energy bar I have reserved for a midafternoon snack.

"You smoked that section," Jimmy says when he arrives.

"Blame it on 'Jumping Jack Flash,'" I reply, handing Jimmy his player and headphones.

It was fun pulling my cart in time to the Stones, and for the last few minutes I was even regretting not bringing music myself. Now that I've handed back Jimmy's MP3 gizmo, however, I'm just as happy to return to my no-batteries-needed earworm. I'm also realizing my burst of energy has been at the cost of what is a limited amount of calories available to burn, and suddenly I'm feeling even more ener- vated than I was yesterday. I'm not the only one. Galen is still another quarter mile behind, and it takes several minutes before he arrives.

"I don't know what's going on," Galen says. "No matter how hard I try I can't keep up."

"What's going on," Conrad answers, "is that for a month we've all been burning more calories each day than we've been taking in."

"Yeah, you're doing great," Jimmy says. "Don't worry about it."

"I just don't understand," Galen repeats as though he hadn't heard Conrad's explanation or Jimmy's encouragement. "I tried as hard as I could."

I glance at Jimmy and then Conrad, but we all avoid each other's eyes, and no one says anything. I suspect by their silence they are hav- ing the same thought I am. We are standing in our harnesses, and Galen's head is hanging while he catches his breath. We have all vis- ibly lost weight, especially this last week, but Jimmy and Conrad less so. I can feel my own frame much thinner than it was at the outset, but the last three days Galen has thinned at an alarming rate, espe- cially in his upper torso. I have no worry that he can make it the remaining distance—he could do that just on his reserves of mental strength—but I am concerned that he is at a transition, that this may be the first time he has had to confront that inevitable reckoning in all our lives when our bodies no longer respond to what our minds tell them to do. I say "concerned" because I don't think Galen, who is the strongest man for his age I have known—and who looks younger than his years perhaps more than anyone I have met—imagined he would have to face that reckoning for a long while.

JUNE 26

WE PULL OUR CARTS ALONG the top of a corrugation that rings a salt lake and marks the high water of some past age when this desert was perhaps not a desert at all. Last night we camped at the very west end of this lake, and as we set up the tents a ten-knot breeze rippled the water and also created a headwind for a pair of shelducks that had to paddle harder to open a distance from us with which they were comfortable. At that point one of the ducks simply stood in the middle of the lake, revealing it to be nothing more than a shallow pan. Once our tents were up the wind increased, and while Galen and I worked on our notes, I kept glancing outside because the wind was pushing the water closer and closer to our tent.

"It's ten feet away," I told Galen.

We went back to writing, and in a few minutes I looked out again. "Five feet."

"We might as well get it over with," Galen said, putting away his notebook.

We pulled on our boots, took some of our supplies out of the tent to lighten the weight, pulled up the stakes, and carried it a hundred feet to higher ground. Conrad and Jimmy, perhaps showing more sense— or more luck—had pitched their tent farther from the shoreline and were still okay. Once we had our tent staked in its new position, Galen and I went to their tent for dinner. Galen took a reading on our GPS, and Conrad plotted the day's travel.

"Thirteen miles," Conrad reported. "Pretty good for the malnourished."

Now this morning, at the north end of the lake, we leave the terrace of this ancient shoreline and cross a wide floodbed that then

narrows as the rift begins to constrict. At midmorning we see a solitary female chiru that first runs but then stops and turns to scrutinize
us. This is the first chiru we've seen in over a day, and she is behaving
in the same manner females in the calving grounds did when they
were with newborns. We unbuckle from our carts, Galen and Jimmy
ready their cameras, then we spread out across the hillside and walk a
grid searching for the calf.

"I can see the mother, just over there," I call to the others. "See
her ears?"

The mother chiru's ears are just visible above the crest of the hill
where she watches us while remaining as hidden as possible from
our view. We complete the grid, then move uphill and begin to sweep
the hillside at a higher level. The mother continues to watch, confirming the calf's presence, but the young one remains secreted from
our view, perhaps in a shallow, perhaps behind a ceratoides bush.

"Maybe we shouldn't hassle them anymore," Jimmy suggests. "The
little one is probably missing its mom."

"I'm thinking the same thing," Conrad agrees.

Galen and I also concur. Even if we found the calf, it is unlikely we
would get better shots than the ones we already have. On the other hand,
that is a judgment about which you can never be certain, and consequently, as an operating principle in documentary photography and
filmmaking, you take every opportunity to improve on what you already
have. In this case, however, that has to be weighed against the stress we
are causing to this chiru and her baby, and that in turn is a trade-off
that wildlife photographers—as well as wildlife biologists—are wise
always to be reassessing.

That brings to mind an article by William Bleisch I read before
leaving on our trek, in which he defended the tactics of Wong How
Man—the photographer and adventurer who had partnered with
him to organize the first expedition to study the calving grounds of
the central chiru herd in the Arjin Shan Nature Reserve—against an
editorial that had run in Hong Kong's South China Morning Post crit-
icizing Wong for chasing kiang, chiru, and gazelles in his vehicle to
get good photographs. Bleisch defended Wong—and at the same

time his own fieldwork when, in the chiru's calving grounds, he had fastened plastic identification tags to the ears of newborns—arguing that the benefit to the chiru from both the photographs and the science outweighed whatever stress it caused the animals.[iii] Wong How Man was even more explicit. "Having been a photojournalist for the *National Geographic* for many years," he wrote in another article, "I understand the power of photography. [In Arjin Shan] I vowed to bring home both the pictures of the magnificent live antelope and the gruesome images of the remains of the slaughtered pregnant females and full-term fetuses the poachers had left in their wake. These photographs will not only bear testimony to the antelope's plight, they may also send a chill up the spines of the beautiful people who seek to wrap themselves in fine shahtoosh."

Both the Bleisch article and the Wong piece were printed in *China Explorers*, a handsomely produced quarterly published by the China Exploration and Research Society. Commonly known by its acronym CERS, the organization, based in Hong Kong, was founded in 1987 by Wong, whom the Asian edition of *Time* magazine called "China's most accomplished living explorer." In addition to staging expeditions to China's most remote regions, CERS—with backing from multinationals like IBM, Coca-Cola, and Shell, and brand names like Land Rover, as well as contributions from wealthy Hong Kong business personalities—also funds scholars preserving China's archaeological heritage and wildlife biologists protecting its natural history. In the Arjin Shan, for example, Wong's group provided vehicles for wildlife biologists studying the chiru in their calving grounds. The officials there were so pleased with his support they have given him the title of Chief Advisor of the Reserve.

CERS also sponsored the expedition to Arjin Shan in 1998 when William Bleisch made the first survey of the calving grounds of the eastern population of chiru, and they supported subsequent expeditions that returned to the calving grounds each summer for the next three years. After that the Arjin Shan Reserve—with additional funding from the International Fund for Animal Welfare—began to step up the number of wildlife patrols it sent into the field. On his last survey in 2001—the same year Schaller mounted his camel and donkey caravan to search for the calving grounds of the western population— Bleisch could see the results. "The Chiru population of Arjin Shan Nature Reserve," he reported, "seriously depleted by poaching in the past five years, appears to be safer now. In past years when we have arrived on the calving grounds, tell-tale tire tracks have indicated the poacher's routes and circling vultures and ravens have led us to the piles of female chiru carcasses stripped of their pelts and left to rot. This year, we found no sign of poaching on the calving grounds and the chiru were able to give birth in relative peace."[iv]

At the same time, encouraging results also were reported farther to the southeast, in the Kekexili Nature Reserve (also known by its Tibetan name as the Hoh Xil Reserve), a seventeen-thousand-square-mile area that encompasses much of the eastern population's migratory route and calving grounds. In Kekexili, efforts to contain the chiru poachers had started ten years earlier—before the nature reserve was created—and they were initiated not by wildlife officials but by a local forty-year-old Tibetan named Suonan Dajie who lived in an adjacent region close to the headwaters of the Yangtze River. Suonan headed a committee that was charged with exploring the possibilities of alternative economic development in the region, including Kekexili, a mostly unoccupied area that at that time was under the administrative control of the prefecture and the county in which Suonan lived. Suonan knew that in the early 1980s Muslims, most of whom were from the northern half of Qinghai Province, had discovered gold in Kekexili, and thousands of them were in the area prospecting illegally. With two other members of his committee—including his personal secretary, a thirty-year-old Tibetan named Zhaxi Duojie—he made a trip to the remote region to investigate.

क

"AT THAT TIME, in 1992, the economy was really difficult for the local people," Zhaxi told me when, months after our trek, I met him in the restaurant of a four-star hotel in Beijing. "People still had not recovered from the terrible snowstorm in October 1985 when so many of the domestic animals and also the wild animals died. There was famine after that for several years."

We were in a lounge called the Jet Bar, surrounded by shiny brass, red granite, custom-woven carpets, and indoor plants. Most of the patrons were businessmen in suits. Young Ya Ya, the primate biologist from Fauna and Flora International, had volunteered to help as translator. Zhaxi wore denim pants and a plaid shirt, and had a hand-embroidered pouch, presumably for his valuables, looped across his chest. He was of medium height and build, with scraggly chin whiskers and bright eyes. He held his back straight, and as he looked around the lobby at the businessmen in their business huddles, his bemused grin suggested he did not feel out of place.

"We took a long detour to get to Kekexili," he explained. "In those days there was no road. When we arrived we found out that the miners were killing the wild animals. They were killing the wild yaks and the donkeys [kiang] for their meat. They were poaching the chiru, so that is when Suonan Dajie decided to change direction, from thinking about mining to conservation, to saving the animals."

"Why did he do that?" I asked.

"He was like me," Zhaxi replied. "We both grew up with the wild animals, and we have natural emotions attached to them. My father died when I was one year old, and my mother died about the time my permanent teeth came. After that I was a free boy, and I went to the north side of the Tongtian River [the upper Yangtze] to herd sheep. In the Tibetan language, the name for this area means 'the place of the Tibetan antelope.' There were many antelope, and also wild yak and donkeys. Everyone hunted, but not so much the antelope because the meat was not that delicious. We hunted yak and donkeys, but we only hunted weak animals, not ones that were pregnant. And we only hunted for ourselves, so it was sustainable.

"But the gold miners [in Kekexili] were hunting the wild yak to sell the meat, and also the antelope to sell the wool, in the cities. They didn't know that Kekexili belonged to our prefecture. At that time Kekexili was a place with no laws and no police station, and the poachers were very well organized. So Suonan Dajie decided to use the committee to start arresting the poachers. In the first year we were very successful. We captured many poachers who we then turned over to the authorities for prosecution.

"Then one day we encountered a gang of eighteen poachers," Zhaxi continued. "We were on the western border of Kekexili, near Arjin Shan. A gun battle started, with everybody shooting at each other. We captured the poachers, but some of our group was shot, so we took them back to get help while Suonan Dajie and two others stayed to guard the poachers. While we were gone the poachers took over Suonan Dajie and there was another fight and Suonan Dajie was killed.

"This was January 18, 1994, an important date for me," Zhaxi said, nodding to Ya Ya in a gesture that suggested he wanted to make sure she translated this part accurately. "The reason I am here talking to you now is because after Suonan Dajie died, I had a great responsibility to continue his work. This is why I am doing my work today."

"Did you take over his work arresting the poachers?" I asked.

"No, I decided that was very dangerous work. For a while I got a government job, but I wanted to do work that would continue what Suonan Dajie wanted to achieve, so I decided to start this NGO."

"The Snowland Great Rivers Environmental Protection Association," I said, reading the business card Zhaxi handed me at the beginning of our interview.

"Yes, that is my NGO."

Zhaxi then told me, with Ya Ya translating, that his organization, working with Fauna and Flora International as well as other conservation groups, was trying to develop programs to improve the livelihoods of communities in his homeland by introducing better livestock management and care, by developing cottage industries such as handicrafts, and by promoting ecotourism so not only would there be more income for the people, but also they would be encouraged to protect their wildlands and wildlife.

"This work is long-range, and this is what Suonan Dorji wanted to see happen for his people," Zhaxi said, looking at Ya Ya again to make sure she was translating. I don't need words, however, to see the conviction in Zhaxi's eyes, to understand his resolution to keep alive his mentor's flame, or to sense the place that a mentor must hold in someone's life whose father died when he was too young to remember, and whose mother died before he had all his permanent teeth.

क

THE DEATH OF SUONAN DAJIE was widely publicized in China, and when I was doing research for this book I even found an article about it—and about what next happened to his vigilantes—in the *Wall Street Journal*. Most of these articles told how Suonan Dajie's body was frozen by the time he was found, one hand on the trigger of his rifle and the other on the bolt. His brother-in-law, Zhaba Duojie, then took over the band of anti-poachers and, presumably owning an instinct for publicity, changed the name of the group from the Zhiduo County Western Working Committee to the Wild Yak Brigade. "Wild yaks are ferocious when they're attacked," the *Wall Street Journal* quoted one of Zhaba's lieutenants as saying, "but peaceful otherwise. Just like us."

The authorities in Zhiduo County had issued a decree allowing the Wild Yak Brigade to sell any pelts they confiscated to finance their operation. Zhaba was paying his men a monthly salary, and they were becoming increasingly effective apprehending poachers. Then, in 1998, the Brigade made a potentially important contribution to the understanding of the chiru's natural history when they happened upon another of the birthing grounds of the eastern population of chiru. However, just as happened to William Bleisch when he and his group would make a similar discovery of the other calving area of the eastern population, the vigilantes arrived only to find the poachers had beaten them there. The scene was as devastating as it was heart wrenching: There were carcasses of some eight hundred female chiru with dozens of baby chiru still trying to nurse their dead mothers. The Brigade members tried to feed the calves with powdered milk, but the effort failed and all the newborn chiru died.

Meanwhile, spurred by the national publicity following Suonan Dajie's martyrdom, the government approved Kekexili as a regional reserve (and two years later it would upgrade it to national status). The reserve eventually began to send wildlife officers into the field to chase poachers, and at the same time the Wild Yak Brigade continued its own patrols. Soon the vigilantes developed a reputation for being more effective than their official counterparts: By 1998 the Brigade had captured over four hundred poachers and confiscated nearly four thousand chiru hides.

Assisted by its catchy moniker, they were also enjoying worldwide attention in the press. This incurred the jealousy of some officials in the local prefecture who criticized Zhaba publicly, and at the same time blocked his efforts to win public funds to support the Brigade. For Zhaba, this exacerbated an increasingly worrisome problem: Despite having sold some of the pelts they had confiscated, his group had a growing debt. Then, hearing about the Wild Yak Patrol's success, and wanting to aid the effort to save chiru, Friends of Nature, the environmental NGO in Beijing, and the International Fund for Animal Welfare—known by its acronym IFAW—invited Zhaba to the capital, and they arranged for the press, including China Central Television, to cover his visit. Zhaba brought some hundred rolls of film the Wild Yak Brigade had exposed but had never developed. Friends of Nature paid the lab costs, and then exhibited the images in Beijing: the bodies of skinned chiru, the stacks of freshly fleeced hides, the Brigade members trying to keep orphaned baby chiru alive. Many of the photographs would later be reproduced in newspapers and environmental publications around the world.

Zhaba then had a private meeting with Liang Congjie, the founder of Friends of Nature, and Grace Gabriel, the China director of IFAW, and explained that the Wild Yak Brigade needed money to pay their old debts, to make their payroll and to obtain better vehicles. He told them the poachers, using their earnings to buy late-model SUVs and modern weapons, were now able to run down entire herds of chiru, killing as many as five hundred at a time. In the past, with less capable vehicles, they were limited to hunting in the winter—when the ground was frozen—but now not only were they shooting the animals year round, they were hunting at night, using high-powered lights to blind the chiru. Liang and Grace both pledged to support Zhaba's organization, but Grace could see a potential conflict if IFAW and Friends of Nature were to support the Brigade and the Brigade then sold the chiru pelts it confiscated. Liang agreed with Grace's concern, saying that if the skins were sold into the international market, it would only make matters worse by feeding the demand for shahtoosh wool.

"There is a saying in Chinese," Grace told Zhaba. "You are lifting a rock to drop it on your own foot."

Zhaba agreed wholeheartedly. He returned home and told his fellow Brigade members, who affectionately called him Secretary Zha, that from here forward they would destroy all the pelts they confiscated. He was now confident he had a way—even without selling confiscated hides—to keep the Wild Yak Brigade operating. All he needed was to win official sanction. He was optimistic he would achieve that when, shortly after his Beijing visit, the vice governor of Qinghai Province asked him to assist in drafting a plan for Kekexili's preservation. Everything, it seemed, was going in the right direction. Then something happened that none of Zhaba's friends could have foreseen. His body was found in his house with a gunshot wound to the head, and the cause of death was officially listed as suicide.

Despite the raised eyebrows of many who knew Zhaba, the remaining members of the Wild Yak Brigade pledged to keep working, and Friends of Nature and IFAW made good their promise: Friends of Nature contributed two jeeps and IFAW donated $10,000. "We even got permission to have [the jeeps] outfitted as Public Security vehicles," Friends of Nature reported in its newsletter, "complete with flashing red lights....When the Wild Yak Brigade took delivery of the jeeps, they wept."

The Wild Yak Brigade also honored Zhaba's pledge to destroy any chiru skins it confiscated from poachers. A few months later the Brigade invited Liang and Grace to witness the burning of an enormous stack of chiru skins. In turn, the environmentalists brought reporters from Beijing Radio and TV. With cameras clicking and VCRs whirring, Liang, Grace, and the new leader of the Wild Yak Brigade, each holding a flaming torch, set fire to a mound of gasoline-soaked hides that in the local black market were worth over $30,000.

Just before this event, the State Forest Administration, which officially oversaw Kekexili, had organized one hundred seventy policemen who spent three weeks in the field pursuing the poachers in Qinghai, Tibet, and Xinjiang. One officer was killed in a vehicle accident, but the China Daily reported that during the initiative, called The Number One Action, wildlife police confiscated one thousand six hundred fifty-eight chiru hides, seized eighteen vehicles, fourteen firearms, and twelve thousand bullets, and arrested fourteen poachers, who all received prison sentences from two to nineteen years. Not to be outdone, the officials then had their own chiru hide-burning ceremony a few days following the Wild Yak Brigade's event.

Over the next few months the Brigade continued to field more patrols, capturing fourteen more poachers and seizing an additional one thousand sixty-one skins. A China television crew accompanied them on one patrol, and the Brigade enjoyed even more publicity and acclaim.

"It's not that we do nothing and the Wild Yak Brigade does everything," the leader of the official wildlife patrols complained to the press. "We spread a lot of propaganda, and people don't sell chiru skins in the markets anymore."

The growing conflict between the official wildlife officers and the vigilante Wild Yak Brigade was perhaps inevitable. The officials were critical of the Brigade because it was technically an illegal organization, as only four members were Forestry Department policeman who, by law, were allowed to carry weapons and wear uniforms. It didn't help, either, that both the officials and the Brigade were headquartered in the same small town; several of the Brigade were converted poachers who had joined the other side, and these men in particular had reputations as being both fearless while on patrol and hard drinking when off duty. The people I interviewed regarding the history of the Wild Yak Brigade also intimated there was an element of jealousy because the Brigade was more effective than the officials. Even with GPS and good maps, the official patrols would sometimes get lost trying to navigate across Kekexili, but most of the Brigade members were former herdsmen who knew the land intimately.

"We saw it coming," Grace Gabriel told me when I talked to her. "We tried to convince the government to recognize the Wild Yak Brigade, and get the group the recognition they deserved. But by then it was too late. There was too much bad feeling between the officials and the Wild Yak Brigade. In early 2001, the Brigade was disbanded."

When I interviewed William Bleisch, he had another insight. "I think it's easier to understand the Wild Yak Brigade if you also understand the tradition of raiding that has always been part of the culture in eastern Tibet. This tradition of one group raiding another was clearly described by Ekvall, and it is also a trait common to most nomadic cultures.[v] Viewed from this perspective, the Brigade was true to its cultural history: They were a band that organized raids against outsiders—the gold miners—who were interloping in their territory."

From my perspective, I came to see the Wild Yak Brigade as a missed opportunity, an example of a community-based conservation initiative that, had it been legitimized, would have been perhaps unique in the world.

क

WE PULL OUR CARTS ALONG THE BASE of sand dunes that have drifted against a lateral moraine that extends along the floor of the rift like a miniature range of mountains. The dunes have been rippled by wind as a sandy sea bottom is by currents, and the wheels of our carts break the surface crust, leaving parallel tracks that seem to violate the purity of the dunes in the way that footprints do when they track virgin snow. When we reach the end of the dunes Conrad, who is in the lead, stops.

"Do you hear something?" he asks.

We all stand silently and listen. It sounds as though there is a faint hum, but it is nearly imperceptible.

"I think it's natural," I say. "I've heard it before in places that are totally silent, like in the Haleakala Crater and in Antarctica, and even when I was in the Chang Tang the first time, in the Aru."

"I don't know," Jimmy says. "I think I can hear it oscillating."

"That's what I thought," Conrad adds.

"It could be our imagination," Galen says. "It happens to pilots crossing continuous areas with no features, like rain forests and oceans. You start to hear noises in your engine that aren't there. It's called 'auto rough,' and maybe this is the same phenomenon, our perception filling in noise that isn't there."

Jimmy and Conrad remain skeptical. We continue, and in a half hour we stop again and listen.

"I can still hear it," Jimmy says. "Like a really distant train."

"There couldn't be any vehicles or motors," I reply. "Remember what the guys in Schaller's party told us about the rift?"

Members of Schaller's party said that not only is this part of the rift uninhabited, but parts of it are cut with gullies deep enough they thought we might have trouble getting our carts through. So it seems unlikely, or even impossible, anyone could get a vehicle in here.

"Still, I definitely hear something," Conrad says in a questioning tone.

In another half hour we pull our carts across the stream, and my theory about vehicles is suddenly and alarmingly disproved when, on the opposite mudbank, we cross tire tracks.

"They're too narrow to be a Dong Feng," Conrad says.

"Maybe a Land Cruiser," Galen offers.

"Whatever they are, they're fresh," I reply. "Maybe even in the last day or two."

It has been nearly a month since we left our own truck and Land Cruiser on the other side of the Chang Tang, and none of us are ready for this abrupt return to the artifacts of our civilization.

"Maybe they're a Chinese survey," I say. "Geologists or something that somehow managed to get a vehicle in here."

"I have a feeling we'll find out soon," Conrad replies.

Conrad's hunch proves accurate when, a quarter hour later, he stops abruptly and points downvalley.

"There's a building."

Even at a half-mile distance we can all distinguish on a bench above the riverbed a rectangular structure. I retrieve my binoculars, focus on what appears to be a tin-roofed shed, and then see more than just the building.

"There're also people," I say. "Someone is standing in front of that shed."

"Are they drokpa?" Jimmy asks.

"No, I think they're miners. There're fresh tailings just below him."

We continue, and as we near the hut we can see indeed it is a mine. In the erstwhile streambed a bulldozer has dammed two ponds where a large diesel-driven pump feeds a hose that climbs the gravel bank to a large sluice with a dozen men on each side shoveling dirt onto it. Spotting us, one of them signals in a welcoming gesture for us to ascend a trail that cuts up the tailing. We park our carts and ascend the path, and when we arrive the miners stop working; soon we are surrounded by two dozen men in patched work clothes who appear to be Central Asian Muslims, and who also appear to be as startled as they are excited to have four foreigners appear out of nowhere.

"Where did you come from?" one of them asks in Chinese. By his army surplus overcoat and comparatively clean pants, he appears to be the foreman.

"From that direction," Jimmy answers in Chinese, pointing to the southwest.

"There is no road that way," the foreman replies.

"Yes, no road," Jimmy confirms.

Jimmy's answer initiates a murmur among the crowd

"Are you from Pakistan?" another miner asks, revealing perhaps the limit of his frame of reference.

"No, we are from America."

There is again a murmur as the group absorbs this news.

"What are they saying?" I ask Jimmy.

"I don't know. They're speaking Uighur or something. But I'm guessing they're wondering what planet we dropped in from."

The foreman speaks again to Jimmy in Chinese.

"He wants to know if we're hungry," Jimmy translates. The foreman then indicates an adjacent camp of canvas tents. We follow him to what appears to be a second placer operation, where we are introduced to a middle-age man in clean work clothes. He wears a brimless white cap, and he has an undershirt whose white collar is visible above the neck of his tunic, giving him a clerical look. Behind his large tinted glasses his bright eyes are noting our appearance, which, even to these hardy prospectors, must look scrofulous. He motions us to a canvas tent where inside there are four metal-framed beds, a table in the middle, and a pot-bellied stove with a kettle of steaming water on its top-plate. He motions us to sit on the beds, and then serves us tea.

"Would you like something to eat?" he asks Jimmy in Chinese.

"We have food in our carts," Jimmy replies.

Jimmy turns to us and translates, but the hesitancy in his reply to our host's question has apparently belied his attempt at politeness because our host smiles and, reaching under his bed, retrieves a summer melon he then cuts with a large knife. He hands each of us a substantial slice, and I hold mine under my nose, breathing the fragrance of the peach-colored flesh that smells like a cross of honeydew and cantaloupe.

"Oh my god," Jimmy says as he takes his first bite.

Our host watches in apparent amusement as we finish our slices of melon. With a smile he cuts each of us a second portion.

"Ask him how long the mine has been here," I say to Jimmy as I eat my next slice.

"Three months," Jimmy translates. "It took twenty days for bull-dozers to cut the road to get the equipment in here."

"How long will they be here?" Galen asks.

"Five years. They expect to take a total of sixty thousand kilos of gold."

"How many miners are here?"

"Just over a hundred. They're all related, from an extended family in the Qinghai Province."

क

I ALREADY KNEW FROM THE READING I had done before our trek that Qinghai was home of the poachers who had been raiding the chiru in their calving grounds in the Arjin Shan and Kekexili Nature

Reserves, blinding them at night with high-powered lights, shooting them with late-model rifles, leaving the skinned carcasses in the heaps that William Bleisch would describe to me when I later met him. I would also learn later, when I interviewed Bleisch, that the white cap with no brim or embroidery worn by our host at the mine is the head-wear characteristic of the Muslim Hui people from the northern part of Qinghai, the same ethnic group who were slaughtering the chiru in the Arjin Shan Reserve.

There is no way to know if our host is aware of the poaching by the gold miners in Arjin Shan and Kekexili, but we guess that he must be; it seems likely he could even know some of the poachers personally, or that either he or his comrades could once have been poachers them-selves. Whether this is true we have no way of knowing, and we also decide not to ask them, as any discussion about our interest in chiru might lead them to suspect there are animals in this area.

What is undeniably true is that our host and his crew have been very gracious to us, and to show our appreciation we give them two sets of the balloon tires tied to the backs of our rickshaws that we have carried for over two hundred and fifty miles. The miners are sincerely thankful—the wheels will no doubt make excellent carts or wheelbarrows—and our host holds my hand with both of his as we thank him again for the melon. We gather for a group photo, and then we depart.

Below the mine we strain to pull our carts over berms of loose dirt bulldozed to make holding dams for the sluice ponds. We cross the river that this morning was clear and delicious when we dipped from it with our drinking cups; now it is turbid and unpotable. We have to double-team the carts—one pulling and one pushing—to get them out of the riverbed and onto the beginning of the gravel road that the miners told us, with unabashed pride, they managed, with their two bulldozers, to cut through the Kunlun Mountains in only twenty days. These Qinghai equivalents of Texas wildcatters are testament to how the embrace of private business initiative by the government these last twenty years is transforming at what seems a logarithmic rate not only most cities in China, but also much of the country's remaining wildlands. Our host told us he and several of his relatives had pooled their money—presumably made pursuing other schemes—to capitalize the gold mine. With so much invested in heavy equipment, and limited by weather to operating the mine only in the summer months, he told us they work round the clock in two twelve-hour shifts.

We struggle to pull the carts up the road as it ascends a steep hill, and once on top we decide to pitch our tents. It is bare and rocky, and the sky is dull and leaden. In the middle distance we can see the mine. By the time we finish dinner it is dark, and standing outside our tents as we sip our evening cocoa, we can see, illuminated by floodlights, the gray scar where the two bulldozers are scoop by scoop removing the hillside. There is a slow drift of air downvalley that brings with it the muffled clanking of the machines. This is not how we imagined returning to the civilization we left behind only a month ago, although that month even now seems measured best not by calendar days, but by a diurnal rhythm imprinted with the kinesthetic memory of walking sunrise to sunset across a wild open where there is yet no muffled clanking of machines.

JUNE 27

IT IS ALREADY LIGHT WHEN WE WAKE, but we feel no rush to break camp, as we plan to pull our carts at a slow but even pace down the road until near dark. When our carts are packed, we glance one last time at the gold mine, then leave. In an hour we stop to use the satellite phone to call the home number in Kashgar of the travel agent with whom I had arranged months before to have two vehicles waiting to meet us at a remote village on the north side of the Kunluns. Schaller's party had told us that if for any reason the vehicles were not there, we should take care if we then decided to walk out, because crossing the Taklimakan could be risky.

"There would be a chance you wouldn't make it," one of his party had warned us.

The travel agent's wife answers the phone, and Jimmy has a brief conversation with her in Chinese.

"He's in Urumchi today," Jimmy says, "but his wife gave me his cell phone number."

Jimmy then waits to get another three-satellite fix, enters the mobile number and in a few seconds is talking to our agent, who apparently is standing at a busy intersection between high-rise office buildings in the largest city in Xinjiang Province.

"It's all set," Jimmy says when his conversation is finished. "The vehicles are already on the way, and I have the GPS coordinates of the village."

"That's a little different than when Deasy was through here," Conrad says.

"But I like knowing I don't have to walk across the Taklimakan," Galen replies as he packs the satellite phone in his cart.

As for me, my sentiment is more in line with Conrad's, but I also share—as I know we all do—Galen's relief that our rendezvous is confirmed. We stop for lunch where a small clearwater stream crosses the road. Galen reports the elevation reading on the GPS is eleven thousand five hundred feet. Conrad starts our stove and is brewing coffee when we see in the distance a large orange truck crest a rise, disappear into a dip, and reappear close enough we can see it has two sets of double rear wheels. We conclude it must be a late-model Dong Feng even larger than the standard-issue truck that we used to transport our gear to the base of Tavr Kangri. When it reaches us the truck slows and stops, and the driver leans out the window while his two passengers lean over him, all three craning their necks and wearing on their faces expressions of disbelief.

"Ni hao ma," Jimmy says.

"Ni hao ma," the driver replies.

He asks where we are from, and Jimmy gives him the Cliff's Notes version of why we are sitting on the edge of this remote road, next to these bizarre-looking carts, drinking coffee. In reply, the driver explains to Jimmy he has contracted with the miners to truck drums of diesel fuel and other supplies to the operation, making two round trips a week. The driver and his companions wave as they depart, and when we finish our coffee we also leave, pulling our rickshaws into motion with the same ingrained reflex with which a donkey resumes hauling a cart.

We travel another hour and then stop again when Galen notices near the road the circinate horns of a blue sheep. These wild mountain sheep range from the central to the eastern Himalaya, and north across Tibet and the Kunluns, and the size of these horns suggests they once belonged to an old ram. We rest while Galen positions the horns in a bed of blue wildflowers and photographs them. I am surprised we haven't seen any of these animals on our trek, but then they favor the kind of steeper terrain that we, encumbered with our carts, have striven to avoid.

"The mine may also be a factor," Galen says, "Like we said, if there was any wildlife around here the miners have probably shot it for food."

Galen refers to an earlier conversation when we had concluded the most likely reason we had seen no wildlife in the vicinity of the mine was that the miners had hunted out any animals. We knew that in Kekexili and Arjin Shan the gold miners had, in addition to chiru, also shot hundreds of wild yak to supply meat to their work camps, and later to sell in Golmud and Xining, the two cities closest to the reserves. We also knew that in 1978 and 1979, in Arjin Shan, wild yak were shot extensively by the government geological survey, which sold the meat in local markets. Between 1958 and 1961 wild yak were hunted to supply meat against the famines that resulted from the devastating policies of the Great Leap Forward, and going back to the 1930s they had been hunted by nomads once they had acquired more sophisticated Russian, British, and Chinese army rifles.

At the turn of the previous century many of the explorers, including William Rockhill and Sven Hedin, described huge herds of wild yak. "The hills…were literally black with yak," Rockhill wrote in 1894; "yaks were remarkably numerous…occasionally we counted them by the hundred," Hedin noted in 1903. As I described earlier, in the Aru Basin, in 1990, Schaller was still able to find 681 wild yak; when Conrad, Jimmy, Galen, and I passed through at the beginning of our trip, we saw one. "Excessive hunting in this century has caused such a rapid decline in wild yak," Schaller wrote in *Wildlife of the Tibetan Steppe*, "that it is reminiscent of the decimation of bison in the American West."

Just as the bison have become an icon of the great grasslands that once covered the Midwest, Schaller has described the wild yak as the symbol of the "boundless space of the Chang Tang." Unlike the American Midwest, however, most of the alpine steppelands of the Tibetan Plateau have not been parceled and tilled, and if the number of drokpa allowed to graze in the Aru Basin—and elsewhere in the Chang Tang—were controlled to a minimum, and hunting were eliminated, it seems to me that the herds could still be restored—if not to their historic numbers, then at least to a population that would ensure they continued to roam the Chang Tang.

If this were to happen, it is likely to begin with the control of hunting, as this is the easier of the threats to the wildlife of the Chang Tang to contain; more challenging is to protect and save from development the animal's habitat. Elsewhere in the world, the loss of habitat is the dominant threat to endangered species. In North America, eighty-five percent of the over one thousand species currently on the endangered species list are there because of habitat loss; only seventeen percent of them are there because of overharvesting.[vi] In the Chang Tang, in addition to managing the movements of the drokpa, it will be arguably more important to prevent mineral exploitation—gold mining and oil drilling—with the attendant construction of roads and the ancillary consequence of drawing even more people into the area, including nomads who now own trucks purchased with money made from poaching chiru. If there is a lesson to be learned from North America, it is that habitat loss is incremental, and the war to save it is won by fighting one battle at time, oil concession by concession, gold mine by mine.

क

As GALEN LOWERS TO HIS KNEES to get another angle of the large horns of the blue sheep ram, I wonder whether the animal had fallen over at this spot in the floor of the rift from old age while grazing peacefully in this little meadow—maybe with the blue sheep equivalent of a stroke—or whether he had been shot. Somehow the latter seems the more likely possibility. Yesterday at the gold mine we tried to engage the miners in a discussion about wildlife—to see if we could find out whether they were hunting—and asked them if they had seen many wild animals in the area. Our host then told us there weren't any wild animals, and then he hastily changed the subject and asked us if we had seen any sign of gold in the area through which we had passed.

"There's no sign of gold anywhere but here," Galen replied just as quickly. Once Jimmy had translated Galen's answer, Galen had turned to us and said, "Fortunately it's true. I haven't seen any signs of mineralization until we got to this place."

Even if Galen is right and there isn't any gold beyond the location of the mine, the concern is that the miners, despite our report, will continue to push their vehicles, assisted by bulldozers where needed, deeper into the rift. If they were to do that, and if then they were to reach Shor Kul, it would take only a few hours to drive across the basin from one end to the other. Then if they were to continue their search for gold into the foothills on the south side of the basin, they would likely happen upon the same flat-bottomed streambed that had given us such easy access to the calving grounds. And we knew all too well that if that were to happen, the miners would discover gold of another sort.

Galen finishes taking his pictures, and we continue down the gravel road, following a terrace that extends for miles above the bottom of the rift. We arrive at the edge of a *nullah*—a deep gully sliced through the terrace by a lateral stream descending from the high mountains that border the north side of the rift—and we are impressed to see how the miners, with great skill, have bulldozed the road up and down the steep sides. We begin the descent, and without brakes on his cart it's a sketchy challenge for Conrad to get his rickshaw to the bottom of the gully. Then for all of us it's a leg-burning exercise to pull the carts up the opposite side, but I make each step without thinking about the effort because my mind is occupied with the speed with which the miners built this road, and consequently the ease with which they could extend it past the mine.

Schaller had told us at the outset of our adventure that it was important to document the calving grounds so the area could be protected before any poachers discovered it. In an unexpected way that possibility has taken a new and unforeseen urgency.

क

IN LATE AFTERNOON we arrive at a very deep nullah, and once we reach the bottom we find the road, instead of climbing the opposite side, continues down the gully until it reaches the river that flows down the floor of the rift. The road then follows the river's edge, and we take care not to torque the carts more than necessary to pull them over the rounded stones. By day's end we reach a point where the road once more leaves the river and begins a long ascent up another nullah toward the top of the terrace. We no more begin the climb than we pass a small bench covered in spring grass cropped by domestic goats to a lawn.

"What do you guys...think?" I ask between huffs.

"Looks good...to me," Jimmy replies.

"Me too," Conrad adds.

Galen agrees, and we park our carts and set up what will be, assuming tomorrow goes as planned, our last camp.

"What do we call this one?" Conrad asks.

"How about Golf Green?" I ask, and everyone agrees the name fits. When the tents are pitched I crawl in my shelter, spread my sleeping bag and lie on top, stretching the muscles in my back. Galen lies down and like me also seems to enjoy, at least for a few minutes, doing nothing.

"You know," I tell him, "for me, anyway, this trip is turning out to be one of the most physically demanding expeditions I've ever been on."

"Same here," he replies. "It's up there with the winter ski traverse of the Karakoram I did back in 1980. But if this one ties with that one as the hardest, it's in a class by itself when I think of everything together—the adventure, the team, the migration, the birthing grounds, the conservation component. I can see someday I might look back on this as the best trip of my life."

"I might too," I reply, pressing my left knee over right leg until my back pops. "Although right now the key word for making that judgment is 'someday.'"

When people ask me what it takes to be a mountaineer, I often reply that the only requirement is a short memory for pain. I might say the same for pulling two-hundred-fifty-pound rickshaws for a month across uninhabited steppelands with an average elevation over sixteen thousand feet. Often an expedition like this one looks good only on reflection, but that this adventure, even before it is over, is already one of Galen's favorites, bodes well for how the rest of us will judge it in the future when we think back on our days following the migration of the chiru.

It helps, of course, that we have achieved our main goal—locating and documenting the calving grounds—and for that we can pat ourselves on the back; but any self-congratulating needs to be counterpoised by the reminder that our effort is still a small part of a much larger international endeavor that, if it were to succeed and the chiru were again to multiply, would be an achievement for which the kudos should go less to those like us whose contribution is combined with a chance to work in the field than to those individuals devoting so much of their lives to saving an animal none of them have seen outside of George Schaller's photographs.

After our trek, when I traveled once more to China and then to India to talk to people dedicating their lives to saving chiru, I began to appreciate the irony of them working so hard to save an animal they are unlikely ever to see in flesh and blood. There are no chiru in any zoos in the world, and, because they have evolved so specifically to live in a habitat as rarefied as the northern half of the Tibetan Plateau, Schaller thinks it unlikely they will ever be held successfully in captivity.[vii] Other than a few hearty people willing to camp for weeks, often in snow, and to drive over rough roads that require them every few hours to dig out their vehicles from mud wallows at elevations of sixteen thousand feet—and with resources necessary to pay for such transport—no one in the world is going to see these animals. Yet around the world people like Ashok Kumar's team in India and Ian Knox and his associates in London are devoting much of their lives to this campaign to save chiru.

As so many of our planet's species eclipse into the sixth great spasm of extinction—what some conservation biologists have labeled the Pleistocene-Holocene Event, a name that for me, anyway, places the "event" in a geological context that invites the imagination to move forward into some millennial future when whatever perplexed hominid descendants survive this self-inflicted destruction may be looking back in an attempt to reconstruct how we could have so fouled our own nest—all of us concerned about the fate of the Earth reach out for any good news we can grab. As I did research to learn what I could about this international effort to save chiru, I began to see the people behind it as a ray of light in the penumbra that is expanding ever more widely across the Earth's formerly wild places. If there is hope for the chiru—and by extension, hope not only for others of the planet's endangered animals but, just as important, also for the wild places they inhabit—it resides increasingly in the efforts of this growing army of foot soldiers, individuals who, as David Brower described, "are like travelers lost in the wild, who want to go back to the last recognizable landmark and look again for the next."

Brower said that these individuals seek to restore wild places not in an effort to stop the clock, but rather in the knowledge they must keep the clock running. "There is nothing more important," Dave Foreman, the front-line environmentalist has stated, "[and] there is no greater ethical demand." In my own backyard, where my house is a short walk to the edge of the Los Padres National Forest, my neighbor, who is an expert birder, told me excitedly he recently saw a California condor "that was about as hard to spot as a low-flying B-52" fly over the neighborhood. In our small town I sometimes run into the individuals working on the condor restoration project, and they tell me about their setbacks when a bird dies from lead poisoning or is shot by a hunter. But they also tell me about the thrill of seeing these birds in the sky above our forest. Sophie Osborn, the woman in charge of the introduction of condors into the Grand Canyon, described being on the South Rim "when the sun was setting and the light was spectacular and five adult condors were circling around before heading down to roost, and several hundred park visitors began clapping...there is nothing more beautiful than a condor overhead, with the wind in its wings."

Around the world programs small and large are striving to save the Chinese alligator, the golden lion tamarin, the Yuma clapper rail, the Mediterranean monk seal, the Saker falcon—the list goes on—from the sixth spasm of extinction. Recently in Abu Dhabi a meeting of Arabs, concerned about the plight of the Saker in the wild, issued a declaration stating their policy to encourage the use of captive bred birds and discourage the importation of birds captured illegally or, even if technically imported legally, taken from the wild in ways that are unsustainable to the Saker populations. The meeting was hosted and funded by the heir apparent of the United Arab Emirates.

In Madagascar the aye-aye, a large lemur with batlike ears, is the only living representative of its family of primates. Like other lemurs on the island, it is threatened principally by destruction of its forest habitat, but in this case also by villagers who kill it because they believe the animal is a harbinger of bad luck. The plight of the aye-aye—and its unique taxonomic status—has been published widely by international conservation organizations, and a captive breeding program has increased the animal's population, allowing researchers to learn more about its habits, and at the same time to increase awareness among locals of the animal's unique attributes.

In the United States, the black-footed ferret, a mustelid (the family that includes weasels, badgers, otters, and skunks) that preys almost exclusively on prairie dogs, was by the late 1970s feared to be extinct. Then in 1981 a small population was discovered in Wyoming only nearly to die off a few years later from disease. As happened with the California condor, the surviving animals in the wild were captured and placed in a breeding program. Despite turf wars between the state and federal agencies involved, the program is succeeding, and the animals have been reintroduced successfully near prairie dog colonies in Montana and South Dakota.

When I was a kid, reading in the *Weekly Reader* the article about Martha the passenger pigeon, I also read about the efforts to save the nene, the Hawaiian goose that in the late 1950s was facing extinction. Over the next forty years, more than two thousand birds were bred in captivity and released into the wild. After our rickshaw trek, when I visited Ian Knox at the Wildlife Crime Unit in London, I left Scotland Yard and walked back to my hotel through St. James's Park, across from Buckingham Palace. On the greens opposite the pond I spotted a medium-size goose with a distinctly erect posture and a telltale series of brown-black stripes on its neck. Taking my binoculars from my daypack (you never know, even in a city, when you might see an interesting bird), I brought into focus a healthy-looking Hawaiian goose.

None of these stories should be misconstrued to conclude that any of these animals are safe. The aye-aye will have a future only if deforestation in Madagascar is stopped. The black-footed ferret can survive into the future only if the attitudes of ranchers and others in the Midwest toward prairie dogs change, and only if the stakeholders agree to preserve the habitat of both predator and prey. Even though over two thousand Hawaiian geese have been released to the wild, their populations are not self-sustaining because they continue to be preyed on by feral cats, dogs, and rats. It is accurate to conclude, however, that if not for the focused effort of individuals committed to the survival of these species, they, and so many hundreds of others worldwide, might exist today only as inanimate museum relics alongside Martha the passenger pigeon.

"Hope always is beyond optimism," Schaller told me. "As long as you have some options and choices for an area or for a species, the hope remains that you can help it. That's number one. Number two is, if you focus on a limited goal that you know is achievable, then you can see progress. But one doesn't get up in the morning, stretch one's arms and say, 'Today I'm going to save the world.' No, you say, 'Today I'm going to focus on trying, step by step, to protect some very specific part of it.'"

JUNE 28

WITH CAMP DISMANTLED and our carts packed, we once more trudge up the gravel road that now climbs steeply toward the top of the terrace. It is a struggle to advance the rickshaws each step, and I feel about the way I would waking early to start the day with a five-mile run up a steep trail.

"It's not the year," I tell myself as I strain against my waist harness like an ox pulling a plow, "it's the mileage."

To the side of the road the old camel trail is in places still visible, like the vestige of an older civilization underlying a new one. We all realize that had we been here a year ago pulling our carts along the camel trail, we would have been forced to portage our loads down and then up some of these nullahs, and this gully alone could have taken a half day; as we have little more than a one-day supply of food remaining, we may have been even hungrier than we are now by the time we reached our vehicles. Still, given the choice, I know I speak for the others in saying all of us would prefer to have the camel trail in trade for the gold mine.

We reach the top of the terrace and once more the road is nearly flat. I pull my cart alongside Conrad, and he gives me an affirming nod. This morning the sky is clear and the air is cool. Perhaps because of the denser air, or perhaps because of the fresh food at the mine, or perhaps because we have confirmed the vehicles will be waiting for us—or perhaps because of a combination of these things—we seem rejuvenated. Even Galen, despite his still-thinning upper body, seems to have more energy, and on one long section of the road that declines at a gentle grade we playfully trot our carts like horses pulling buggies on a fresh spring day. In the distance I see a small herd of animals that triggers an initial reaction to group them with kiang. Then I remember we are on the edge of civilization, and with binoculars I can see they are a group of five domestic donkeys. Soon we pass a motley collection of domestic camels that are losing their winter coats in wide sheets that in places hang off their sides as though they have been flayed by some colossal predator.

Studying the map, we estimate by late afternoon we can reach the vehicles waiting for us. We know it will then take several days to drive across the southern margin of the Taklimakan to Kashgar, but we also anticipate we will be comfortable in our vehicles, and there will likely be an oasis or two along the way where we can purchase fresh fruit and vegetables, and probably cold beer, although it seems unlikely any beer could taste as good as the cans Conrad had secreted in his cart.

The journey is nearly over, and even without the perspective of hindsight I know already I share Galen's opinion that although it may compare with perhaps one or two other expeditions I have done as one of the most physically demanding, it will stand alone, as Galen said, as the most fulfilling. My mind returns to the calving grounds, and, curiously, not to the female chiru and their newborns that I saw with my own eyes, but to that video clip Jimmy showed me our last evening in Maternity Ward Camp, the one where the baby chiru, blissfully unaware of Jimmy's presence, runs across the hillside then stops and looks directly into the camera as though it were a freeze-frame, its wide eyes circumscribed by its long lashes as though it were a Tibetan Bambi.

I continue to pull my cart down the gravel road, and the image of the baby chiru stays with me. All four of us know that nominally our journey is a success, but now I realize perhaps we will succeed in our larger goal if we can get our images, and our descriptions of the long migration the female chiru make year after year to have their babies in a safe haven, to stick in people's heads, just as this image seems to have stuck in mine.

"A mindworm instead of an earworm," I tell myself.

I no more than have the thought, however, and my earworm returns. Now I hear Ravel's Bolero and, at the same time, see the baby chiru run up and down the hillside, its colt legs gamboling in time to the flute and the clarinet and the muted trumpet.

"Not a bad way to finish the trip," I tell myself, smiling as, in my imagination, I watch the chiru and listen to the music, like a video clip that keeps playing over and over.

EPILOGUE

क

TWO WEEKS AFTER WE RETURNED HOME, following a long flight from Kashgar to Urumchi to Beijing and back to the United States, I drove to Galen's house in Bishop, California, to meet with George Schaller. Jimmy and Conrad couldn't make it, but Conrad had collated all the numbers and locations of our chiru sightings, and Galen and I were to review these data with Schaller so he could prepare a report for the *Gnusletter*, a periodical published by the World Conservation Union (IUCN) and distributed to antelope specialists around the globe.[1] Schaller then intended to draft a brief of the report to submit to the Chinese that would include a proposal they create a new nature reserve to encompass the calving grounds, and as soon as possible dispatch a wildlife patrol to the gold mine, to make sure the miners stayed in the mine.

Driving alone, I crossed the High Sierra over Tioga Pass, stopping in the Yosemite backcountry at Lake Tenaya to have a picnic. The evening before I had dinner in San Francisco at Zuni Café, noted for its signature dish of free-range chicken oven-roasted over a bed of sourdough tidbits marinated in a vinaigrette mixed with currants and mustard greens. Thinking ahead, I had ordered two chickens, one of which I ate in the restaurant, and the other which, at lake's edge, I arranged on a cloth spread over a flat-topped granite boulder. I also had a small ice chest with a half-full bottle of 1997 Sanford Chardonnay that I finished off, drinking out of the bottle with one hand while I ate the chicken with the other. When I finished I went for a swim, floating on my back while I watched a group of beginning rock climbers ascend a granite dome next to the lake, following a route that I remembered ascending when I had started climbing over thirty years before.

I was gaining weight, but still I had five more pounds to go before I was back to normal. For the three days we spent driving across the Taklimakan, and for the three days we then spent in Kashgar, we ate for lunch and dinner great platters of roasted lamb shish kabob with attendant fruits and vegetables, and drank prodigious amounts of beer. Our gluttony culminated our last day in Kashgar in a private dining room where we reclined on Persian carpets around a low table heaped with fruits and nutmeats while three young women brought dishes of lamb and various fowls while another woman with black oval eyes and pomegranate-colored lipstick, dressed in a pomegranate-colored gown with a belt of embroidered gold that wrapped tightly around her trim waist, performed just for us a traditional Uighur dance.

"Should I be taping this?" Jimmy asked.

"I don't know. It might not go down that well at headquarters," I replied, referring to National Geographic's budget office.

"Not to mention our wives," Conrad added while lowering to his mouth a large bunch of claret-colored grapes.

Back home, Jimmy submitted the tapes to National Geographic's Television Division, Galen expressed his films to the Illustrations Department, and I started to organize my journal entries to write the article for the magazine's editors. Then, in mid-July, we were lucky to fit into our busy schedules this two-day meeting with George Schaller. He was on the West Coast with his wife, Kay, visiting their son, and he was able to return via California before leaving on another trip to the grass plains of Mongolia, where he was overseeing a long-term study of the region's wildlife. Galen and his wife, Barbara, were also scheduled to leave the day after our meeting, to teach a two-week photography workshop in Alaska.

We spent the two days huddled over maps and reviewing carefully all of our major chiru sightings, and also the route of the migration and the probable paths the various arms of the migration took beyond Dispersion Camp. George was very appreciative of our effort and told us our findings—and our documentation of the calving grounds— were a substantive contribution to the understanding of the chiru's natural history, and would be important to his proposals to the Chinese to create the new reserve. To celebrate, Galen woke me up the next morning before dawn to go on a five-mile trail run. He was still skinny, and I wasn't sure he would ever regain his upper-body muscle, but he ran like an antelope, bounding down a steep hill at a pace that would challenge a thirty-year-old marathoner.

Two weeks later—a month after we returned—I was home outside in our patio celebrating my birthday with several neighbors. One friend who is a celebrity television chef showed me how to grill oysters in their shells on the barbecue. I was in the kitchen preparing coffee when the phone rang, and even though I had intended to let the answering machine pick up calls during our party, for some reason I felt motivated to lift the receiver. It was David Breashears. His voice was high and broken, as voices always seem to be when I get calls like that one, or on the occasions when I have had to make the calls myself.

"Who was it?" I asked.

"Galen and Barbara. A small-plane crash...late last night...just outside of Bishop...coming home from their trip to Alaska."

I carried the butler's tray with the cups of coffee to my guests, and whispered the news to my wife, who covered her mouth with her hand. I excused myself and went to the small study I keep in the corner of our property, where I write. I sat in my reading chair and sipped my coffee. Galen and I had been tent mates each night of our trek. When you lose somebody so suddenly after having spent so much time with them, it creates a surreal sensation in which you try to fill their absence with a palpable presence. I was back with Galen and Barbara, sitting on their patio with George and Kay, the last evening of our rendezvous. The Rowells had invited several wildlife biologists from the area to a fine dinner that Barbara had organized with a local caterer.

Barbara was bringing a butler's tray of coffee to her guests, just as I had done for mine only minutes before. I was sitting next to Galen, and we were both watching her cross the lawn. She wore a light cotton summer dress, and she was tan. She carried the tray with poise, for she owned what my wife refers to as natural style. Galen turned toward me, and I leaned my ear to him.

"Isn't she beautiful," he said.

My memory of our adventure will always be bittersweet, framed as it is by the loss of Galen and his wife, who was such a large part of his life. Fortunately I think Shakespeare had it wrong when he wrote, "The good (that men do) is oft interred with their bones." Perhaps Shakespeare would have felt different had he witnessed how, in Galen's case, a man's good is memorialized forever in a body of stunning visual work.

Our story came out the following April in NATIONAL GEOGRAPHIC, and who from our team could ever have imagined that on the cover the title of our piece would read "Galen Rowell's Final Trek." In a tribute to Galen in the back of the issue the celebrated wildlife photographer Frans Lanting, a close friend of Galen's for over twenty years, wrote that Galen "infused landscape photography with a whole new energy. He was so physically fit he could become part of the wild landscapes he photographed, hiking through them at great speed or hanging from a rock wall while photographing as no one had before. Now there are hundreds of photographers following him."

To both inspire and guide the generations that follow you is the only legacy that has substance. I found solace remembering that while our crossing of the Chang Tang was Galen's final trek, it was also, as he had told me that evening in our tent, his most fulfilling. By that he meant, of course, that instead of a mountain climbing expedition whose goal is necessarily framed by ego-driven endeavor, our journey had a goal that was beyond simply trekking where no one had trekked. As George Schaller had told us, we had made a true contribution.

क

THROUGH THE CHINESE REPRESENTATIVE of the Wildlife Conservation Society, Schaller submitted to government officials in Xinjiang Province the findings from our trek, along with the proposal to create the new reserve, to "prohibit all guns and traps in the gold mining camps and elsewhere in the region" and to "place an anti-poaching unit and guard post in the Serak Tus valley (the "rift")…from at least mid-May to mid-August to prevent poaching and disturbance of antelope at the calving grounds."

"Now we must wait and be patient," he told me. "These things take time."

At National Geographic, as the Television Division edited the video we had turned in, they had the idea to expand the story by covering the efforts in China to capture the poachers and in India to arrest the dealers. They sent Lisa Ling, the on-camera host of *Ultimate Explorer*, and Gary Scurka, the segment's producer, to New Delhi, where the two filmmakers met Ashok, and with his help devised a plan to pose as an American couple in the market for shahtoosh scarves.

"It was my first undercover work," Lisa told me after they returned, "and I was a little nervous."

Ashok and his group had been watching a high-end shop in the five-star Meridien Hotel in Delhi that they suspected was trafficking in shahtoosh shawls. Gary modified Lisa's handbag so that it contained a video camera with a tiny lens that on the outside looked like a button or a rivet; she was also wired with a hidden tape recorder connected to a radio transmitter that Ashok would monitor. Lisa took a deep breath, and she and Gary entered the shop. She set her handbag down so that the video camera could capture the transaction. To gain the shopkeeper's confidence, she and Gary first bought a carpet. Then she said she was in the market for shahtoosh shawls, and she was interested in purchasing at least five. To her surprise the shopkeeper replied that he had twenty, and produced one that he had on hand.

"I knew immediately it was shahtoosh," Lisa said. "I have felt shahtoosh before, and truly there is no fabric like it."

The shopkeeper asked the couple to return the next day and he would have an assortment of shahtoosh shawls from which they could choose. Lisa and Gary returned to their hotel confident the shopkeeper would soon be facing a minimum jail sentence of three years. Then next morning the *Times of India* ran an article announcing the government seizure of a large shipment of shawls. Lisa called the shopkeeper to confirm their purchase, and he said that because of the report in the newspaper he didn't want to sell the shawls. He told Lisa he hadn't known they were illegal.

"Yeah, right," she said when she hung up the phone.

Lisa was about to give up, then decided next day she would return to the shop one more time. She told the owner she and Gary were still interested in the shawls, but that they were leaving India that afternoon. To her surprise, the shopkeeper said he could still get the shawls. Lisa then told him that since she was leaving, she would have a friend of hers come by to close the deal.

Working with the CBI—India's equivalent of the FBI—Ashok and his associates arranged for an undercover agent to pose as Lisa's friend. For her security, they decided not to give her a camera but to wire her with a tiny microphone and radio transmitter. The police would be waiting outside the shop, and when the undercover agent said, "These are real shahtoosh," that would be the signal for the police to swoop in.

The agent entered the shop and introduced herself. The shopkeeper wanted her to come to his warehouse, where he had the shawls and she could select the ones she wanted. She told him she wasn't comfortable doing that, and wanted him to bring the shawls to the shop. He said okay, and she waited. Finally he returned with the shawls, and when she felt them and said, "Yes, these are real shahtoosh," the police moved in. Then somehow, in the confusion that followed, the shopkeeper managed to escape, and the police were left to arrest only the store's two assistants. Lisa and Gary were devastated.

"We were emotionally wrung out," Gary said. "The shopkeeper, who had twenty or thirty shawls, got away. It's not an easy thing to do, to see [the two assistants] led away by the police, knowing you had some involvement in it. Lisa and I looked at each other and said, 'I don't like this.'"

The television show ended with footage National Geographic obtained from a Chinese cameraman that showed a wildlife patrol in the eastern Chang Tang pursuing chiru poachers. There was grim footage of the skinned carcasses of females who had been shot shortly after they had given birth to baby chiru that were then condemned to die. There was also footage of Chinese officials interrogating poachers they had caught. The sequence ended with a scene of a tall young man with short-cropped hair facing his interrogator. His eyes were downcast, and he was scared.

"How old are you?" the interrogator asked.

"Fifteen."

"How old?"

"I'm fifteen years old. I came here to catch antelope."

"How many antelope have you caught?"

"On the truck there are more than thirty skins. They promised to give me seven hundred yuan every month."

"What does your family livelihood depend on?"

"It depends on me," the young man answered nervously. He avoided eye contact, and he looked as you would expect any frightened fifteen-year-old to look who was in serious trouble, probably for the first time.

"My whole family depends on me," he said again, his voice cracking as he wiped tears from his eyes with his coat sleeve.

When I went to National Geographic's headquarters in Washington, D.C., to tape the interview for the TV show with Lisa, she said this had been one of her hardest assignments.

"There's no black and white answer," she told me. "You see these people trying to make a living, and many of them aren't really bad people, but still they're caught in this web. Then you see the piles of skinned chiru carcasses, and then you see the footage you guys got of the mother chiru and their babies, and you know if nothing's done these animals are going to be extinct. So you just take a deep breath and tell yourself, okay, this is tough, but this is how it's got to be dealt with."

क

IN ADDITION TO FIFTEEN-YEAR-OLD KIDS in China and young assistant shopkeepers in India, the lives of the craftspeople in Kashmir were also caught in this web when Ashok and the Wildlife Trust of India finally succeeded in their long campaign to persuade the Kashmiri legislature to ban the weaving of shahtoosh shawls. I was curious to learn firsthand about the livelihoods of these Kashmiris, so after our trek, when I visited India to meet Ashok and Belinda, I took a few extra days and traveled to Srinagar.

Ashok had been monitoring the political situation to judge whether it was safe for me to make the trip, and as it had been several weeks since there had been any firefights or bombings, he thought I could get in and out without incident. The taxi ride from the airport to the hotel was nevertheless disquieting. Using the skills I had developed making quick counts of chiru, I tallied over nine hundred heavily armed soldiers lining the streets. There were tanks and armored personnel carriers parked downtown, and at one busy intersection soldiers on top of a sandbag bunker tracked my taxi with a turret-mounted 50-caliber machine gun as my driver, complaining about the drop in tourism, nonchalantly sped around the corner.

Other than that, the timing of my visit was good. Ashok and the Wildlife Trust had just completed their two-year effort to survey every individual in the Vale of Kashmir involved in the shahtoosh industry.[ii] They had done this both to bring a realistic assessment to counter the Kashmiri government's claim that "hundreds of thousands of people" would be out of work following the ban, and also as a first step to encourage the Indian government to assist finding alternative incomes for those Kashmiris who were indeed affected.

When I arrived at my hotel I was met by a young Kashmiri named Riyaz who had assisted in the survey. He gave me a copy of the forty-eight-page report just off the press that was then being distributed in Delhi to politicians and law enforcement officers, and in Kashmir to trade representatives of the weavers and wool buyers.

"We surveyed about forty-five thousand people in the wool and weaving industry here in Kashmir," Riyaz said, "but we found only about fifteen thousand of those were directly involved in shahtoosh production."

Looking through the booklet, handsomely printed with photographs of various craftspeople attending their tasks, I was surprised by the degree of specialization required to make the shawls. In addition to weavers and spinners, there are workers who apply a special starch to strengthen the yarn that otherwise is too fine to weave, washermen who remove the starch after the shawl is woven, sorters who divide the yarn by strength—with the stronger yarn strengthened even more with a resin so it can then be used in the warp, and the finer but weaker yarn going into the weft—other men who make the warp, women who then guide the yarn into the warp to prepare it for the weaver. There are specialists whose only job is to clip the finished shawls; others to darn any imperfections; others to dye the shawls that are colored; and others to embroider the finest shawls that then sell in Milan and Paris and London for more than $15,000.

We finished our tea, and then it was time to begin my own survey, but I was concerned. I was the only Caucasian in the hotel, and thinking I might make an attractive target for insurgent kidnappers, I wanted to remain as inconspicuous as possible. Like a fish finding security in a large school, Riyaz and I hired one of the thousands of three-wheel "auto-rickshaws" that congest the streets of Srinagar. To remain out of view, I hunkered down in the enclosed cab as we sped through the old part of town on our way to visit one of Srinagar's most accomplished master weavers.

"I am Gulum Rasool Mir," the weaver said when we were introduced. He appeared to be in his mid-fifties with short-cropped gray hair and a manicured salt-and-pepper beard. He had large deerlike eyes behind thin metal-frame glasses and wore a long sleeve white shirt that was crisply laundered and framed by a fine-woven wool vest. His hands were lean yet strong, and his fingers looked like a pianist's. Everything about him—his slow but purposeful walk, his gentle yet firm handshake, his open eyes that looked directly at me—suggested the calm focus of a master craftsman.

We ascended the stairs in his house to a small workroom that held his loom, its wooden parts polished from the years of use and gleaming in the light of a side window overlooking a courtyard. The loom held a partially completed shawl, and Mr. Mir sat down and demonstrated how it worked.

"Is this shahtoosh?" I asked.

"No, this is pashmina, but it is the finest pashmina that is made. There has been no shahtoosh wool now for over a year."

Mr. Mir explained that in addition to his weaving, he is currently the general secretary of the Kashmir Valley Shahtoosh and Pashmina Shawl Weavers Association. Recognizing that shahtoosh is illegal, his group is working to develop what is effectively a brand name for the finest pashmina, and following the release of the survey that Riyaz and his workers completed, Mr. Mir was hopeful the government would give his group a grant to promote the idea of branding pashmina.

"We are thinking of calling it 'Kashmir Pashmina Special.' What do you think?"

"I think it might be better to have one short word," I replied, trying to be polite while still letting him know what I thought. "Kind of like the French have developed the brand Champagne. It might not be as effective if it was 'Northern France Bubbly Wine.'"

"Yes, we realize the name is too long," Mr. Mir replies with a smile and nod.

He explained that even with a good brand, he and the weavers he represents don't expect to make as much money weaving pashmina as they could with shahtoosh, but they are also hopeful—again with government help—to create a cooperative that would purchase pashmina directly from Tibet or Mongolia, eliminating the middlemen from whom they now obtain wool.

I thanked Mr. Mir, and then Riyaz and I continued in our auto-rickshaw through the narrow alleyways of Srinagar's old town to the office of a wool merchant. He was an older man, perhaps in his late sixties. His feet were bare, and he wore a knitted cap and ankle-length caftan. He served us tea while in one corner of the room an assistant, sitting cross-legged behind a large balance beam, weighed small clumps of raw wool that he then handed to Muslim women dressed in black burkas, while another assistant noted in a large ledger their names and the weights of the clumps of wool they received.

"The women are the spinners," Riyaz explained. "They take the wool home and spin it into yarn, then bring it back and it is weighed again.

They have to return the same weight of wool they receive. Then they are paid for the spinning."

With Riyaz translating, I asked the wool merchant how long he had been in this business.

"He says his family has been wool dealers going back to his great-grandfather," Riyaz translated. "Before that, he doesn't know."

"Does he believe that chiru are killed to get shahtoosh wool, or does he still think it is collected from bushes and rocks?"

"No, he has seen the pictures of the dead chiru, so he believes it, and he says they do not support the killing of animals. But he says in the old days, before the demand was so big, the wool they received was collected from what the animals shed naturally. Fifty years ago no one killed the animals."

"Explain that everyone believed that, but the truth is the animals have always been killed, only now there are so many being killed that soon there may not be any more animals."

"He still thinks there is some way the wool can be collected," came the reply. "Maybe they can be raised."

"Tell him people have tried that but it didn't work."

"He says there must be an alternative of some kind," Riyaz translated. "They cannot make as much money from pashmina as they can from shahtoosh."

"Explain that if they keep weaving shahtoosh all the animals will be killed, and then there won't be any shahtoosh or any animals."

Riyaz didn't need to translate the old man's answer, because there was no answer. The old man sipped his tea, and unlike Mr. Mir the weaver, he did not look me in the eye.

क

ALL THE WEAVERS AND WOOL MERCHANTS I met in Srinagar told me that since the ban became official they were no longer weaving shahtoosh or selling shahtoosh wool or yarn. After I returned from Kashmir, however, a reporter for the Indian newspaper The Pioneer went undercover in Srinagar, posing as a buyer interested in shahtoosh. She found a shop that offered to sell her several shawls, and the shop owner even arranged for her to visit weavers who were making two shawls. The weavers told the reporter there were still thousands of shahtoosh shawls a year woven in Srinagar, making me suspect that on my visit to Kashmir what I had been told by the weavers and wool traders I met was what they thought I wanted to hear. Even if the number is exaggerated—as seems likely—and even if there are only perhaps a thousand shawls a year still being made, that nevertheless represents the lives of between three thousand and five thousand chiru, and that is more animals than we saw that morning after the snowstorm on the plain next to the calving grounds.

"The problem has not gone away," Ashok wrote me after I returned from my visit to India. " The Indian state wildlife department has just made the biggest seizure in their history: 215 kilograms of pure shahtoosh wool that had crossed the porous border from Nepal to India. This quantity of raw wool would represent the killing of nearly three thousand Tibetan antelopes. Just as bad, there is evidence that a large consignment of raw shahtoosh has crossed over from Tibet to Nepal, waiting to be smuggled into Kashmir."

Despite the bad news, the ban on shahtoosh in Kashmir has forced the manufacture of the shawls to go underground, and that can only make it more difficult for the trade to continue. Also, when I talked to the weavers and wool merchants in Srinagar, some of them, at least, seemed to have a genuine empathy for the chiru—now that they knew the true origin of the wool—and they were committed to developing as a substitute a high-grade pashmina.

There is also good news from other fronts of the anti-shahtoosh campaign. The enforcement division of the U.S. Fish and Wildlife Service told me that the cases of shahtoosh coming through their office was declining. In one of their more recent seizures, a shop in West Hollywood was fined $175,000 for selling shawls—one of the biggest fines ever in an endangered species case—and the owner was forced to run public service ads exposing the source of shahtoosh in Harper's Bazaar and Vanity Fair. The fashion magazines were also on their own joining the chorus to save the Tibetan antelope: Vogue published a sidebar promoting environmentally sustainable alpaca shawls as "anti-shahtoosh" and "ecologically correct."

The news from China is also encouraging. The summer after our trek the number of wildlife officials on patrol in Kekexili was increased to over a hundred, and for the first time since the reserve was created there was neither evidence of any poaching nor apprehension of any poachers. Arjin Shan reported the same positive lack of encounters. The following spring Schaller returned to the southeastern quadrant of the Chang Tang Nature Reserve, and in an area where in the early 1990s he surveyed just under four thousand chiru, this time he counted over six thousand.

"This area is going in the right direction," he told me. "Patrols are searching for poachers, guns are being confiscated, and education is creating awareness about wildlife laws among nomads and officials. The Tibet Forestry Department has obviously made a dedicated and successful effort to protect the wildlife. But in the other areas of the Chang Tang that are still uninhabited, where there's no patrols, poaching is still continuing in a big way. I would say, as a whole, the population is still probably going down. But that in some areas the numbers are going up shows you what can be done."

Then, after he had returned from his survey, Schaller received a press release stating the Chinese were considering making chiru the official animal when, in 2008, they host the Olympic Games. If that were to happen, the chiru might enjoy a prominence as ubiquitous as the panda bear.

क

MEANWHILE, IN THE UNITED STATES, Lisa Ling told me our TV show, called "Deadly Fashion," had one of the highest ratings of any recent program in the series. After the magazine article in NATIONAL GEOGRAPHIC appeared, Jimmy, Conrad, and I were interviewed on "All Things Considered," and the NPR producer later told us it also had elicited an unusually high response from radio listeners. The National Geographic Society built an exhibit about our expedition that was displayed in the central foyer of their Washington, D.C., headquarters, and it also was well attended. There were several large-format prints of Galen's images, a shahtoosh shawl behind glass that was on loan from the U.S. Fish and Wildlife Service—who had confiscated it—and my rickshaw, loaded with my gray duffel, tent, water bladders, my ice ax secured to the side and my filthy jacket tied to the top. Before leaving Kashgar we had packed the rickshaws in cardboard boxes, taken them to the Chinese post office, paid $1,200 for postage, and mailed them home. Five weeks later a clerk in my little hometown post office called and said I had a box from China I needed to come down and claim because it was too big to deliver.

When I was in Washington to tape the TV interview with Lisa, I stopped by the exhibit to have a look. A group of school kids on a field trip were walking through the display. I was standing in front of my trusty rickshaw when the kid standing next to me said, "Hey mister, aren't you the guy in these photos?"

"Yeah, that's me."

"Is that your cart there? "

"Yeah, that's my rickshaw."

"Wow, it's pretty cool."

"It's like a good friend. It took care of me when I needed it to."

"These animals are cool, too. They walk a long ways, don't they?"

"Yeah, a long ways," I replied.

"You think they're going to be okay?"

"It's hard to say for sure," I told him as I looked at the exhibit, at my old rickshaw, at Galen's photos, at the kids studying them. "But I think so. Yeah, I think they're going to be okay."

POSTSCRIPT

AS THIS BOOK WAS GOING TO PRESS, George Schaller received an e-mail from the Forestry Department in Xinjiang that they were actively considering his proposal to make a reserve to encompass the calving grounds of the western populaton of chiru. The outdoor clothing company Patagonia, Inc. generously offered to fund for the first year a team of wildlife officers who will be positioned at the gold mine. In future years, this patrol will greatly appreciate help from outside contributions. If you are interested in supporting this effort, please make contributions payable to the Wildlife Conservation Society, and send them to WCS, 2300 Southern Blvd., Bronx, New York, 10460, Attn. International Asia Program for Tibetan Antelope Conservation.

ENDNOTES

PROLOGUE

[i] See my book describing this journey, *Below Another Sky* (Henry Holt, New York, 2000). This adventure was more a pilgrimage, what Peter Matthiessen calls "a journey of the heart": I was taking a nineteen-year-old woman, Asia Wright, on an adventure across Tibet designed to summon memories of her father, a close friend who had died in my arms following an avalanche on a remote peak in Tibet when Asia was only a baby. Asia and I eventually reached that mountain and together scaled the flank of the peak where we found her father's grave and together reburied his exposed bones; along the way I had also taught Asia about the father she never knew. I took her to the Aru Basin because I wanted her to see true wilderness; I knew that was something her father would have wanted her to experience had he lived.

[ii] Only three of these early explorers passed through or near Aru Basin: H. Bower in 1891, H. H. Deasy in 1897, and C. G. Rawling in 1903. Many of these early explorers were attempting to reach the forbidden city of Lhasa, and all failed. For further reading, consult Peter Hopkirk's *Trespassers on the Roof of the World* (Jeremy P. Tarcher, Inc., Los Angeles, 1982).

PART ONE
THE MIGRATION
CHAPTER ONE

[i] I learned after our expedition there is an initiative in Wyoming and Montana to convert cattle ranches to wildlands that is called The Big Open. My apologies to anyone who finds my use of the name confusing with its association with eastern Montana, but I found no other phrase that reflected the sense of vastness I felt in the Chang Tang.

[ii] Schaller has written two books describing his studies in the Chang Tang. *Tibet's Hidden Wilderness, Wildlife and Nomads of the Chang Tang Reserve* (Harry N. Abrams, New York, 1997) is a larger

format book with color photographs. The reference here is from the more academic *Wildlife of the Tibetan Steppe* (University of Chicago Press, 1998).

iii In the 1930s Terry Moore and three companions from the Harvard Mountaineering Club made the first ascent of Minya Konka, on the eastern margin of the Tibet Plateau. It was one of the more significant climbs of the era: It took the four of them over a year to travel to China by steamship, cross the country by train, and ascend the Yangtze by boat, then walk overland, through territory controlled by warlords, to the peak. Then, because of war and revolution, the region closed to outsiders. In 1980, when China next opened to mountaineers, I was fortunate to be on a team returning to Minya Konka, as we were the first foreign visitors to the region around the peak since Moore had been there fifty years before.

iv In an early draft of this book I used the word "sanctuary" in this sentence to describe the Aru, but Schaller, proofreading with his characteristic focus on accuracy, objected. "It may have once been a sanctuary," he said, "but as it is now, you need another word." "Stronghold?" I asked. "Yes, that will work."

v This is from Schaller's *Wildlife of the Tibetan Steppe* (page 283), where he also observed that the chiru, "isolated on the Tibetan Plateau, [have] evolved there and adapted to the rigors of the Chang Tang, needing only space to roam, scant forage, and special places to give birth and spend the winter. In the coming century, when saving biological diversity will be humankind's most important challenge, special taxa, such as the chiru, must remain the focus of conservation."

vi When Galen first presented this image to the public, in a slide show at the American Alpine Club, photographers sitting near me whispered "sandwich"—suggesting, in the days before Photoshop, that Galen had overlapped two photographs—but the truth is he saw the rainbow forming, then sprinted several hundred yards and scrambled up a hill to position the rainbow so that it arced into the Potala.

vii There is now evidence that my musing may actually be inaccurate regarding our species' cultural evolution from hunters and gatherers to pastoralists to agriculturalists. "It's the reverse of what people commonly think," Schaller told me. "Agriculture and animal husbandry developed at the same time in the Near East. People took their animals seasonally up high for better grazing, and then they just stayed there."

viii The Norwegian survey team, from the University of Tromso, Norway, who visited the Aru in 2000 and again in 2001, estimated that nomads in the Aru had about 15,000 head of sheep, goats, and domestic yak in the basin. At the same time, once the females and newborns had returned from the calving grounds, the team estimated there were 9,000 to 11,000 chiru in the basin, but only seventy wild yaks.

CHAPTER TWO

i In my interviews for this book with George Schaller, he cautioned me to make a clear distinction between the conservation work he was doing (and that we were assisting him to do) and what he felt were the more polemic positions of the animal rights advocates. "I think wearing furs of endangered species is a complete no," he said. "The spotted cat fur craze in the eighties, for example, led to the extirpation of jaguars in several areas of their range. But wearing a mink coat, to my mind, is fine if the mink comes from farm-raised animals."

CHAPTER THREE

i See *Where Have All the Birds Gone?* by John Terborgh, Princeton University Press, 1989.

ii In view of Galen's death one month after our return, I was at first reluctant to include this anecdote, but then I changed my mind, realizing it reveals one of Galen's strengths: his tireless capacity for hard physical work. I also realized it was an attribute to inspire us all.

iii The drokpa nomads are not the only group poaching chiru. In the early 1990s much of the poaching was done by corrupt officials and army personnel, and beginning in the late nineties and
continuing today, the worst of the poaching is by organized gangs from the Qinghai Province.

iv The summit of the caldera is already above 6,000 meters, so it seemed to me possible that the
prehistorical summit could have been higher than Everest. I asked George Schaller his opinion,
and he thought this very unlikely. He is probably correct, as the geology of the Tibetan Plateau
is in main part a secondary reaction to the collision of the Indian and Asian continental plates,
and intuitively one would suspect the most dramatic uplift of this geology to be found along the
frontline of the event. Still it would be somewhat easy to calculate with a surveyor's theodolite
the prehistoric height of this volcano, assuming at some stage of its geological life it was an
unbreached cone, so I leave it here as a carrot for some future geologist.

PART TWO

THE BIRTHING GROUNDS

CHAPTER FOUR

i In World War II both Mackiernan and Bessac worked in China and central Asia for the Office
of Strategic Services—OSS—which after the war re-formed into the CIA. By then Mackiernan
was posted vice consul to the U.S. Consulate in Tihwa—later renamed Urumchi—as a cover to
his real mission: to spy on the Russians' nascent program to develop an atomic bomb and their
accompanying effort to mine uranium in northern Xinjiang. Bessac was allegedly in China on
a Fulbright scholarship, but very probably working undercover to assess the political situation
in Inner Mongolia. As the Communists in China became increasingly victorious over the
Nationalists, both men found themselves fleeing Tihwa along with three white Russians who
had been working for Mackiernan. The five men headed south by camel and horse across the
Taklimakan, then from November 1949 until March 1950 wintered on the north side of the
Kunluns. With improving weather they began an arduous trek with camels and horses across
the eastern Chang Tang toward Lhasa, surviving on chiru, kiang, and wild yak they were able to
shoot. By then Mackiernan was almost certainly under orders to reach Lhasa and assess whether
the United States should support Tibet in what seemed an inevitable confrontation with China.
In what was probably a delay caused by internal friction between the State Department and the
CIA—disputes that in turn were linked to the paranoia from Senator McCarthy's accusations
that Communists had infiltrated the United States government at high levels—the commu-
niqué to Lhasa requesting safe passage for Mackiernan and Bessac was late arriving. Tibetan
border patrols, under orders to shoot any outsiders, attacked the caravan, killing Mackiernan
and two of the Russians. Bessac and the surviving Russian reached Lhasa, where Bessac was
received by the Dalai Lama and the ruling regents as a possible hope for American support
against the pending Chinese invasion.

George Schaller originally told me this story, when I was planning my first trip to the Chang
Tang, and later I found an article about it published in 1950 in Life magazine. The Life piece was
misleading, however, but in 2002 Thomas Laird published Into Tibet, describing this adventure
and suggesting that Bessac's interactions with the theocratic government in Lhasa could have
spurred the timetable of the Chinese invasion of Tibet, motivated by Peking's desire to establish
hegemony before the United States could arm the Tibetans. In researching his book Laird was
able to obtain some CIA and State Department documents under the Freedom of Information

Act, but found most either destroyed or otherwise unavailable, and the CIA still refusing to discuss Mackiernan's true mission, other than to admit he was the first CIA agent to be killed in action. Bessac, today living in Montana, where he is a retired university professor, still insists he was only a Fulbright scholar, and according to Laird gets testy when anyone suggests otherwise.

[ii] After we returned I found this quote in *Roughing It*. Mark Twain actually said "This solemn, silent, sailless sea." He may have coined that last word to reflect his frustration trying to sail a boat across the lake with no wind. Galen may also have forgotten Mark Twain, in the same paragraph, called the area surrounding Mono Lake a "lifeless, treeless, hideous desert," and the lake "this lonely tenant of the loneliest spot on earth." Galen was accurate comparing Heishi Beihu with Mono Lake in that they are both saline desert lakes with no outlets, but I found Mark Twain's dismissal of Mono Lake and our awe of Heishi Beihu representative of the evolution of the American moral attitude toward the natural world, from disregard for any landscape that didn't have an obvious value to our own species, to a regard for the intrinsic worth of any wild land and its wild animals that is increasingly becoming more common, albeit in fits and starts, in America's attitude toward the wild earth.

iii Ladakh is the small region in the Himalaya in the eastern half of Indian Kashmir. There is a small population of chiru that wanders into Ladakh for two or three months, in the spring, and this group is the westernmost extension of the animal's range.

CHAPTER FIVE

[i] This quote was taken from an article by Judy Mills, a senior program officer with the World Wildlife Fund formerly based in Hong Kong, who was one of an increasingly large cadre of journalists working to publicize the plight of the chiru. Her article was published both in *Zoogoer* magazine and the WWF TRAFFIC bulletin titled "Fashion Statement Spells Death for Tibetan Antelope."

CHAPTER SIX

[i] Schaller thinks there may have been a French geological party that traversed the Shor Kul Basin in the 1990s. There was definitely a Japanese party of mountaineers through the Basin on reconnaissance in 1999 that returned with a full expedition in 2000.

CHAPTER SEVEN

[i] While I was writing the article about our expedition that appeared in the April 2003 issue of NATIONAL GEOGRAPHIC, Bill Allen, the editor in chief, addressing the same concern about tipping off any would-be poachers, suggested keeping the map that showed the calving grounds vague.

[ii] When in 1999 I drove from the far edge of West Tibet through the Aru and back to Lhasa, I encountered, in the south-central section of the Chang Tang Reserve a large open-pit gold mine excavated with the help of several bulldozers, cranes, and dozens of trucks. Since then China has introduced The Great Western Development Program, which calls for more surveys of remote areas, more roads into former wildlands, and more development of natural resources, even in nature reserves. Writing about this in *China Explorer*, wildlife biologist William Bleisch noted, for example, that "Hanasi, a national-level nature reserve in Inking, has been downgraded to a county-level reserve and turned over to the local government for management," with the increased possibility it will be developed. Even with reserve status, there are several active gold

mines inside the Arjin Shan Reserve, and Bleisch considers those mines, and the roads that service them, to be the biggest threats to wildlife in that area.

[iii] See *Birds of Heaven* and the chapter titled "On the Daurian Steppe."

[iv] See *Heaven and Earth and I, Ethics of Nature Conservation in Asia*, edited by Vivek Menon and Masayuki Sakamoto, Penguin Books, India.

PART THREE

THREAT AND HOPE

CHAPTER EIGHT

[i] This is the photograph of Galen that NATIONAL GEOGRAPHIC published as an afterword in the "On Assignment" section of the April 2003 issue that included the article describing our expedition. I was pleased the editors chose this image because, with only ten steps left to the top, it captures that intense drive that was so much part of all summits, literal and metaphorical, that in his life Galen strove for and usually reached.

[ii] Later I would measure on our map the distance to the Aru Range and find those mountains were 135 miles to the south, and that Ulugh Muztagh was 230 miles to the west.

[iii] The International Fund for Animal Welfare also assisted in paying for anti-shahtoosh booths, as well as printed handouts, at the fashion shows. Combined with their efforts in China, Europe, and the United States, IFAW has now contributed over $500,000 to the campaign both to ban shahtoosh and to contain the poaching of chiru.

CHAPTER NINE

[i] This was from a conversation with the naturalist Anne Rasa, one of the world's authorities on mongooses. She came to Africa as a young woman to study its wildlife and never left. Now in her sixties, she lives alone near a settlement of Bushman in the Kalahari where she passes her days studying scorpions.

[ii] Once on an expedition to Antarctica (when I filmed Conrad and Alex Lowe making the first ascent of a big wall on the frozen continent), we were traversing the icecap on approach to our climb when I spotted on the white expanse a dark object perhaps a quarter mile away. Recalling that on the icecap any dark object is foreign, and thinking it might be a huge meteor, we diverted our route and discovered the desiccated remains of a seal. We were about eighty miles from the coast, and it has remained a mystery how the seal could have come to rest at a position that far inland.

[iii] Before starting this tagging program, Bleisch had checked with a number of other field biologists who had similarly tagged other species, and all of them assured Bleisch they had never lost an animal. Even then, Bleisch lost seven chiru, and he decided to discontinue the tagging. He's still not sure why chiru are so sensitive, but the inability to tag them has left gaps in what otherwise would be a more complete understanding of their migration routes and calving grounds.

[iv] See "Success for the Chiru! Now What" in the Autumn 2001 issue of *China Explorers*, the quarterly newsletter of the China Exploration and Research Society.

[v] Robert B. Ekvall was born in Gansu, China, in 1898, to missionary parents, and raised there until he was thirteen, when he traveled to the Unites States for his studies. He returned to eastern Tibet in 1928, and—fluent in Chinese and Tibetan—lived among the local people, including the nomads, until 1936, when he returned to the United States. In his writing he is perhaps best known for his book Tibetan Skylines, a lyrical description of his experiences living intimately among the nomads of eastern Tibet, including time spent on horseback riding with a band of raiders who included the inimitable Stretch Ears Jamtzen, Fence Teeth Wanjur, and Slab Face Rinchin, characters Ekvall developed with the skill of a novelist. In describing the tradition of raiding among eastern Tibetans, Ekvall illuminated a tradition common to nomadic groups that up until the Communist hegemony following World War II prevailed across Central Asia, including Mongolians and Kazaks, the latter who conducted not only internecine raids but also forays south into Tibet. Ekvall taught at the University of Washington from 1958 to 1974, and he died in 1978.

[vi] Additional factors include the invasion of alien species (49 percent), pollution (24 percent), and disease (3 percent). These factors add to more than 100 percent because many times species are threatened by a combination of factors, or initially by one factor that then opens the door to an additional threat. For more information on this topic, see Rebuilding the Ark: Toward a More Effective Endangered Species Act for Private Land. (1996, the Environmental Defense Fund, Washington, D.C.)

[vii] In 2003 Schaller was told the Chinese are planning to spend $3.5 million on a captive breeding program to raise chiru for their wool. "Captive breeding is highly unlikely to be economically viable, and may well cause the death of many chiru through inexperience in handling the species," Schaller reported in the IUCN publication the Gnusletter. William Bleisch also told me the zoo in Urumchi had tried to keep several chiru, but they had all died, apparently unable to adapt to the change in altitude and temperature. Just as this book was going to print, however, Bleisch told me he had heard that two young male chiru have been successfully held in captivity in the Kekexili Nature Reserve. He also said a university in China is working to genetically splice chiru and pashmina goat genes, in an attempt to create a domestic animal that, the scientists hope, would then be able to produce the finest wool in the world.

EPILOGUE

[i] Gnusletter, Volume 21, Number 2, 2002, pages 21–23.

[ii] The survey was made possible by grants from the International Fund for Animal Welfare and the Rufford Maurice Laing Foundation. If crediting these institutions in this book sounds like the kind of attributions you hear on public radio and television, my apologies, but I do so because I think it's important to recognize these groups; although I have tried in this story to recognize the individuals who work so hard on campaigns such as the one to save chiru, they could not achieve what they have without grants that fund their efforts.

ACKNOWLEDGMENTS

WITH A SCIENTIST'S SCRUTINY, George Schaller read this manuscript, and after earmarking my many errors, approved it. The only thing he didn't read was this Acknowledgments section, and if he had, he never would have permitted what I am about to say for several reasons, not least because I have no way of proving it. But here it is, anyway:

When you consider the increased understanding that today we have of so many of world's most charismatic species—lions, pandas, gorillas, tigers—as well as the more plebian but no less important animals including myriad species of wild sheep, goats, and antelope, all because of the lifetime work of George Schaller; when you consider that in Tibet alone, by his suggestion, counsel, and persuasion, about one hundred thirty thousand square miles of the plateau is now a nature reserve; when you consider that he has, in his capacity as director of science for the Wildlife Conservation Society, at any given time approximately seventy of the world's foremost wildlife biologists under his direction and, more importantly, under his mentorship; when you consider that many of those biologists he has inspired will go on to inspire in a similar way hundreds of conservation biologists of future generations; then you can argue that he has done as much as any person working on the front lines of conservation to save what remains of the wild creatures of this Earth.

Without George's inspiration I never would have had the idea for this journey, and without his continued support the western population of chiru would never be as close as it is today to winning protection.

I want to thank National Geographic for their early endorsement of this project. Here Rebecca Martin of the Expedition's Council deserves my and my companion's heartfelt thanks. A partial list of the other people at National Geographic who supported this project and worked hard on the various media "products" that together have so successfully broadcast the plight of the chiru include Bert Fox, Kevin Krug, Peter Miller, and Kevin Mulroy.

My companions and I give our appreciation to the Kelty Pack Co., and to their Korean partner Dong-In, for donating the cost of the development and construction of our rickshaws. Special thanks to the staff at Galen's office, Mountain Light, who, in his absence, helped organize the photography that graces this book. William Bleisch, Zhaxi Duojie, Grace Gabriel, Nan Kempner, Ian Knox, Ashok Kumar, Ritu Kumar, Riyaz, Michael Sautman, Belinda Wright, and Ya Ya Zhang gave me their time so I could better tell the parallel story of the effort worldwide to save the chiru by containing the poaching, banning the weaving, and controlling the sale of shahtoosh shawls.

As the book's editor, John Paine did a superb job helping me organize the manuscript. Others who read the manuscript or provided advice, research, or in other ways contributed, include Kenneth Brower, Bill Burnham of The Peregrine Fund, Bob Colacello, Andy Fisher of the Metropolitan Police at Scotland Yard, my literary agent Susan Golumb, Erin Harvey, my daughter, Carissa Ridgeway, my wife, Jennifer Ridgeway, Johnna Rizzo, Kay Schaller, Carl Thelander, and Jim Thorsell.